A Fire to Kindle: Harris County Schools & Education Before 1950

A - H

Mike Vance

Dos Dogs Press

Library of Congress Cataloguing-in-Publication Data

Name: Vance, Mike 1959 – author

Title: A Fire to Kindle A – H

Identifiers LCCN

ISBN (hardback) 978-1-965272-09-1

ISBN (paperback) 978-1-965272-10-7

ISBN (ebook) 978-1-965272-11-4

Also by Mike Vance

Please enjoy these other titles by Mike Vance. They are available
where books are sold and also at www.mikevancewriter.com

Non-Fiction

Undertold Texas Volume 1
Getting Away With Bloody Murder
Mud & Money: A Timeline of Houston History
Murder & Mayhem in Houston (with John Nova Lomax)
Houston Baseball: The Early Years, 1861-1961
Houston's Sporting Life
Stand-Up Stories Tales from Behind the Microphone
Brenham

Fiction

The Devil's Lease
Wingo: The Remarkable Story of an Unremarkable Man
Wingo's Redemption
Zeke Gets Glasses. Jungleburgh Children's Reading Community (with John Swasey)

Contents

Dedicated to Gloria Rinehimer, Charlotte Moore, Spencer Haygood, Marcella Howze, Joan Batcha, and Martha Wetzel who stand out among my public school teachers who inspired a love of language, history, and research.

About the Photos

There are plenty of photographs and other images included. I've tried to credit them all. One of the two biggest sources is the fine Houston History Research Center, Houston Public Library. It is located in the historic Julia Ideson Building across McKinney Street from Houston City Hall. It is worth a visit just to admire the wonderfully preserved structure if nothing else. I began getting images from there for this project twenty years ago. You'll find more about that in the Acknowledgements in the second volume. Photos from there are credited HHRC.

The second large source is the Houston Independent School District. They came very late to the idea of preserving their history, and much of what might have been saved was long since destroyed by the time my search began. Still, there were some nice finds, plus the annual reports were filled with images. Those were scanned from pixilated printed matter, so they are not always sharp, but I thought them well worth including. Photos from there are credited HISD.

One other source which I have abbreviated is the Harris County Public Library photos found at the always undervalued Harris County Archives. Several of those were the only images of a given school I was able to find. They are marvelous, and I am so grateful they were saved and digitized. Photos from there are credited HCPL.

I visited many historical societies, other school districts, and several individuals. I also bought a few dozen old class photos here and there. I love those pre-WWII photographs. They were the lifeblood for many a commercial photographer across the nation.

A quick mention about the endnotes, too. The *Houston Post, Houston Chronicle, Houston Press,* and *Galveston Daily News* are abbreviated as *Post, Chronicle, Press,* and *GDN* respectively. That *Houston Press* was the Scripps Howard daily which published from 1911 to 1964. The *Telegraph & Texas Register* that was published in Columbia briefly before moving to Houston is noted as *Telegraph*. That primarily refers to the daily edition or tri-weekly since the publishing frequency changed more than once.

A Fire to Kindle:

Harris County Schools & Education Before 1950

A Fire to Kindle Preface

This book has been well over fifteen years in the making. In its pages, you will find a bit about (almost) all the schools that existed in Harris County in 1950 or earlier. That includes both private and public schools, a journey that is outlined within. The reader will be able to follow the demographics of the county as it switched from rural, with numerous county districts, to largely urban and suburban. There is so much to learn about the small communities that now live on only through street names, but were once vital and somewhat self-sufficient. At least of equal importance to the schools entries are the sidebar pieces on the origins and evolution of education in Texas and some of the quirky and instructive goings on in our schools along the way.

Getting here has been a long road of research that has proven to be an extremely informative window into how public records are kept and maintained. One of an historian's absolutely favorite things is following rabbit trails, finding a mention of something slightly off topic that sounds interesting enough to follow. Sometimes there are nuggets that cry for inclusion in your work, and often there are dead ends. In a time of segregation and racial disdain, White newspapers rarely bothered to cover important stories about what was happening in the African-American or Hispanic communities. Chasing those minority stories was tough because an exponentially smaller written record remains.

Going back into the 19th century public records is a frustrating exercise indeed. Alexander McGowan was Harris County Treasurer in the 1880s, and, if he was alive today, I'd like to buy the man a sandwich and a beer. He or his clerks carefully entered details of all schools under the county's purview - names, locations, changes in the status of schools. His successors, well, not so much. Over the decades, governments and school districts employed bureaucrats who felt like free space was more important than the stack of the dusty old ledgers that was filling it. Storage is a problem for most of us, but when those by-gone records are tossed into the dumpsters of the officials who are tasked with maintaining them, many stories are lost to us forever. A more responsible and creative solution was in order.

The task undertaken here is large, and the cut off year of 1950 was chosen with much thought in an attempt to make the number of schools included at least somewhat manageable. It includes the schools that came from the first bond elections after WWII, but not the explosion of new campuses that were built in the following decade to educate the Baby Boomers. It does not include the early Sunday Schools because those offered mostly religious instruction and generally lasted only a couple of hours a week. They do not meet the standards of education that I set for the project. I tried to place the most emphasis on schools that impacted the largest numbers of students in the years prior to 1950. Mostly, I tried to keep the stories as entertaining as possible.

There were plenty of surprises along the way. Some related to how school districts tend to reuse land, and one school gave way to another then to a parking lot then back to school use. It wasn't until the end of the 20th century that HISD started letting go of big parcels of real estate.

While I hope that I've amply documented the inequality and injustice of Jim Crow and entrenched racial prejudice, I did not delve into the important stories of desegregation in Harris County schools because those have been covered extremely well in other books. A good place to start is with *Make Haste Slowly* written by my good friend, Bill Kellar.

I can guarantee that, as much as I tried to include everything, there are going to be some early schools missing from this book. The 19th century private schools were often a seat-of-the-pants operation. Names changed, buildings were moved, and records have disappeared. I'm sure, too, that some entries are shorter than what some readers would like to see about their old schools, but only so much room exists in a book, even one of two volumes. Hopefully, taking the entire body of work into consideration, I have covered a great deal about the schools as well as the communities they served and the changing values and priorities that they conveyed to the students and parents who were their patrons.

Of all the rich and informative stories to be found in this book, the biggest and most powerful is the tale of two cities, Black and White. We all learn about the Civil Rights movement to some degree, and the institution of slavery. We have seen grainy black and white footage of marchers getting sprayed with fire hoses and helmeted Alabama state troopers blocking the Edmund Pettus Bridge. But for those who did not live through the era of legal segregation, myself included, it is difficult to grasp the day-to-day pain of it. This struggle was not lived through a series of protests and Freedom Rides. It was lived seven days a week from the minute you tied your shoes to leave the house.

I firmly believe that nothing illustrates the intractable roots of racism as well as the detailed chronicle of education. The nickels and dimes tell the story. Fully seeing the sub-standard facilities, the unequal expenditures, and the denied opportunities will hopefully offer at least a glimpse of the frustration that faced an African American or Latino parent who wanted nothing more than a fair shake for his or her child.

Institutionalized is a powerful word. It conveys something that has dug itself into every little nook and cranny of a being. Like Brooks Hatlen, the fictional inmate who becomes institutionalized at Shawshank Prison to the point that he can no longer function on the outside, the racism in so many American school systems, and most every other aspect of daily life, was institutionalized throughout the years covered by this book. When the doors of previously all-White Kashmere Gardens Elementary School were opened for Black children in September of 1960, there was no switch flipped that suddenly made everything equal and fine. It took HISD ten more years and a fair measure of figurative biting and clawing in opposition before they fully integrated all of their school rooms. The struggle to reach a balance remains part of our national dialogue to this day.

By reading the little stories that make up the history of the Houston and Harris County schools, one gets a sense of the bigger picture. There were thousands of triumphs and plenty of hesitant progress. There is heartbreaking injustice, to be sure. Most of all, we should all never, ever lose sight of the fact that our public school system is the most valuable resource we have as a society. All of the solutions to our future problems are found behind those schoolhouse doors. Our schools belong to each of us, and we must remember that it is not there for private agendas or individual gain. The intellect of every child is a fire to kindle. I hope future generations take that job seriously.

Mike Vance

March 7, 2025

The Start of Free Public Schools in Texas

Texas President Mirabeau Lamar and his administration talked a big game. In 1839, he followed up on one of the causes for separation named in the Texas Declaration of Independence three years earlier. That revolutionary complaint was made in spite of the fact that there were public schools, free to some of the poorest residents, set up by municipal or church authorities at San Antonio, Nacogdoches, La Bahia, and Gonzales during the Spanish and Mexican Texas years. Citizens at Bexar had a non-mission public school as early as 1748, so the tradition of Spanish schools was well-established. Alcalde J.B. Elguezabal even proclaimed compulsory attendance in 1802, and later civic leaders reinforced the edict. After the advent of the empresario system, there were also several tuition-based school houses in the Anglo colonies at places including San Felipe, Brazoria, Matagorda, and Stafford's Point, and overall, the state government of Coahuila and Texas passed regular laws to provide for educating its citizenry.[1]

Under Lamar and the Texas Republic, a law was passed setting aside almost 15,000 acres of land in each Texas county to be leased as a finance mechanism for public schools. A later law designated another league which the county could sell. The problem was that land was "so abundant and... so ridiculously cheap that no funds could be secured either from sale or lease." As one Houston historian noted in the 1960s: "Although it might be an honor some writers like to bestow upon President Mirabeau B. Lamar, that he was the "Father of Public Education in Texas", it is applicable only in the sense that his intentions may have been in that direction."[2]

The school lands in Harris County, surveyed in 1839 and early 1840, were located roughly 36 miles northwest of downtown Houston near the present day town of Hockley. The revenue from the lands appears to have provided rather negligible funds over the years compared to the cost of operating public schools.

Though the Republic, and later the state, dragged its heels on creating an education system, the City of Houston jumped on it as a primary order of business. An 1838 city charter gave Houston the right to buy and sell property, and a scant two weeks later, Mayor Francis Moore, Jr. and the council set out to build a school, even before the market house or the jail. Though the school charged tuition to all but a handful of qualifying indigent children, and though the entire effort was abandoned before the Republic would breathe its last, the effort was there, at least for a while.[3]

Mayor Moore was a leading part of a movement in January 1846 to establish public schools throughout the newest state in the union. A convention was held in Houston to organize and form committees with an eye toward lobbying the new legislature, going so far as to form a newspaper called the *Public School Advocate*. The difference might have been in the fact that, unlike the majority of settlers in more rural areas of Texas, Mayor Moore, city founders Augustus and John Allen, and other key Houstonians hailed from the Northeastern United States, an area that had repeatedly shown an affinity toward book learning for the masses.[4]

Like many innovations concerning American education, the North outpaced the South. Most places in America provided some sort of mechanism for the basic schooling of those who could not afford it, and there were even sporadically located public county academies in the South, though those charged tuition. The first American instance of free education for all came in the form of the Boston English High School in 1820. Seven years later, Massachusetts expanded the concept for all grades of public school in the Commonwealth. By 1851, education in that state was compulsory.[5]

The flip side was true in Houston that year. An 1851 visitor to the city wrote a letter to the editor of the *Telegraph and Texas Register* complimenting the town's business community and churches, then remarked "I was astonished to find that in a city some sixteen years of age, containing a population of between three and four thousand souls, and much wealth and intelligence as there is, there was not to be found one single edifice built for Educational purposes – not even the most common school house!!"

The first real attempt at establishing a system of public schools in Texas came in 1854 when two million dollars of the money that had come to the new state from the sale of lands to the United States were set aside as a school fund.

The man behind this push for public schools was Connecticut native Elijah Pease. A newcomer to the state in 1835, he quickly built up his Texian credentials. He fought at the Battle of Gonzales, took part in the convention at Washington that drafted a Texas Declaration of Independence, and became the Republic's first comptroller of public accounts.[6]

The 1854 "Act to Establish a System of Schools" handed the duties of doing so to the counties, and it did so without much funding. A year later, the state treasurer, who also served as Superintendent of Common Schools, wrote Governor Pease that it "imposed a heavy duty on the Assessors and Collectors of the different counties without making any provision for their payment." He added in correspondence to those county officials that thought the legislature had failed to fund their "time and labor," that he was certain that in the next session, they would provide "liberally." That term would never become applicable.[7]

The officials in Harris County performed a scholastic census as required by the law, reporting a school age population of 1,370 in 1854 and 1,449 the following year. The surviving 1855 listing showed a total of 17 districts, aside from Houston, at the communities of Harrisburg, San Jacinto, Galveston Bay, Cedar Bayou, Dunman's, Willow Creek, Spring Creek, Little Bayou, Habermachers on Buffalo Bayou, and at various German settlements at Spring Branch and on Greens, White Oak, and Brays Bayous. It is unclear how many of those districts actually formed schools to take advantage of monies offered under the new law. It is known, thanks to a report in a far off Pennsylvania newspaper, that on November 1, 1854, only 83 of the City of Houston's roughly 700 school age children were attending classes.[8]

After the school system had a year under its belt, State Treasurer James H. Raymond sent a request to the various Chief Justices of the counties, akin to today's County Judge, asking for their thoughts. Only 28 of them responded "quickly". Harris County's chief executive was not among them.

Reports from other counties, however, likely indicated circumstances found statewide. Overall, only 89 counties made an effort to take part in the new school system in 1854 and just 74 the following year when the first disbursement of funds was made. Much of the trouble was due to a lack of organization. In Bastrop County, for example, there were 29 common school districts formed, but in 1855, only three of them went so far as to elect trustees. Brazoria County was even worse. Only one district elected trustees. In Fort Bend, not a single district organized to make claim to the monies available under the new law. Dallas County seems to have had one of the very best results in Texas, reporting in 1857 that the state funds were paying almost "two-thirds of the tuition for those who attend school." The *Houston Telegraph* remarked that Dallas' efforts were "better than it does generally." The most frank and dismal assessment came from the Chief Justice in Nacogdoches who reported that "There is but little interest taken in the school law."[9]

Many of the Harris County records have been lost, but a payment of $849.40 out of the school monies for the year 1854 was received by the county treasurer over a year later. One thing that Harris County was doing with the money was paying for the education of indigent children. The minutes of Commissioners' Court show multiple payments "out of the school fund" for this purpose in the late 1850s and the 1860s.The subsidized students, however, the only ones getting a free education, were often taunted so mercilessly by their paying classmates that many came to prefer ignorance over the harassment.[10]

Harris County did set up a mechanism to certify teachers in May 1858. Dr. Ashbel Smith, Rufus K. Cage, and Dr. William H. Howard were named as examiners and ordered to hold quarterly examinations to certify those wanting to teach. Each examiner was paid three dollars a day for the time they worked. Though the county was paying some teachers of the indigent children, the schools that employed these teachers were not recorded. Their names, however, were listed that summer and fall: I. Leffingwell, John A. Hancock, J.A. Lyons, A. Ruber, John Tate, John Buckley, Mrs. M.A. Coward, Mrs. M.L. Capshaw, O.H. Perry, Thomas McMillan, Miss

Henrietta Sawyer, Mrs. Hawkins, Mrs. Abby, Miss Maher, Mrs. H.L. Cotton, Mrs. Wyam, Miss Van Alstyne, C. Braun, Mrs. Green, S. A Bolinger, Samuel Barron, W.P. Cunningham, Rudolph Boehr, E. Ruckward, and A.D. Burdick. Several of them are known to have run small private schools, and they were receiving public funds that year and the next. The highest totals topped $200 in some terms and were drawn by Casper Braun at the German Lutheran School.[11]

In 1860, there were still funds being sent from the state comptroller to the Harris County Treasurer for school purposes. There was $3,282 received that year and added to over $3,000 already on hand. Even during the Civil War, a semblance of school districts were maintained in the county, though the only government supported students were those who were proven to be indigent, in which cases the teachers were directly compensated by the county.[12]

Among Treasurer James H. Raymond's many other suggestions to the governor about the 1854 school law was that the state make actual use of the school funds rather than trying to live off interest. "Are we to keep it," he asked. "As the university and county lands are kept, by the present provisions of the Constitution, for the benefit of succeeding generations? Or will we throw off the appearance of suspicion that attaches to the present system, and show by our acts that we have confidence in the honesty and integrity of the present generation?"

Unfortunately for the future of Texas education, the Pease administration placed an equally high value on seeing Texas gain new railroads. Soon after the start of the schools program, the bulk of the "set aside" fund was loaned to the railroads in the state to bolster construction. The interest on those loans was to further augment the public schools.[13]

As with any other corporate ventures, especially those in what was for Texas at the time an emerging technology sector, many of the railroads went bankrupt, undermined by poor and greedy management and the upheaval of the Civil War. Texas Governor Sam Houston, returned to that job from the U.S. Senate, praised the common schools and said that "the nucleus of a complete system is already provided." His successor, Pendleton Murrah, was less enthusiastic, saying in December 1863 that the distribution "to the schools for the last two years is insignificant." Specifically, he noted that the railroad companies then owed the school fund about a quarter of a million dollars with another $166,000 in interest due, as well. Much of the school fund had vanished with the trainmen's dreams.[14]

Famous Texas historian Eugene Barker summed up the mid-1850s attempt at schools thusly: "It proved a miserable failure. Doubtless it contained some element of merit but the enormous loss that accrued to the School Fund is eloquent testimony to the fact that not all finely conceived theories work out in practice."

As half-hearted as the 1850s school laws were, the wartime budget realities of the early 1860s brought an end to the effort entirely. One and a quarter million dollars was taken out of the two million dollar school fund principal and transferred to the Texas military board, and investment income in general withered like rye grass in summer. A law setting aside all revenue from the sale of public lands for education was repealed. On top of it all, the few railroad companies which were keeping up with at least a portion of their interest payments began doing so in Confederate currency, an instrument that depreciated until it was used as wallpaper.[15]

After serving his two terms as Texas governor, Elijah Pease, the architect of the 1854 school law, remained in Austin, vocally opposing secession. When the war ended and Union forces occupied the state in 1865, General Phillip Sheridan appointed Pease as provisional governor. It was his elected successor, Edmund J. Davis, though, who would be successful in finally bringing free schools to the Lone Star State.

Davis was the governor, but the Federal authorities wielded considerable power, as well. As a matter of policy, Washington was appalled at the abysmal state of literacy and education across the conquered South. Texas had a 17% illiteracy rate among Whites and 90% among Blacks. Crime was high. The homicide rate was double any other of the 37 states. In 1870, the National Bureau of Education called Texas "the darkest field educationally in the United States."[16]

With Texas politicians of most all stripes paying at least lip service to a state education system, Davis set about making it so. He signed a schools act into law on April 24, 1871. Provisions included common statewide curriculum, a system of teacher certification, establishment of grade levels, continuing education for teachers, and central administration of schools.[17]

Davis appointed Jacob Carl DeGress to be the first Supervisor of Public Instruction. The Prussian-born DeGress was young, only 23 when he came to Texas in 1865 as a brevet colonel with the Freedmen's Bureau. Youth did not mean untested in the least. He was a twice-wounded commander of Union cavalry who had fought at Vicksburg and in Louisiana before traveling as a staff officer on Sherman's march through Georgia. With the Freedmen's Bureau, DeGress served at both Houston and Galveston in multiple civil affairs capacities, seeing firsthand the operation of the Bureau's schools. While in Houston, he met and married Betty Buckner Young, a Confederate war widow. After two years as a bureaucrat, he was stationed to West Texas as a regular Army captain in command of the Ninth U.S. Cavalry, a troop of African American veterans then being dispatched against Indians.[18]

When Davis tapped DeGress to run his schools, there was little opposition to the appointment, though it was a job that came with much authority. The governor, attorney general, and supervisor of public instruction were in charge of the system all the way down to selecting county school boards and teachers and setting their salaries. A subsequent head of the state schools said that the 1871 statute was "only a few sections and less than three printed pages... but it gave to the Board of Education powers that might well excite the envy of the autocrat of all the Russias."[19]

If the ex-Confederates, then a minority in terms of political power, did not grumble about DeGress personally, they certainly did so about the law itself. They railed against centralized oversight at the state level, asserting that from district school boards all the way down to teachers, appointees would be Republican friends of Governor Davis and would be receiving exorbitant salaries in a system rife with fraud. The Democratic newspaper in Austin went so far as to suggest that most of the school money would end up in the pockets of the Republican politicians. Judge Benjamin C. Franklin of Galveston, a San Jacinto veteran, said public schools were unconstitutional and that taxes collected "will be squandered without any proportionate public benefit."[20]

Jacob DeGress

Harris County was placed by DeGress in District 1 under the supervision of Erastus Carter along with the counties of Austin, Brazoria, Brazos, Galveston, Montgomery, San Jacinto, and Washington. In June 1871, a few weeks after his own appointment, Carter in turn named J.G. Tracy, who enjoyed a contract as state printer, Captain J.E. Whittlesey, James Mitchell, Henry Clay Ferguson, and Lewis Bartess to be the Board of School Directors for Harris County. They held their first meeting on July 13 of that year with the initial order of business being to set the local property tax rate at 95 cents per one hundred dollars valuation, augmented by state money.

Whittlesey was elected board president and Ferguson, an African American, was named secretary. His successor, Charles Schmidt, later complained that Ferguson was "not a good scribe," though whether his statements were based on fact or prejudice is unknown. Nonetheless, Ferguson's notes written "on loose sheets of paper which were 'stitched together'" are the first record of free public schools in Harris County.[21]

Henry C. Ferguson was born a slave on the Ferguson Plantation in Jasper County in the mid-1840s, but rose to political prominence as a leader of Black Republicans, along with his brother Charles Ferguson and Walter Burton, in post-Civil War Ft. Bend County. He served as sheriff and tax collector prior to moving to Houston to work for the school board, returned to Richmond to take a lucrative job as tax assessor, and was run back to Houston in the aftermath of the brutal Jaybird-Woodpecker War of 1888. Though he represented Ft. Bend at the Republican state conventions in 1894 and 1898, by 1900, he was living with his wife and three children at 1110 Polk in the Bayou City.[22]

The taxes Ferguson and his fellow board members approved were not universally well-received, to say the least. Citizens of Harris County called them "unconstitutional, unnecessary and unwarranted." Writing about the history of those times some 80 years later, a *Post* reporter told that "The City Council was amazed by the opposition which arose, first because people compared public schools to charity schools; second because the well-to-do objected to the mixed social conditions public schools would create. They were able to educate their own children... and thought it unfair that they should be taxed to educate the children of others."[23]

Governor Davis defended the taxes, pointing out that the overall tax burden in Texas was lower than just about any other state. Speaking in Galveston he said, "If you live in a hut and sleep under Mexican blankets, it will cost you less than if you fabricate an expensive building. If you have no government, it will cost you nothing. If you have public schools and law and order, you must pay for it."[24]

Initially, Governor Davis was having none of the protests and non-compliance. He ordered Attorney General William Alexander "to threaten seizure of their properties if payments were not made, with some seizures actually being made." The man responsible for those actions in Harris County was A.B. Hall who served in the dual job of county sheriff and tax collector. Hall, however, was not known for either his diligence or his honesty according to many.[25]

The opposition was not all economic. A good part of the tax protests and vociferous squawking was rooted in simple bigotry. That meant deeply held prejudices against both the newly freed African Americans and against the Yankee interlopers who dared to finally bring public education to Texas. Forget the fact that Houston was founded by New Yorkers and that over half of its first leading families hailed from the North or from Europe.

The idea of educating Blacks, though never illegal in Texas as it had been in a handful of other Confederate states, was repugnant to some Whites. When the Freedmen's Bureau had first opened schools in 1865, one editorial stated that: "This is a novel school among our people, they never having been used to anything of the kind, and the novelty is not pleasing, not being en rapport with the tastes and habits of Southern people."[26]

The sentiment had not changed in those particular quarters in the ensuing five or six years. The White press was still adamant, and sometimes virulent, about maintaining segregation. The *Houston Telegraph* opined: "We may let our children work in the fields or shop with the children of our former servants. They may hunt or fish or play together, but to attend the same school never!" The *Galveston Daily News* was less giving: "Colored children are not sufficiently advanced in civilization to be fit companions for White children."[27]

Most pro-Union politicians understood the landscape they faced. Texas Secretary of State James P. Newcomb flatly said that the state's Democrats "fight the public schools because it will be the means of educating the colored children as well as the White." Despite rampant rumors to the contrary, Supervisor DeGress pledged to keep the schools segregated, and he honored his word, likely afraid of potential consequences both violent and political.[28]

Not everyone in Texas was grousing. There were definitely voices on the other side who pushed for complete integration and equality just as the new Federal laws of the time required. Mathew Gaines of Brenham, one of the two Black Texas state senators, remonstrated against the segregated schools.[29]

Other protest groups had their own blatant self-interests at heart, too. Germans, prevalent across Texas, were afraid the public schools would be used to "de-germanize" them, a goal that was openly stated by some who favored assimilation of foreign minorities.[30]

Catholic leaders opposed the public schools as an infringement upon their rights. They refused to allow teachers in the church schools to take the state oath, even though the new law mandated that all teachers in any school pass a competency test. In San Antonio, the bishop even went so far as to refuse the sacraments for parents who sent their children to public school. It is unknown if the Catholic DeGress was ever denied communion. Eventually the church gave in, and Catholic teachers were certified, though some grumbling continued.[31]

The Baptists were equally aggrieved, if not more so. The president of Baylor University called the idea of Texas public schools "the most absurd, blundering and monstrous system of free schools ever adopted on this continent," adding that examining teachers for competency was humiliating.[32]

In the end, a large number of Texans couldn't afford both public school taxes and private school tuition, so they brought their children into the state system. In the neighborhood of 1,100 private schools closed or joined the state system in 1872.[33]

Any and all religious instruction was prohibited in the public schools, and violations resulted in teacher termination. It was a popular stance, with newspaper editorials urging that teachers not be publicly affiliated with any religion and that they be individuals "who feel themselves first as citizens."[34]

In spite of all the whining outrage, Houston and Harris County schools opened as planned. Throughout the first school year, more and more new classrooms came into the fold. By June 1872, heading into the first summer break, "there were twelve public schools in the city and eighteen in the county presided over by sixteen men and fourteen women."[35]

The *Telegraph* of September 25, 1872 ran a spare listing of some of the various Houston public schools. "A boys' school was taught by Mr. Hammond, with eighty pupils and one assistant. Mrs. Neyland had a boys' and girls' school. Another school of about thirty-five boys and girls was Mrs. Sutor's, while Mr. Chapman presided over a school of forty-six boys and girls and Mrs. Long, thirty; a Mrs. E. M. Tucker also had a school for boys and girls." The primary African American school was Gregory Institute run by four teachers for 140 pupils. Mr. J. T. Fisher, a White man, ran a school for 55 students and employed one Black woman as his assistant. Sarah Wren, an unmarried Black woman, had a school with 64 pupils, and "Miss Sarah North from New Orleans also had a Negro school." The *Telegraph* reported that teachers were "greatly needed" in the city's Black schoolhouses.[36]

Teachers of the Black students were subject to "continual insults, social ostracism, threats of injury and all the annoyances that malice can invent." Finding places for the White teachers of African American students to board was also problematic, oft times only a few families were willing to house them. Still, Harris County could claim the highest number of Black school children in Texas under the new law: 760 girls and 734 boys.[37]

Salaries for teachers were generous, ranging from $75 to $110 a month. School principals salary ran from $115 to $150, and all were obligated to teach Monday through Friday for six hours a day "excluding hours of recreation". The total salary figures far outstripped the money budgeted in the legislature.[38]

There were also facility costs since very few of the buildings, if any, were owned by the government. In May 1873, Sheriff Hall reported that the county had spent $2,956.09 for renting the various school buildings for the previous nine months.[39]

At one brief and fleeting juncture in the first year of the new school law, Republicans felt reassured that common sense and a desire for education would prevail. DeGress said in 1871 that problems had abated around the state except in the districts of Galveston and Houston. The self-interest of politicians, however, did not rest.[40]

Texas Democrats, seeking a wedge issue against the Northern-led Republicans, made the Republican schools one of those, especially targeting the people who did not believe Blacks should be offered education of any kind. Democratic campaign rhetoric also charged that Texas children would be learning manners and morals at odds with those of their parents.[41]

It did not take long for the ex-Confederates' efforts to turn personal. The Texas Senate convened hearings aimed at DeGress and his alleged party favoritism. Some of the school appointees, a minority, said that they had never been asked about their political leanings at all. Others told a different story, one said that DeGress instructed him to "select good men, sound Republicans, as Democrats as a class are opposed to free schools."[42]

There was at least a little fire to be found in the smoke the Democrats were fanning. The Third Congressional District, which included Houston and Galveston, was the most Republican in the state, but also featured a volatile Republican primary in 1871 in which incumbent James T. Clark faced Louis Stevenson, a Union League member who had been active in organizing Black voters. At his party's urging, in hopes of moving Black votes from Stevenson's column to Clark's, Superintendent DeGress appointed several Black school board members including Henry Ferguson in Houston and George Ruby, Norris Wright Cuney, and Nathen Patten in Galveston.[43]

DeGress forced Stevenson supporter and district school supervisor S.A. Waldron out of his job, fearing that Waldron was "a spy in the camp." Waldron complained to the Democrats in the Senate that DeGress was asking for kickbacks from school building contractors and from sellers of school books and the slate boards that students used. The investigating committee called dozens of witnesses, including book depositor E.H. Cushing of Houston, a strongly pro-secessionist leading citizen of the city, and found no wrongdoing on the part of DeGress. Still, some Democrats stated that even though they'd found nothing, he was probably guilty.[44]

The Democratic minority on the investigating committee took particular offense at DeGress' characterization of them and stated in that report that "no sane man who is at all acquainted with our people will deny that the great mass of them, Democrat and Republican, are favorable to education... The people cannot be intelligent and virtuous unless they are educated. Many are too poor, many are too ignorant and many are too vicious to educate their own children." Nevertheless, the Democrats continued their vehement attacks on the Republicans for having passed the free schools law, and the charges were enough to plant thoughts of corruption among some voters with the end of the investigation, and the clearing of DeGress, not coming until after the election.[45]

Democrats also painted the tax rate of $1.50 per $100 valuation as exorbitant, even though the rate was much higher in other states. Illinois was $4.50, but even southern states like Arkansas and Mississippi were over a dollar higher than Texas.

The budget for the 1871 free public schools in Texas was $504,500 with the biggest items being $450,000 for teacher and administrator salaries and $40,000 for books.[46]

Some Republicans complained that the largest expense of the system was the duplicate facilities and personnel for the segregated White and Black schools, but they knew that as bad as the tax backlash was, that if they integrated the schools, the racist backlash would be even greater. With an ever greater number of ex-Confederates re-entering the political fray, they knew integration was not going to happen.

Democratic politicians, cherry-picking Democratic judges in some districts, got an injunction to stop collection of property taxes in 1872. The injunctions were later overruled on appeal and the property taxes declared constitutional, but meanwhile the school finances fell further into arrears. In the next Congressional elections, Republicans lost all four Texas seats. Republicans at the state level responded by cutting school costs, eliminating 23 of the 35 district school supervisor jobs, increasing class size to at least 35 students, and cutting teacher pay. The top pay was reduced to $100 a month, the third level all the way down to $50 a month and a new fourth class level that applied to most rural schools getting only $25 a month in salary.[47]

As 1872 continued, Democrats filed more and more injunctions to declare the free schools law unconstitutional, all of which were shot down by the Texas Supreme Court. Nonetheless, Governor Davis and Superintendent DeGress continued the cost cutting. For the 1872-73 school year, the number of school inspectors was slashed and the position of school principal was eliminated entirely. Teachers in some parts of the state began to be paid with treasury warrants which merchants often discounted by as much as 25%. That was way better than Houston where many teachers went without pay entirely.[48]

At a teachers institute held in Houston on April 5, 1873, many of those attending were so fed up that they drafted a petition: "To the Honorable Senate and House of Representatives of the State of Texas: We, the undersigned teachers of Harris County, do most respectfully report to your Honorable Body that having received nothing for our services since the month of May 1872 and most of us being entirely dependent on our salaries as a means of subsistence, we are therefore in distress, while many of us are in destitute circumstances. In view of these facts, we most earnestly petition the Legislature to take into immediate consideration our deplorable condition and devise some means for our speedy relief." Among the teachers signing were veteran instructors including: Mrs. M.J. Young, S.B. Gore, Mary C. Halsey, M. Hammel, K.R. Jones, C.L. Gillespie, Carrie Lovell, Frances Carley, M.A. Gilbert, Z.M. Noble, E.W. Neyland, C. Raun, H.M. Abbey, C.M. Dunbar, S.G. Yancey, Kate Dillon, Mary K. Marshall, and Edith Triplett.[49]

Not long after the submission of this petition, Harris County Sheriff A.B. Hall issued a statement covering the period from September 1, 1872 to May 1, 1873, showing that he had disbursed $18,591.42 as "teachers' salaries" and it is presumed these 'destitute circumstances' had been somewhat alleviated.

Statewide politics continued to work against the free public schools. By the summer of 1872, Democrats were using the school law as their top campaign issue. It worked. Voters in 1873 sent a Democratic majority to the legislature where they promptly sacked the statewide curricula, gave control to locally elected school boards, and greatly curtailed tax collection, even though that had already been happening in many locales including Harris County. They kept the requirement of compulsory attendance, but eliminated all fines and penalties against violators. Even the Democratic *Galveston Daily News* said that the old Republican-devised system was "infinitely preferable." Governor Davis' veto of the new schools bill was overridden.[50]

In 1872, fifty-six percent of school age Texas children attended school, the following year, under the revised law, attendance had dropped to 48%. Even more significant, the average school year had gone from nine months to six. Expenditures per student fell from $9.65 to $6.48 over the two-year period of the transition between the laws. Soon the system that began in 1871 disappeared entirely.[51]

With new Governor Richard Coke in charge, Supervisor of Education DeGress found himself out of a job in February 1874. Though he had been branded a Yankee carpetbagger, he remained in Austin and was elected alderman and then mayor in the late 1870s. The summer of 1880 was devastating to DeGress; a lawsuit successfully challenged his eligibility to serve as mayor, and his wife and two of his three daughters died. Two years later, he remarried to a cousin of famed Confederate General Joseph E. Johnston, and re-emerged in Republican politics. Presidents Garfield and Harrison each appointed him to terms as postmaster of Austin, and another lawsuit reinstated his service as alderman in the interim. From 1885 to 1888, he even served on several committees concerned with construction and dedication of the Texas Capitol. Jacob C. DeGress died of complications from his war wounds on St. Joseph's Day in 1894.[52]

For a brief time after DeGress' 1874 dismissal, free public schools in Texas seemed dead, as well. In 1875, a new constitutional convention took place, producing a document ratified in 1876 that is still in use today. The 1876 system that was created was less centralized and limited taxes. Citing the need for a "general diffusion of knowledge", it set down "public free school" funding as coming from "one-fourth of revenue from state occupation taxes" and the poll tax on males between 21 and 60. It was not until 1949 and the Gilmer-Aiken Laws that created the Texas Education Agency that the tax basis for school funding was restructured.[53]

The school law that emerged was even weaker than what a committee of Democrats, recently gaining the majority of elected offices, had recommended. There were no supervisory positions at all. The State School

Superintendent's spot in the Texas Board of Education triumvirate had been replaced by the State Comptroller. Compulsory attendance was eliminated and would not return for over a generation. School taxes were only allowed in incorporated cities and towns. Statistics for the 1878-79 school year told the tale. Using the same criteria as the Reconstruction Republican law had laid out, only 39% of Texas children were in school. Expenditure per student had plummeted to $4.03. Monthly teacher pay, equal for the sexes under the Reconstruction law, now averaged $48.13 for men and $28.31 for women, and in some locales, the school year was allowed to drop to only 72 days.[54]

On August 19, 1876, the Texas legislature passed "An Act to Establish and Provide for the Support and Maintenance of an Efficient System of Public Free Schools in the City of Houston." Houston followed up by passing an ordinance that let the city assume control of all "public schools and school houses" then existing within its corporate limits on May 4, 1877.

Specifically, the schools were free to all Houston children between the ages of 8 and 14. Those below or above that age were required to pay tuition. The monthly cost was $1.50 per student, and the teacher was allowed to keep up to five dollars per month total with the balance going to the school fund. In 1881, the top age was raised to 18, and the school year increased from eight months to nine.[55]

The law handed Mayor J.F.D. Wilson and city council control of the previously private schools within the Houston city limits. In turn, they created a three-person board of trustees and a three-person board of examiners to oversee the school operations. The inaugural school board consisted of Captain E.W. Taylor as board president along with Robert Cotter and B.C. Simpson. Professor H.H. Smith was hired as the superintendent at an annual salary of $2,000.

The school year opened on the first Monday in October 1877 with three primary grades and four grammar grades being offered. City council appropriated $15,000 from the general funds to maintain the schools, and additional capital was donated by the Peabody Fund, an annual gift that continued for the next few years.[56]

A reporter from the *Houston Age* set out to visit the new schools, managing to get to eight of them accompanied by Superintendent Smith. After listing some specifics, the reporter offered this observation: "We can candidly say that, despite all that has been urged to the contrary, we have never witnessed a more refined and intelligent-looking class of pupils than we found yesterday in our public schools. The schools are patronized by our best and most prominent citizens and are conducted by some of the most intelligent ladies in Houston. In short, the public schools of Houston are pervaded throughout with a spirit of refinement seldom found in institutions of a like character. In our most pleasant journey with Prof. Smith, we found that gentleman fully alive to the onerous labors attending his highly responsible position."[57]

Not everyone was equally impressed. The *Houston Telegraph* wrote: "Free schools commenced all over the city yesterday. What a farce they are under the present law—or rather what a farce the law is. Teachers get ten cents a day for each day that each pupil attends. When it rains and only half the children attend school, the teacher has to work just as hard as usual on half rations of pay. And they won't last over two or three months at most."[58]

Superintendent Smith prepared the first courses of study and chose the books which would be used, taking into account the volumes most likely to have already been purchased by the city's parents. Smith's tenure as school boss was brief. He resigned in November 1879 to take over as principal of the State Normal School in Huntsville, today's Sam Houston State University. He was replaced in Houston by Professor E. N. Clopper.

There were 28 teachers that first year, 14 in White schools, and 14 in the African American ones, receiving between $30 and $50 per month. Their salaries made up 90% of the money spent to educate the city's youth. The school year consisted of 160 teaching days. It would increase to 178 school days just eight years later. The teachers were serving 1,565 White pupils and 1,296 Black. One report charged that 61 White children and 279 Black children enrolled could not yet read.[59]

Harris County also set up a new school system under the law in 1876, and the county began selling off small portions of the school lands near Hockley, though not enough to support the schools. A three-man county school board was formed with Dr. Ashbel Smith, Professor Horace Clark, and the same Captain E.W. Taylor who served with the city.[60]

Beginning in late September 1876, the county began establishing school communities, or districts. Trustees from an existing rural school petitioned the county judge, C. Auden Jones, who certified that they had a sufficient school house then assigned district numbers on a first come first served basis. Number one went to the Westfield School Community.

Overall, schools under the new Democratic imposed law were not institutions that garnered much praise. Thomas Gathright had recently come to Texas from his native Mississippi to be the first president of the new Agricultural & Mechanical College near Bryan. He traveled Texas as much as he could in order to get acquainted with his new home, and in summer of 1877 came to the State Fair at Houston. He reported on the visit to a leading newspaper back home, using the pen name of William. On the subject of education in Texas, he offered this: "In conversing with persons from various portions of the State, I find that although educational interests are seemingly much cared for, the standard of culture is not high and teachers are worse paid than in any other civilized community. This is to be accounted for upon many hypotheses, but specially and chiefly upon the circumstance that so many parties, with little culture, have come from the older States, looking for something to turn up, and having spent what little means they brought, have resorted to teaching to keep in the shade. The school-room in Texas is the charnel house of extravagant hopes. The free school system is no system at all but is a factor in killing all private enterprizes, and in rendering it madness for teachers in other parts to come here to make a living or a reputation."[61]

History in Black and White

Racial inequality in early Harris County schools was not confined to facilities and expenditures. Time and again, books and articles purporting to be "histories" of local schools turned out to be the history of White schools and White pupils and teachers. In 1936, for example, in honor of the Texas Centennial, HISD commissioned a history of its schools. It apparently never went into circulation, but a small handful of typed copies exist today in libraries and archives. Only the White schools are included.

One of the two authors of that study was L. L. Pugh, by most accounts the solid and forward thinking superintendent of the Harris County School System in the 1910s, and the man who pushed for consolidation of county schools from a one or two-room frame model to up-to-date brick buildings with great educational resources. He was truly devoted to a good education for all students, just not apparently on an equal basis.

In the annual reports of county schools from Pugh's tenure, it was not uncommon to find a one paragraph report for a given rural district using a phrase such as "they have one White school", when, deeper research into the pay records reveals that there was also an African American school. Or in a few cases, a report flatly stated that such and such district "has five schools" when the list of teachers showed that there were in fact six schools in that district, just that one happened to be for Black children.

One of the most amazing items, when viewed from a modern perspective, is a nice map of city schools that HISD produced about 1930. On a detailed city street map were hand drawn circles for elementary schools, triangles for junior highs and pentagons for high schools. The White schools are only outlines against the backdrop of the White map and the colored schools are, quite literally, colored in. What is most striking, though, is that all the White schools are carefully named in small hand lettering, while the colored-in shapes are identified by their location alone.

Such is the historical legacy left to us from a time of institutionalized racism. As much as a large number of people from those days could not envision an integrated and diverse society, they likewise could not imagine how much poorer they would leave their children and grandchildren by preserving only a portion of the story of their times.

Schools A

ABBEY SCHOOL

The co-educational school at Walker and Travis that was run by Mrs. H. M. Abbey and her daughter, Florence, started in the immediate years following the Civil War, operating by at least 1867. Though it began as a private school, it was one of the institutions taken into the first public school system in 1871, and by the following year had an enrollment of 36 boys and girls.[1]

Ella Smith Hickman shared this note about the Abbey School: "A unique way of discipline is reported of Mrs. Abbey's school. When little boys became too mischievous she would make them sit on a low block of wood and keep their eyes ahead of them. If the culprit turned his head, Mrs. Abbey would kick the block from under him while the class laughed at his embarrassment."[2]

ABBOTT SCHOOL

The community of Chaneyville was centered around a junction of the Houston & Texas Central and the GH&SA Railroads and named for Thomas R. Chaney, the manager of the huge Howard Cotton Oil Mill that opened there in 1880. It was the start of an industrial boom that employed hundreds in the area. Though the worker population was more Black than White, there were schools for both of the segregated races in County District 25. The White school was operating at least by 1891, and in 1895 was located on a narrow lot at the southwest corner of Barnes and Abbott. It was quickly the largest schoolhouse in the district, employing two teachers and utilizing four cords of wood to get through the winter.[3]

The wooden building was made available for the use of a community church, though other meetings were banned in 1899 after neighbors' complaints over rowdy night meetings during the week. By 1910, the district badly needed a new building. A temporary fix divided it into three rooms, but in 1912, the district opened a new brick structure, one year before the Chaneyville School was annexed into the City of Houston. The name soon changed to Abbott School in honor of Newton C. Abbott, a New York born lawyer who moved to Houston in 1900, where he was part of the group that founded the Riverside addition.[4]

Originally opened for the first four grades, it employed three teachers by 1914, its first full year as a city school. One year later, Abbott received four new indoor toilets and was taking part in a neighborhood gardening program. Boy Scouts and Wolf Cubs met weekly at the building. It was not long, however, before Abbott began to receive annual criticism in the Mother's Club inspections. By 1918, it needed lighting, a teacher's restroom, and was sorely lacking in sufficient ground space.

Abbott School, 1st & 2nd Grade class, 1916. Mike Vance Collection

In the early 1920s, the four room brick building had almost 200 children and was listed flatly as "in bad repair" and "not modern in any way." It scored the lowest of any White school in the city on the Strayer-Englehart scale, and most of the students were moved to the new Cleveland Elementary nearby. Abbott may have remained as a special education facility. The school closed in 1959 and was sold by HISD in February 1962. Roznovsky's Hamburgers ran a burger restaurant in the lower/basement floor of the building for several years. The old building was finally demolished in the 1980s.[5]

ADDICKS H S

Harris County District 10 replaced four one-room, single teacher schools that only went through eighth grade with a new $10,000 brick high school that opened on October 2, 1912. Carrie Fox, the first principal, reported that the 40 students who filled the 11 grades were short on books, and the grounds were not yet complete, but a fundraising entertainment helped. A piano was purchased on the installment plan, and the three-teacher faculty was enthusiastic.[6]

Maybe Addicks HS. The same exact image also appears in a county report as Hillebrandt. It is likely that the same design was used from both. HHRC

As the years went on, high school students from both Cypress and Spring Branch attended Addicks High since their community schools were limited to only grades one through eight. In spite of the need, things did not always go smoothly in Addicks ISD. A school bond election in 1938 carried by five votes out of the 97 total votes cast, and opponents began a protracted court battle to overturn the verdict. Though almost certainly not related, the 28 Addicks High grads of 1941 had to receive their diplomas in the dark due to a power blackout.

The district finally gave up the ghost in 1948, and state funds were used to provide tuition and transportation for the pupils to attend school in Katy.[7]

ADDICKS SCHOOL

Most Houstonians today know Addicks as the name of a flood control reservoir just north of I-10, but it started life as a railroad stop near the older German community of Bear Creek. The names Latitia and Bear Hill were also used, but first postmaster Henry Addicks had the moniker that stuck. The town had its troubles, a smallpox epidemic in 1891, and almost total annihilation in the 1900 storm, yet it became the commercial center for the area's farmers and ranchers when the Missouri, Kansas and Texas Railroad placed a stop there in the early 1890s. With the railroad in place, locals no longer needed to overnight with friends or relatives in Spring Branch on their shopping trips into Houston.[8]

Other one room schoolhouses preceded the one at Addicks, which was in place as early as 1910. After disastrous Houston floods in 1929 and 1935, the Harris County Flood Control District was created, and one of the remedies to the problem was the creation of dams and reservoirs upstream on Buffalo Bayou, in what were then rural areas, to control the release of water into the city. Just after WWII, the roughly 200 residents of Addicks were relocated, and by 1947, forty homes and buildings had either been moved or destroyed as the original townsite of Addicks and her school ceased to exist. [9]

ADDICKS COLORED SCHOOL

The Addicks area, first as County District 10, then as an ISD, maintained a school for African American students for much of the first half of the 20th century. In the first decade of the century, it operated a six month term which was longer than many other rural Black schools.[10]

One-Room Schools

In 1912, Harris County schools were in the midst of a building boom, but there were still eighty-three one-room schoolhouses in operation, fifty-eight for Whites and twenty-five for African Americans. Superintendent Pugh was hoping that someday all common school districts could afford nice brick buildings with libraries and modern conveniences, but in the meantime, he offered a host of suggestions to make the wood frame one-room schools more palatable to teacher and student alike.[11]

He spoke of cleanliness to "place the children in the best mood and frame of mind." The one-room school was also a one-person operation, and it fell to the teacher to provide the janitorial services, as well. It was up to them to keep the building cheerful with tidy curtains and little touches such as flowers. Pugh also suggested enlisting the help of the students in sprucing up the place.

Outhouses did not go unmentioned. Some of the country schools' privies were filthy, he stated, and that "counteracts all the endeavors of the teacher to develop a finer taste for literature, music, etc." He added that "there is no reason why the outhouses in the country should not be kept as clean as in the city."

Within the week prior to the opening of school, Pugh commanded that each school ground should be mowed and cleaned. There was even a $50 prize offered for the best school grounds in the county with the money to be spent on adding to the school library.

"Think for one moment of a boy full of life and vigor who has been roaming the prairies and the green pastures, wading the streams, and picking the flowers of the summer, entering into a school building in September with barren walls and with school grounds barren and unsightly," he wrote. "Do you then wonder why many boys and girls have dropped out of school never to return again?"

Lighting and ventilation were of vital importance. "On account of poor light in the one-room schools many of our former pupils are wearing glasses today," he opined, and "stupifying foul air has ruined the health of many pupils." One culprit was uneven heat in the winter caused by the wood burning stoves.

Pugh laid out a list of equipment that was needed to make the one-room school an efficient place to learn. He suggested bookcases and a well-selected library both for school and home loan, at least three levels of dictionaries, a good globe, wall maps and pleasant pictures as well as "crayons, erasers, broom, fire shovel, wash basin and waste basket... Pint, quart and gallon measures" and a thermometer.

A good desk with locking drawers for the teacher was a must, and desks of all sizes for the children. He noted that "Pupils are sometimes cramped in seats that are too small, or so high that their feet dangle, and the pupil is made nervous, restless and unfitted for study."

Lastly, Pugh called for an ample length of Blackboard "so explanations can be given by the teacher so that all can understand."[12]

ADLONG SCHOOL

The Adlong School was at the southwest corner of what is today Highway 90 and the Adlong School Road near the T&NO rail line. It was opened about 1907 and served as an intermediate school in County District 17 until it, along with Gum Gully and Krenek, was consolidated into Crosby in September 1925.[13]

ALAMO E S

Alamo School opened at 207 E. 27th and Courtlandt in 1927, sharing grounds just east of the older Sunset Heights School which had been built by Harris County District 25. That district was later incorporated into HISD at the urging of its trustee Thomas H. Dixon. When the new eight classroom building and a lunch-play-room were constructed with roughly $75,000 from the bond election of 1926, the entire campus was renamed Alamo Elementary. HISD sold the property, which had been used solely as a maintenance yard for well over a decade, in 2010, in spite of several energetic attempts to preserve and repurpose the historic buildings.[14]

Alamo School. HISD

ALAMO E S, BAYTOWN

The Alamo School at 6100 North Main in Baytown opened in 1930 and received additions and remodeling in 1937 when it had grown to 16 classrooms, then more work was done in 1956, 1969, and 1979 before moving to a new building.[15]

ALAMO SCHOOL, SHELDON

See Sheldon School

ALDINE SCHOOL

The town of Aldine started life as a railroad stop called Prairie Switch, getting a post office under the name of Aldine 23 years later, in 1896. True development began around the turn of the century with many out-of-staters moving south to farm satsumas or figs, choices that later gave way to vegetables or dairy cattle. School was held first in a small one-room structure that doubled as a community building, then a two-room frame school was built by County District 29 on Aldine-Bender Road about 1910 to handle grades one through seven. It continued to be used even after consolidation of four small schoolhouses and the formation of Aldine ISD in the 1930s, and was moved to the site of the new school near the corner of Aldine-Bender and Aldine-Westfield to be used for the primary grades. The old two-room building burned in November 1948.[16]

ALDINE E S

After their three-year-old high school became overcrowded enough to necessitate building a new one, the 1933 building in Aldine was converted to an elementary school. It sat on the big plot at the corner of Aldine-Bender and Aldine-Westfield Roads. The school was later used as an alternative education center and in 2017 was operating as the Ellen Lane School.[17]

Children line up at Aldine School. HCPL

ALDINE H S

When County District 29 voted to consolidate all of its White schools into a centralized campus in 1932, the plan was to offer grades one through nine. Prior to that, Aldine area students who wanted more education, something not compulsory in Texas past age 14 at the time, had to commute to Jeff Davis High in Houston. The high school opened in February 1933 at Aldine-Westfield and Aldine-Bender and was immediately at capacity. One year later, grades 10 and 11 were added. That same year, the school was named in honor of the recently deceased S.M.N. Marrs, a former state education official. Overcrowding caused the auditorium to be divided into three classrooms and the old wooden school to be moved in for relief, as well.[18]

After the district reorganized as Aldine ISD in 1935, a bond was passed to build a new 10-room junior/senior high building next door, and the Marrs name moved with it. For a while, the Marrs name was attached to both the elementary and the new high school. A separate gymnasium/auditorium was also constructed, and in 1939, a six-room wing was added. By 1948, yet another new high school rose at the complex, this time named Aldine High, and the 1936 Marrs building became the junior high school.

By that time the scholastic population at Aldine had grown more than 800 percent since consolidation, a fact that was getting press around the state. Months later, on the day of the Homecoming Dance in November 1948, the wooden gym and the old wooden school burned to the ground. An even more serious fire, six alarms, struck six Novembers later when the 1948 main high school was destroyed. After attending classes in the junior high on a split shift, the Mustangs moved to yet another Aldine High in 1956, this time at Airline and West Road, and the previous high school site was given permanently to the junior high.[19]

ALEXANDER SCHOOL

See Brunner School

ALIEF SCHOOL

The small community of Dairy opened a two-room school in District 10 in 1896 on farmer Nancy Elizabeth Lloyd's property. By 1910, the district was busy enough to warrant separation, and County District 46 was established, replaced by Dairy ISD seven years later. Months after that, the town and school district were renamed to honor its first postmistress, Alief Ozelda Magee, and the following year, a new multi-story brick schoolhouse with basement opened, celebrated with homemade ice cream in the new auditorium on the top floor. The cornerstone and some of the original brick were reused in a new gym at 7th and H Streets about 1940. In 1947, a merger between the adjacent Alief and Addicks districts was proposed, but voters in both areas overwhelmingly voted no. In Alief the count was 37 to 6 against. It meant the senior high students from Alief would continue to travel to either Missouri City or Sugar Land for their schooling.[20]

Boarding Rural Teachers

Harris County School Superintendent L.L. Pugh felt that the county was having a teacher crisis in 1912. Though Houston was a thriving city, and booming oil fields in Humble and Goose Creek had brought an era of virtually unprecedented prosperity to the county, teachers were leaving their positions, lured away by the bright lights of the nearby big city.

"Because they were not able to get a boarding place, two or three teachers gave up their schools," Pugh wrote in the annual report. "Fifteen teachers in the rural schools told me that they had trouble in getting boarding places. This very difficulty causes many a teacher to accept a position in the city at the first opportunity that presents itself. Certain it is, that if the drain of the best blood from the country schools is not to be greater than less, the best families living in the country must consent to board the teacher. The patrons must feel that it is just as much their duty, if they can conscientiously do so, to board the teacher as it is to pay taxes for the support of the school."[21]

Boarding a teacher in a local home was a time honored tradition in America, and that included the area around Houston. Dilue Rose Harris wrote of a teacher coming to her community at present day Stafford in Fort Bend County to start school in June 1835 and "boarding around among the neighbors."[22]

Pugh outlined the problem well: "To find a desirable boarding place in a home where a teacher may have a warm room for herself for study and work, is a very difficult thing, nevertheless it is important. Unless patrons do their duty in this respect, it will become more and more difficult to get teachers of culture and refinement to teach in the country schools."

Part of the reason it was so difficult to consistently find good lodging was the simple question of which families were willing to have a semi-permanent house guest. Josephine Preston might have been in Washington state, but the issue was the same there as in rural Harris County. "The farmer whose home would have been pleasant did not need the money paid for board," she wrote. "The places where the board money was welcome were usually the least attractive in the district."[23]

In places much more remote than Harris County, the problem was acute. A report describing the situation in Arizona in 1917, told of teachers placed in tents, lean-tos and storage buildings. Locally, the common problems were less dire, including large families and no privacy, rooms with no heat, poor food, no room for guests.

One solution came along with the concept of rural school consolidation that was sweeping the nation after 1900 as a means to compete against an exodus from rural to urban areas. One of the reasons people were moving was to give their children access to better schools, and upgraded, consolidated rural schools was thought to be the way to combat that part of the problem. The features that became big selling points in the consolidated schools included gymnasiums, greenhouses and, especially, indoor plumbing, a luxury not found on most farms.

Hand in hand with some of the upgraded rural schools was the teacherage. It was an idea that seems to have been born in Hall County, Nebraska in 1894. The school district would build its own lodging for the teachers. The one in Nebraska was nothing luxurious, a 22' x 28' frame building with seven rooms for teachers plus a screen porch for relaxation. But the teacherage gave dignity and independence to the teachers, and they were financially viable because, in many places, the rent was deducted from or at least offset a reduction in their pay.[24]

The idea was embraced wholeheartedly in Texas. A Department of the Interior study in 1922 reported about 3,000 teacherages across America, and Texas had more than any other state. One reason for that popularity was the preponderance of tenant farmers, who were thought to have a lesser stake in improving the community. Almost half the farms in the U.S. were operated by tenants as opposed to land owners, and the percentage was highest in southern states like Texas.

The newly-built teacherage at Dairy. HHRC

Some Harris County school districts such as Dairy (later to become Alief) and Humble built teacherages to house the single women who taught at their schools. The one in Humble was located in the middle of the several school buildings in town, and the one at Dairy was located behind the school on the prairie.

Clearly there were some local school board folks who were as high on the concept as Josephine Preston in far off Washington when she wrote: "Every teacher must have good wholesome food in order to supply her body with mental and physical energy, and must have congenial quarters in which to prepare and recuperate for the next day's work. Otherwise she cannot hope to develop or maintain her highest efficiency."[25]

ALL SAINTS SCHOOL

This parish school, at the north end of the All Saints Church property at Harvard and 10th in Houston Heights, was in operation from 1913 when it opened in a small two-room structure. The parish, founded in 1909, built a new two-story, grey brick school that was dedicated by the bishop in 1922. Though the All Saints School closed in 1986, the old building is still in use by the church.[26]

All Saints in the 21st Century. Mike Vance photo

ALLEN, CHARLOTTE E S

When Jesse Jones donated a full block of land in his new real estate development in the growing South End of Houston in 1906, Superintendent Horn wrote that "His liberality ought to be commended to the citizens of Houston as an object of emulation. The Houston Schools have not heretofore fared as well in the matter of gifts from citizens of their home city as have the schools of Galveston, San Antonio and some other cities of our State." The resulting school was named in honor of Charlotte Baldwin Allen, the wife of one of the city's founding brothers and a woman who called the city home for almost all of its first 60 years.[27]

The brick building was twelve rooms for grades one through seven, and had two stories plus the basement. From the start it included one of the city schools' first kindergartens, this one maintained by the Parent-Teacher

Association. In charge of the school was principal Lila Baugh, a veteran teacher who had been at Fannin Elementary. When she took the job at Allen in March 1907, she was the first woman principal in a multi-room school in the city, a school that was also the first named after a woman. She remained there for 18 years before leaving for the Texas College of Fine Arts in Kingsville.[28]

Charlotte Allen was in a well-to-do, new neighborhood for its early years, and the school with neat grounds and ivy covered walls had programs to match including one of two, along with Dow, student run savings banks in which children could deposit their own money. Ms. Baugh also encouraged students to be active in athletics, and in 1916, 90% of all pupils above first grade were "enrolled on some one or more of the teams taking part in athletic work. The effort is not so much to win games from other schools, but to encourage games among the numerous teams at the same school."[29]

Children wearing white for Mayfete march out of Charlotte Allen School. HHRC.

In 1956, with a demographic change that the school board deemed undesirable, the Charlotte Allen name was moved to a White school at 400 Victoria Street on the northwest side. The building at Charlotte Allen briefly became an annex campus for an overcrowded Yates High School and then became Will Jones, a segregated Black school. Eventually the 1907 building gave way to a new one. Today the site adjacent the 288 Freeway holds an HISD charter school called the Houston Academy for International Studies.[30]

Prayer and Religion in Public Schools

Three U.S. Supreme Court rulings in the early 1960s affirmed that prayer in public schools violated the establishment clause of the Constitution and was coercing some religious minority students to take part in religious rituals in which they did not believe. The court was then consistent in that stance for half a century while protecting private religious expression. That was far from the first time related issues had appeared, however.[31]

Though there was never any wholesale attempt to insert religion into public schools until very recently, lines were sometimes blurry enough to provoke a small outcry. Superintendent Horn reported on one legal challenge in 1908: "It is not amiss to say, in passing, that our schools are making at least an earnest effort to train our pupils along moral lines as well as mentally and physically. For quite a number of years back, it has been a requirement in the Houston schools that the exercises of the day be opened in every room with Scripture reading. The Supreme Court of our State has, within the last few months, decided a hard-fought case, to the effect, that there is nothing in the Constitution or statutes of our State to forbid such Scripture reading." The results of that ruling did not necessarily translate to the curriculum, however. At the in-service meeting in September 1915, longtime rural Harris County teacher L.D. Washington "made a plea for the teaching of religion and morality." No changes were announced.[32]

There was a later experiment during the 1921-22 school year at the city's Charlotte Allen School that allowed students to be excused on Fridays at 1:00 PM to be "sent under proper supervision to the church of their choice, to be given religious instruction" if their parents desired it. The students lost one lesson per month in each subject at Allen. Just over half the students in school took advantage of the program. Denominations noted were Methodist, Baptist, Presbyterian, and Church of Christ.[33]

In 1934, the Houston Ministerial Alliance, which included five clergymen of Lutheran, Catholic, Jewish, Baptist, and Presbyterian faiths, urged creation of a for-credit Bible course that in which any material that provoked "denominational difference of opinion" would be excluded. The men pointed out that Dallas had such a course. HISD declined.[34]

The United States Supreme Court finally weighed in on the issue in 1948 with their ruling in McCollum V. Board of Education. It was an Illinois case, and the court's decision put a stop to religious instruction being required in public schools on the grounds that it was the use of taxpayer funded institutions to spread particular religious faiths.[35]

ALMEDA E S

The town of Almeda was the product of Illinois land investors who marketed the place as a model community for citrus farming in 1892. A couple of unusually hard freezes started it along the path to being a dairy community instead, but the new settlers needed a school either way. They started one in 1893, placing it in a barn and allegedly having students use hay bales as desks. Roughly a year later, a one room building was constructed.[36]

As the town grew, the school was improved with the digging of a well, a coat of paint, and a new fence, but the County District 36 trustees knew they needed a larger building. In 1914, J.C. Hooper sold a generous parcel of land in the town to the school district for one dollar with the provision that "at least one and a half acres of said land shall be used as experimental grounds for the pupils attending said school for the purpose of training them in the best methods of growing the crops suitable to the country."[37]

Almeda School in 21st century. Laurie Feinswog photo.

The Almeda school was annexed to HISD by popular vote in the district in May 1937, and the town became part of the city in 1959. A new Almeda Elementary school was built around the corner at 14249 Bridgeport in 1981.[38]

ALMEDA COLORED SCHOOL

The town of Almeda also had a school for African American children beginning toward the end of the 19th century. It was still operating with a single teacher, Louise Shanklin, in the middle of WWII.[39]

ANNUNCIATION SCHOOL

The Sisters of the Incarnate Word and Blessed Sacrament had started the Incarnate Word Academy for girls on the ground of the shining, new Annunciation Church in 1878, but the boys of Houston's major parish needed education, too. The first effort by Fr. Quaret focused on preparing the boys for First Communion and Confirmation, and it was briefly disbanded about 1880. The Incarnate Word Sisters soon opened a full school for the parish boys in a frame building on the Annunciation church grounds, with the first graduating ceremony held in 1885. A brick edifice replaced the wooden one in 1903, and in 1910, the parish took over responsibility for the cost of the four-classroom school. They allowed girls for the first time in 1916. By the post-WWII years, the school was enrolling about 250 students a year from first through eighth grades. It closed in 1983, and the building was demolished in 1997 by the nuns who owned it.[40]

ARNOLD SCHOOL

Arnold was a small and short-lived school in the well populated County District 25, appearing in district records in the latter part of the 1890s. its name comes from Mose M. Arnold from whom the school house was rented for eight dollars a month.[41]

ASSUMPTION SCHOOL

The school for Assumption Parish, on the north side near Little York and Airline, was opened in 1948 by the Dominican Sisters and operated only until 1969 before closing. The parish itself dates to the late 1800s and a group of Sicilian immigrant families. The first church building was constructed in 1915. The parish later reopened the Assumption School, and it still operates today.[42]

ATHERTON E S

Chew School, for African American children in the northeastern part of Fifth Ward started as part of County District 25 prior to 1915. It was located just south of Grumbach Street off Cushing where today there is a nearby street called Chew. The building had two rooms and was brick as early as WWI. Annexation by the city brought Chew into Houston schools by about 1920, and later that decade, a new Chew was opened at 2010 Schweikert with a campus running all the way east to Solo Street. Soon after, Chew School was renamed in honor of Charles Atherton, the Jamaica-born educator who had served as the first principal of Colored High School from 1892-1912.[43]

A new 15-room building was constructed in 1935. A decade later, the school petitioned the HISD board for 10 new classrooms along with a cafeteria and auditorium. Those additions came in 1950. Generations of Fifth Ward children attended Atherton including the late, longtime Harris County Commissioner El Franco Lee who once punched his third grade classmate George Foreman and emerged unscathed.[44]

AUSTIN E S

Stephen F. Austin is the Father of American settlement in Texas, so it is not surprising that his name graced a Houston school prior to the famous East End high school that Houstonians know today. The elementary school of that name was a brick and stone building with tremendous personality, on a half block facing St. Emanuel at the northwest corner of its intersection with McKinney. The cornerstone was laid on Washington's Birthday 1902 in what was a decent residential area with various business operations sprinkled in. Given its proximity to Houston largest synagogue, there was a significant Jewish student population in the early years including children of well-known retail merchants such as the Battlesteins.[45]

A remarkably artistic photo of a classroom at Austin ES. Leeman photo

Austin School received a brick addition of four rooms to bring the total classrooms to 12 barely a year after it opened. In 1926, then up to 17 rooms, it was rehabbed inside and out. Changing surroundings finally doomed Austin Elementary in the early 1950s, and the school was demolished and the property sold in February 1963.[46]

AUSTIN H S

Ten-year-old Milby High School was in need of relief by 1937, and that came in the form of the new three-story, red-brick Stephen F. Austin High that opened on 13 acres at Dumble and Jefferson in September 1937 with funding help from the federal government's Public Works Administration. It opened with 44 classrooms, an auditorium, cafeteria, gymnasium, swimming pool, library, science labs, industrial arts shops, sewing, cooking, and home economics rooms. The architects were Maurice Sullivan, Birdsall Briscoe, and Sam Dixon who had collaborated before including on the Petroleum Building downtown.[47]

George Loescher was the first principal at Austin, serving until his death in 1949. He oversaw a thriving school with 224 graduates the first year. The Mustangs even had a live pony mascot named Stevie, and a 120-girl drill team called the Scottish Brigade who raised money to buy a uniform of green coats, plaid pleated skirts, white leggings, hats with a green feather, and bagpipes imported from Scotland.

Like all Houston high schools, Austin students and faculty were heavily affected by WWII with 639 serving and 45 former students killed during the war. The students bought stamps and bonds to purchase three jeeps for the war effort. Today a display at the school honors the 65 Austin grads who have died serving the country in WWII, Korea, Vietnam, and the Middle East.[48]

Austin HS gates in the 21st century. Laurie Feinswog photo

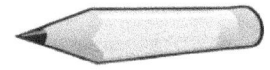

Swimming Pools

Though upkeep and liability ended the practice, most of the White high schools and junior highs in Houston ISD had indoor swimming pools for many years. Some still exist. Others such as an early one at Marshall Middle School, opened as North Side Junior High in 1913, have long since been filled in. The pool at Marshall sits underneath a parking lot.

South End Junior High, which later became San Jacinto High School, had the first such pool in town. It opened when the school did in 1913 and quickly became "a never failing attraction," making the school a social center. The North Side JHS pool, was delayed a few years, but soon served the same purpose.[49]

There were a handful of public swimming options available in town prior to the school pools. The most famous today is the Heights Natatorium that sat a few blocks east of Heights Boulevard on the north side of White Oak Bayou. Most youngsters swam in the cleaner portions of the bayous.[50]

By the late 1930s, there were HISD pools at Sam Houston, Reagan, Davis, Milby, San Jacinto, Austin, and Lamar high schools and at the new wave of junior high schools - Johnston, Jackson, Hogg, Deady, Hamilton, George Washington, and Lanier. They were declared by the district's head physician to be "scientifically constructed and sterile at all times." Pool water was tested every Tuesday and Friday.[51]

The HISD swimming pools were the envy of many. In March 1932, with another hot and un-air-conditioned summer approaching, the student newspaper at Rice Institute ran photos of the women's pool at UT Austin along with an editorial lamenting that "every high school in Houston has a swimming pool of some kind – what is holding Rice behind?"[52]

One custom at the indoor pools would be thought unbelievable today. Boys were made to swim naked. Not surprisingly, girls wore bathing suits. It was policy at high schools and junior highs. When a 21st century *Houston Chronicle* reporter started asking around to see if others had shared his experience, the response was a universal yes. From Johnston, Burbank, Reagan, Cullen, San Jacinto High and elsewhere, men who had grown up in Houston reported that swim time in P.E. was always sans suit. When the policy started in 1913, many Houston youths were undoubtedly accustomed to spending summers at swimming holes along the city's bayous, so raised eyebrows were likely rare. As one interviewee for the article put it: "Never thought anything about it really."[53]

The stated reason was the same nationwide: "fibers clogging the drain." Why that applied to boys' suits and not girls' was unclear to some, but the practice did indeed stem from a day when bathing costumes were made from wool, and the loose fibers played havoc on pool filters. In the early days of pools, many Americans did not even own bathing suits. At pools and seaside bathhouses, wool swim outfits, covering top and bottom, were most often rented. Thus, the idea of boys swimming and taking lifesaving classes in the buff began from a combination of wool fibers and an actual lack of swimsuits in many areas. It persisted in Houston schools for over four decades. The practice ended in the mid-1960s, and boys were allowed to swim covered.

Girls at one time all wore school issued one-piece grey woolen swimsuits with a bathing cap. One student who learned to swim at the Edison Junior High pool during the WWII years, remembers that the suits stretched when they got wet. "So, we would always (get) things to tie our straps together, or big safety pins to pin them together." she said.[54]

The school policy was not even an issue for Houston's African Americans because they simply were not allowed. Houston's Black citizens did not have the luxury of a school swimming pool. There were only a few pay options available such as the "refreshing" pool at Boynton M.E. Church on Dallas Street at Paige.[55]

The *Informer* noted that year after year, when school swimming pools opened for their White neighbors each summer, Black Houstonians were left to swelter.

"When we read about the opening of the swimming pools for the summer months at Johnston and Jackson and Lanier schools, we wonder why it was thought that there was no need for at least one swimming pool in a Negro school," the editor wrote. "It would seem to the *Informer* that the conceivable reasons why swimming pools might be desirable in White schools would almost make a swimming pool for the Negro schools a necessity. We need water, too."[56]

AUSTIN STREET SCHOOL

See Longfellow

AUTRY MEMORIAL HOSPITAL SCHOOL

James Lockhart Autry, Jr., a Mississippian who served as general counsel for the Texas Company, later Texaco, was the grandson of a slain Alamo defender and son of a Confederate officer who was killed in action when James, Jr. was only three. When he died in 1920, he was followed in death only two years later by his son who also shared the same name. Autry, Jr.'s widow, Allie, donated handsomely to Rice Institute where her son had been a prominent student. Three years later, she gifted the city a school on the capacious grounds of the Houston Tuberculosis Hospital which ran from the northeast corner of today's West Dallas and Sheperd down the incline toward today's Allen Parkway. It was a memorial to her husband and son. With a capacity that increased to 50, the children had school from eight in the morning until two in the afternoon with rest periods interspersed. The curriculum was that of HISD who ran the school, so that when they were cured, they could seamlessly return to another school in the city. The TB Hospital closed shortly after WWII when improved medication overtook the need for quiet isolation of patients. Today a large Hanover Company development occupies the site.[57]

Special Needs Children

Prior to 1915, hearing-impaired Houston area children were largely out of luck when it came to special instruction in local public schools. There was not much technological assistance to be found, either. For those who retained partial hearing, there was at least something. The first electric hearing aids, building on technology from the telephone, were invented in 1898, and widespread manufacture began only a year or two prior to the 1915 date. Early models used a carbon transmitter to strengthen the sound signal coming to a person's ears, but there was also a heavy unit larger than a cigar box that must be carried around.[58]

One of the reasons why the Houston school board had not acted to give special instruction to these children sooner was apparently financial. "Instruction for this class will necessarily be much more expensive than for normal children, on account of the much smaller number of children whom one teacher can instruct." Superintendent Horn wrote. "It is considered that eight or ten deaf and dumb children are as many as one teacher can profitably instruct in one class. Nevertheless, the greater need of these children unquestionably justifies the greater expenditure which we are proposing to make upon them."[59]

Though American Sign Language dated to Dr. Thomas Gallaudet in the early 1800s, that was not the path of instruction chosen in Houston. Horn's report summarized the board's thoughts: "These children are to be taught by the oral method, as opposed to the finger alphabet plan. This means that instead of being taught to communicate with their fingers they are to be taught to read the lips of people speaking to them, and to reply by words formed with their own vocal organs. This method is used in practically all places where deaf and dumb children are taught in public day schools. Instead of limiting the communication of the deaf and dumb children to other who are similarly afflicted, it brings them in touch with people of the speaking and hearing world."

Rusk Elementary offered the first instruction for special needs students in 1908 with an ungraded class. There were 19 students admitted, all labeled as "sub-normal." Two years later, a small ungraded class was added at Dow with one delinquent, one blind pupil, one non-English speaker, and one "bright" student "who disliked school."[60]

By 1916, Rusk School, the district's model of cutting edge education and social work, had classes for young "deaf and dumb students." Five years later, the district had a small department for these pupils of whom there were thirteen enrolled in elementary grades levels. All were being taught lip reading along with language and math work as well as "handwork" that included basketry, needlework, and manual training. The youngest children were also taught "corrective speech." Though "larger children (were) taught the regular school branches," there also seemed to be an assumption that a normal career would not be in their future. The department's purpose was stated "to prepare these children for the High School and to prepare them to earn a living if necessary."[61]

Mothers' Clubs actively sought new pupils for the deaf and dumb department. In 1922, there was one new recruit coming, and the women were working with specialists to identify new children who might benefit. The report even named individuals who had prospered under the new program: "One pupil, John M. Arendale, is now attending the Junior High School. One pupil, Mabel Reverie, took typewriting in the night school and is prepared to do copying nicely. One, Sarah Kaldrhen, is attending the public schools in Kingsville."[62]

In the fall of 1924, Dr. T.O. Woolley, the Supervisor of Hygiene for Houston schools, returned from the American Public Health Association convention with news that the organization was calling for "special classes for crippled, blind and defective children in all schools."[63]

Schools B

BAKER'S SCHOOL

In the late 1880s, Houston's Baker Street ran for a few blocks through George Baker's land, part of the old Sam Houston Ranch, along San Felipe Road in Fourth Ward. Baker owned a fair sized parcel of land in the area and was involved in the early cattle business that operated there, just west of town, later branching into other businesses. Two schools in the area, served by County District 23, were named Baker, one White and one Black, and the district bore that name from the mid-1880s until the turn of the century.[1]

BAKER'S COLORED SCHOOL

See Green Pond

BANE E S

The Fairbanks Community sprouted on a patch of prairie that was so populated with sweet gum trees to be known to the railroad men who worked the Houston & Texas Central tracks as Gum Island. Under that earlier name, it was singled out to be part of School District 17 under the new law in 1854, but there is no evidence yet located to suggest that the school was built at that time. The tracks did reach there by 1856. Sporting the moniker of Fairbanks, there was a post office by 1895, and shortly thereafter, a small school that sat next to the railroad tracks. The school became one of seven, five White and two Black, in thriving County District 10, but it was plagued with misfortune where buildings were concerned. The major hurricanes in 1900 and 1915 each destroyed the Fairbanks schoolhouse, and there were long intervals of classes held in a church or a private home.[2]

J.F. Bane was involved as a school trustee prior to WWI, and in 1924, he worked a deal to swap the undesirable little plot by the tracks for a larger parcel near the modern intersection of Tidwell and Little York, just inside the Beltway. In 1936, the district built a new, larger school, adding a cafeteria a few years later. The old one-room schoolhouse was moved to the Carverdale area for the district's Black students. At the outbreak of WWII there were just over 200 pupils at Fairbanks in a building that had electricity, wood burning heat and no telephone. More rooms were added post-war, and the building was replaced with a new one in 1959 and again a few decades later. The name was changed to honor its benefactor J.F. Bane when the 1959 structure opened.[3]

BANMAN'S SCHOOL HOUSE

Banman's School House is referenced as being roughly in the Harrisburg area in 1892.[4]

BAPTIST HILL SCHOOL

Baptist Hill is listed in 1910 County Report in District 4 with Etta as an African American primary school with one teacher.

BARKER SCHOOL

The town of Barker sat about 17 miles west of Houston where Barker-Cypress Road meets I-10 today. At the start of the 20th century, the 80 or so residents there operated a store, inn, brick factory, twine mill, two churches, a depot, saloon, and a school in District 10 that sat perhaps a quarter mile south of the MKT tracks. The one-room school moved to another spot within the town area about 1911 but continued to operate at least through 1915. The Marks Family who had the LH7 Ranch in the area recalled walking three miles to Addicks for schooling after Barker closed.[5]

BARNETT SCHOOL

Professor W.W. Barnett, a native of Bowling Green, Kentucky, had taught at both University of Texas and Baylor and put in four years as superintendent of Houston Public Schools, emerging on top after a legal debacle that saw two rival school boards in the city, one elected (Barnett's) and one appointed.

He opened his own private prep institution at 1315 Main in 1904. The Barnett School and its rather large faculty offered primary, junior, and senior departments at tuition of five to ten dollars a month and instrumental music instruction at $1.50 per lesson. Boarding was also available. Extra activities ranged from an orchestra to a baseball team. When students graduated, they were deemed ready for "any college or university."[6]

Students at the Barnett School came from many of the city's most prominent families. The first graduate was Gladys Hildegarde Bering in 1906, and she was followed over the next few years by students including future attorney and judge St. John Garwood, J.J. Settegast, Louis Stude, and future Harris County District Attorney O'Brien Stevens, who debated at the school against abolishing college football in the U.S..[7]

Barnett's charges had daily recitations of up to forty minutes for senior pupils, along with home study. Class size averaged about 16, and their moral training was designed to develop their best character and hone their study habits. "Going to entertainments on school nights was forbidden and tardiness was pronounced ruinous."

The school moved to Walker Street between Louisiana and Milam in 1907. Professor Barnett died at the end of 1914 and was buried at Glenwood Cemetery on New Year's Eve. The final classes for his school were held the following June.[8]

BARRETT SCHOOL

The area around Crosby supported an African American school at least from the middle 1880s, pre-dating the White school in the town itself. It operated at the Shiloh Baptist Church next to the home of the Barrett family. The patriarch was Harrison Barrett, who settled a freedom colony two miles southwest of Crosby on modern US Highway 90. Barrett had been born into slavery, but saved enough money after Emancipation to purchase a large amount of acreage in 1889. The community had almost certainly already been living on the land during Reconstruction. In addition to houses, there was eventually a sawmill, grist mill, and other mercantile operations near the church/school.[9]

At least part of the time, the Barrett School was receiving funding from Huffman Colored School which indicated those few students were being sent to Crosby. A county report in 1907 listed only one Black school in district 17, a "box structure" that needed new furniture.[10]

Around 1910, a two-room frame school was built on the Barrett property. It was followed by seven expansions, with the early ones, just after WWII, coinciding with the other Crosby area Black schools being folded into Barrett, a school that ran all the way through high school by that time. One of the additions used material from dismantled barracks at Camp Wallace in Hitchcock. In 1949, Barrett School officially graduated its first 12th grade class. One year later, the campus was renamed for Charles R. Drew, an African American doctor best known for his pioneering work in blood transfusions.[11]

BARRICK E S

Barrick Elementary at 12001 Winfrey Lane opened in March 1949 bearing the name of the one-time principal of nearby Burbank Elementary for which Barrick was to relieve overcrowding. It was a six-room white frame building on ten acres of land donated by the Alber family for whom the road in front of it was originally named. It later received an 18-room brick addition.[12]

Barrick ES in 1950. Mike Vance Collection

Teacher Shortage in 1948

"Houston's elementary school children don't always get the kind of teaching they should. School officials, particularly those working in the elementary section, know that some first, second, and third graders get off on the wrong foot. The fault, however, does not lie within the Houston school system, they say. It lies within the shortage of trained elementary school teachers. They say the shortage seems to be getting worse instead of better.

"'What happens when teachers who are not trained for this type of work are given elementary school assignments?" Mrs. Jewel Askew, director of elementary schools, asked. "We have emotionally maladjusted, frustrated children, and many unhappy teachers who quit the profession before they learn how to teach," she said.

Texas' inadequate certification laws are at the root of the trouble, N.K. Dupre, assistant superintendent in charge of elementary schools, believes. Behind the law is the mistaken belief that anybody can teach in an elementary school, he said.

"The old idea that anyone can teach grades one through six is a foolish one," Mrs. Askew said. The most technical teaching that is done in the entire school is done in the primary grades. Can just anyone teach a child to play a musical instrument? No. Neither can just anyone teach a child to read."

Texas teachers are up in arms about the certification laws of Texas. One point in the legislative program of the Texas State Teachers' Association calls for a change in them. Teachers say several things are the matter.

First, elementary teaching certificates are issued only at state teachers' colleges. An education student at the University of Houston or the University of Texas can get only a general or high school teachers' certificate. He cannot get an elementary certificate.

Second, a teacher who has a high school teaching certificate can teach in elementary school, even though she has not specialized or even studied elementary education.

"These young teachers who come to us by the hundreds with high school qualifications are in no sense of the word prepared to teach an elementary school child," Mrs. Askew said. "They are potentially good teachers, for they are very intelligent, most of them are willing to learn and a very large percentage of them make good teachers after they have had two or three years' help."

Here are the facts about teachers in Houston's elementary schools:

Approximately half of them are teaching without elementary school certificates.

Most of them are seasoned teachers by now and doing a good job.

But, Mrs. Askew said, a new crop comes every year, unfamiliar with elementary education, willing to learn, but having to be taught by in-service programs while they are teaching the children. This year, approximately 15 new teachers were hired as elementary teachers who did not have elementary school certificates.

"The colleges aren't turning them out," Mr. Dupre said. "The shortage of elementary teachers is acute over the state. It is much better in Houston because we pay elementary teachers the same as high school teachers." [13]

BARRON SCHOOL

Samuel Barron, who moved to Houston at the age of 52 in the year of its founding, operated a school on German Street, approximately 2204 Canal Street today, in the years prior to the Civil War. That area of Second Ward was one of the more genteel portions of the city at the time, and many of the top families including the Lubbocks, Useners, Ennises, Supers, Fergusons, and Lockharts sent their children to his private school where all grades studied and recited in one room. His granddaughter, Addie Barron, related years later that lunchtime was signaled by a "bell from a nearby plantation sounded, telling the slaves that dinner was ready." The students lunched under a sycamore tree, and others went home to eat. To counteract academic pursuits such as spelling contests, pupils spent the lunch hour playing "games such as bull's eye, jump the rope, and Indian."[14]

BASTIAN E S

Mamie Sue Bastian spent 46 years with HISD as teacher and principal. In 1950, her decades of service were honored by her name being placed on a new school at 7350 Calhoun.[15]

BAUER SCHOOL

The Bauer School, misspelled on at least one map as Bowers, was not located in the area generally thought of as the Bauer Community. The latter was centered around the store and sawmill owned by a family of that name at the north end of modern day Bauer Road. Rather the school was on the Waller-Tomball Road just a short distance west of the town of Tomball. The school opened in the late 1880s, and by 1895, it was the lone school in its own County District 39. Bauer School remained in operation until 1931 when the building was moved to the Hufsmith School campus.[16]

BAYLAND ORPHANAGE

The Bayland Orphanage has one of the longest pedigrees in Harris County history. It opened in 1866, by San Jacinto Bay as the name indicates, for the children of Confederate soldiers. It eventually opened to other orphans as long as they were White and not "defective" or of bad character. Though run by a privately endowed board of directors, the home and school was listed as part of County District 17, and some county expenses were incurred. The first teacher was Rev. C.C. Preston, who had come from Louisiana to tutor the children of John L. Bryan of the small community of Bayland. Preston soon began teaching other children at a building next to the Harmony Grove Church before expanding his vision to include the war orphans.[17]

In 1888, it was moved from the mouth of Goose Creek to a house, with farm attached for the first decade, in what would later become Woodland Heights, and sat at the west end of Bayland Avenue as the neighborhood developed around it. The county portion of the operation, presumably the schooling expenses, were part of District 25. As a matter of policy by that time, children were not released from the orphanage unless they had been adopted. The matron selected for the first Houston location was Keziah DePelchin whose charity toward needy children was well known in the city, and whose name remains connected to the cause.

By 1908, with only 13 charges in the home, the board was looking for another locale. When the orphanage burned to the ground in 1914, a neighbor on Julian Street took the boys in before the home was removed to land donated by Joseph Meyer northwest of the new town of Bellaire. It would set off a rather confusing tangle that culminated in the 1920s with Harris County building a county home for girls on the site and the Bayland board taking back the boys operation. The Bayland Home once again ended up near the bay, this time on a farm near Clear Lake, entwined with the already existing Harris County School for Boys that was tasked with aiding delinquents. The private board dissolved in 1948, and the Bayland Home on Clear Lake closed four years later. The remaining boys were transferred to the Girl's School site back in Bellaire, and the name became Burnett-Bayland.[18]

BAYTOWN SCHOOL

See Wooster

BAYTOWN E S

Baytown Elementary was first mentioned in relation to a bond issue in 1922. The school was located on the north side of today's Bayway Drive west of the Market and Wisconsin Street Y. It was by far the largest elementary in GCCISD by the end of the 1930s with 22 classrooms. Today the property is part of the Exxon complex. Baytown Elementary closed in the 1950s, and students from the area began attending W. B. Travis Elementary.[19]

BAYTOWN J H S

Baytown Junior High School opened in 1929 on ten acres on what is today the south side of Bayway Drive just west of its split into Market and Wisconsin Streets. Another bond election later in the 1930s provided for a gym at the school, a building that was still standing on Exxon property in 2016. At that time there were 25 classrooms, and the school structure was appraised at $200,000. Baytown Junior High today, home of the Goslins, sits at 7707 Bayway, south of Decker Drive.[20]

BAY VIEW SCHOOL

Bay View School, located at Morgan's Point, was a seemingly short-lived educational outpost in County District 13. Originally it shared the district with Red Bluff and Middle Bayou. By the start of the 1892-93 school year, it was replaced on the expense ledger by a school just to the south in the new town of La Porte, and the Bay View schoolhouse was sold.[21]

BEAR CREEK SCHOOL

German immigrants settled the Bear Creek community in the 1850s, and shortly thereafter established a small school for their children. It was one of the original schools licensed by Harris County under the new public schools laws of 1876, overseen by trustees Fred Kobs, L. Koch and Ernst Graschke. The settlement hung onto its German roots, as did many similar communities in the north and west parts of the county. The Bear Creek German Methodist Church held services in that language until it became considered unpatriotic during WWI.[22]

Bear Creek School class. Marie Neuman Gray

Like many other county towns, the small schoolhouse at Bear Creek also served as community center and polling place. Over the remainder of the 19th century, the trustees were consistently German with surnames including Schultz, Weiman, and Hillendahl. The teachers they employed sometimes sported names such as Hilda Gray or Thomas Shannon that indicated they were hired from outside. [23]

BEAR CREEK COLORED SCHOOL

Though Bear Creek was a German community, there were enough African Americans living there by the mid-1880s to warrant a school for these children of former slaves. The school shows up in County District 10 with the White Bear Creek school for the 1886-87 term. The teacher was Martin Stewart, and he received but $19 a month, low pay even by the standard for Black teachers of the day.[24]

The situation was perhaps due to a very low population of school age children to attend. In 1889-90, there was no Black teacher in the district, and the children and the money for them were transferred to the Spring Branch Colored School in district 27. Hy Turpin taught at Bear Creek the following school year, remaining until 1894, but classes for the area's Black students ran only from March through May. The school continued into the 20th century and was eventually replaced, or at least renamed, as Addicks Colored School.[25]

BEAUCHAMP SPRINGS SCHOOL

See Travis ES

A picnic at Beeler School. HHRC

BEELER SCHOOL

Beeler was a one-teacher school in County District 10, along with Fairbanks.[26]

BELLAIRE SCHOOL

See Condit

The "old" Bellaire School that was later used as a residence. HHRC

BENDER H S

When the town school in Humble first added the final two high school grades to its curriculum in 1911, the inaugural graduating class consisted of three students, two of whom were twins. There were no more graduates until 1914, but Humble was one of only three Harris County schools that qualified as a full four-year high school. By 1917, County District 28 was ready for a separate high school building. They hired Oscar Holcombe to create the edifice on Higgins Street. He would soon abandon that line of work and run for Mayor of Houston, but his new Humble High opened in fall of 1918. It was placed on the lot next to the older Humble School that had the word Grammar added to its name at that time. Basking in the patriotism of WWI, the school adopted the motto "Impossible is Un-American." One year later the county districts around Humble were turned into the new Humble ISD. The legislative act had to be repeated in 1923 since language allowing for taxation was omitted.[27]

The red and white brick Humble Grammar School burned in January 1929, and the district replaced it with a new Harry Payne-designed high school named in honor of Charles Bender, still in the midst of the town's school complex. The 1918 high school became the elementary. The new Bender was a slightly smaller version of a building Payne had done in Baytown. By the time it had a few years under its belt in the late 1930s, the school boasted "12 classrooms, a library, office, gymnasium, cafeteria, electric clock, radio, 2 pianos, and an auditorium with a seating capacity of 525 and a projection booth and "a 35 mm movie projection machine." The built in cafeteria was still a rarity at the time.[28]

Bender HS in 1940. Humble Museum

Bender High closed after the 1965 graduation with a new Humble High School opening. The building was used as a junior high, also called Bender, until 1972 when it began service as administration offices for the district. It sat abandoned for decades until the city converted it into a beautiful performing arts center in 2015, and the old band hall became the Humble Museum five years later. Another interesting century-old feature remains. Several live oak trees stand along the street at the front of Bender, planted in honor of Humble area soldiers who died in WWI.[29]

*One of the WWI plaques outside Bender HS. Laurie Feinswog
photo*

BENDER SCHOOL

Bender School was a one room, one teacher building in what was numbered County District 21 in the late 1800s. Louis Bender was a trustee of the district and likely gave the school its name.[30]

BERRY SCHOOL

County District 25 opened Berry School in a "large, beautiful and up-to-date brick building" in the fall of 1910. It arose from a plan to combine the Farmer and McDonald schools on a plot of land donated by James Berry, Jr. and his brother Frank and named in honor of their father, who had fought in the Texas Revolution. There were four classrooms at the building on the Humble Road about a mile north of the HE&WT railroad tracks, but the 60 or 70 students utilized only two of them for the first two years. They were taught by Principal J.M. Synder and Miss Maud McDonald. There was also a library and an auditorium that held 200 people for school or neighborhood events including entertainments in which community members showcased their musical and literary talents.[31]

Growth of the neighborhood led to the opening of a new Berry Elementary at 2310 Berry Road in 1950. Though more modern than its predecessor, the school was un-air conditioned, though at least some former students have memories of a cafeteria with "real plates and real forks and real food." In 2011, a new energy efficient building was opened on the Berry Road campus to house the school which is a magnet for Environmental Science.[32]

School Kids' Special

The school children of Houston, accompanied by parents and teachers, plan to go to Sylvan Beach next Saturday, spend a day's outing at Sylvan Beach, view the Children's Assembly exhibit and scores of tents erected in the Chautauqua grounds to accommodate the campers attending present assembly and that of the BYPU beginning next Tuesday. They form an interesting great white tent city. In addition to the American Indian day program, the assembly exhibition of curios from foreign lands, miniature pianos, musical instruments, typewriters, dolls, World's Fair miniature buildings, and the baby alligator, a great day of pleasure has been planned for the children and others who attend the last day but one prior to moving the exhibit to St Louis. It will be the talk for weeks after its departure next Sunday night. Prof Co's orchestra will provide the music. Prof W W Barnett of Houston will, in course of his address, have something of interest to say to the school children of Houston. Parents, see that your children are there. Numerous amusements, such as Ferris wheel and merry-go-round are on the Pike, but this is the last week day of the grand exhibition of articles collected from around the world, collected at great expense for the children of Texas to view before sending them to St Louis. Swan, the great diver, will plunge head first into a tank of water using a 75-foot ladder from which to spring.

For this occasion, special trains with seats for all.

Large advertisement of the Southern Pacific Line.

Houston Post 17 June 1904

BETH YESHURUN DAY SCHOOL

The orthodox Jewish congregation Adath Yeshurun dates back to 1887 when it was founded as an orthodox alternative to the city's oldest synagogue that had switched to a reformed theology. Though a school is listed at 907 Jackson from 1912 until a mid-1940s merger with Congregation Beth El, the modern school dates its founding as 1949. It is possible that the earlier school was for religious instruction only.

BETHANY LUTHERAN SCHOOL

The Bethany Lutheran Church in Lindale operated this school at the southwest corner of Lazarus and Kings Avenue beginning in the 1930s. The Church closed in early 2016 and was taken over by Oikos Church.[33]

BIG CYPRESS SCHOOLHOUSE NO.2

Northwest Harris County has Cypress Creek and Little Cypress Creek, communities named Cypress and Little Cypress, and in the 19th century, it also had Little Cypress School #1 and Big Cypress School #2. The latter opened at the corner of Telge and Cypress-North Houston Roads in 1884 on land donated by Louis Telge in order to allow the school a place of its own, separate from the nearby church they has been borrowing. Though it was initially in District 7, the schools were in County District 6 by 1890, a fact confirmed not only by records but by the words emblazoned over the door: "Big Cypress School House No 2, Dist. 6."[34]

A second teacher was added at the school in 1920, and with consolidation, in the summer of 1932, two additional rooms were built using lumber taken from the recently shuttered Winkler and Sewell Schools. Among the teachers at Big Cypress was Ernestine Matzke who taught for 48 years, earning recognition by having her name placed on a Cy-Fair ISD elementary of her own.[35]

BINFORD SCHOOL

Binford School, in County District 33, was one of the most northwesterly schools in all of Harris County, sitting on today's FM 1488 north of Kickapoo Creek. It shows up in the county minutes as early as May 1891 when it was already a voting location, meaning that it was almost certainly in operation even earlier. The name comes from the Binford family who at first hosted the building on their property, then sold a one acre tract to District 33 "so long as they shall occupy and use the same for the purposes of a public school." It is possible that this school was the same as Grice which shows up over the same time period but seemingly not in the same years.[36]

BLACK'S PRAIRIE SCHOOL

County District 25 had more schoolhouses over the years than any other since it covered a more populated area of small farms and communities north and west of the Houston city limits. Black's Prairie was one of those close-in schools, showing up in 1886 when it shared a teacher with the North Houston school. The single-room, wood-heated school remained until around the turn of the century, located on the south side of Morris Street, which ran just north of Quitman, three blocks east of Gregg.[37]

BLACKSHEAR E S

By the time Edward Lavoisier Blackshear became the first principal of Emancipation Park School in the 2900 block of Holman in 1916, he had headed schools across Texas including eight years at the helm of Prairie View College. He lost that prestigious, appointed job when he backed a losing candidate for governor in 1914. The Houston schools had been eyeing a location near the park since 1906 to relieve the over-crowding at Douglass. When E.L. Blackshear died in 1919, the school was renamed in his honor.[38]

The single-story school, opened with six rooms, soon had several temporary buildings placed in its yard. By 1935, the bustling Third Ward campus boasted 23 rooms and over 1,000 students. Expansions and remodels continued in 1960, 1965 and 1980, erasing remnants of the 1916 original structure. Today it operates as a Montessori magnet campus.

Blackshear ES in 1950.

BLESSED SACRAMENT SCHOOL

Located where Grace dead ends into Sherman Street, between Drennan and Hunt behind the church, Blessed Sacrament School opened in April 1910, two years after the parish was created. Father J.B. Schnetzer, the first parish priest, went on to head all parish schools in the diocese starting in 1925. He invited the Sisters of the Incarnate Word to run the school which opened with four classrooms, a pastor's study, teacher's lounge, and second floor chapel. The school took over the original church when a new one was built in 1924 and more additions came four years later. Enrollment reached 400 in grades one through eight by the 1940s, but dwindled until the school closed in 1991.[39]

BLOCK'S POINT

See Black's Prairie

BONNER E S

B.F. Bonner, an officer with the Meadowbrook Development company, donated six and a half acres of land for a school in the new neighborhood in 1929, and asked that it be named after his mother, Melinda Bonner, who had been an advocate of education in East Texas. It was, though for a few years after its opening, it was called Meadowbrook Elementary. The small two room school was located on Park Avenue in the new addition with its 32 students and lone teacher in one room and 50 folding chairs and a piano in the other to be used as an auditorium. Roughly $14,000 was spent to construct the building and provide equipment. As the area became a populated suburb, a new building was constructed behind the original brick structure. Today Bonner Elementary at 8100 Elrod is home to over 1,000 students. [40]

The original Bonner ES building. HHRC

BORDERSVILLE SCHOOL

The African American Bordersville community, off today's FM 1960 just northeast of Bush Intercontinental Airport, sat near the boundary of the Aldine and Humble districts, and those entities passed fiscal responsibility for the school back and forth for decades. It was named for Edgar Borders who owned a mill and provided shacks for his workers' housing. In 1934, Humble ISD gave the school to Aldine ISD and would eventually begin paying for Black children in the Humble district to attend class at Bordersville. Humble did not operate a school for Black children after that time, determining that they did not have a population that warranted the expense. When the Borders mill closed in 1941, the community sunk deep into poverty, and after it was mostly annexed by Houston in 1965, it was another 16 years before services such as water and sewers were brought there.[41]

BOWERS SCHOOL

See Bauer

BOWIE E S

See Dodson

BRACKENRIDGE E S

The property at 2814 East Quitman and Jensen, then called Clark Street, first became a Houston school in April 1907, but it took a two plus year ordeal to get there. Colonel Brackenridge of San Antonio had donated the land to the city for school purposes in early 1905, and L.S. Green was quickly chosen as the architect for the two-story building. The desire for a school was high since the closest options for White students were either the very crowded Cascara School or Staples School which was in an area still largely rural.[42]

Almost immediately, the city determined that costs were too high, and "ornamental" items were omitted from the original plans. These included a cupola, columns, cornices, and plumbing. Then, as construction was well along, the city inspectors deemed the building unfit and unsafe, "viable only as material." The ensuing legal wrangle and corrections took such a long time that a four-room Brackenridge Annex was opened in a rented building. Perhaps because of the myriad of headaches, when the school opened, the district abandoned the Brackenridge name in favor of calling it John H. Reagan Elementary. Once all nine rooms of the new school were up and functioning, the streetcar still stopped eight blocks short. The principal arranged for the manager of the streetcar company to ride his line out for an inspection. Fortuitously, it poured rain. "He reached the school very submissive, and very wet, and promised the teachers, while the rain ran down in his shoes, everything they asked for."[43]

Reagan did have successes. A settlement house was formed and a kindergarten furnished by the Christian Endeavor Society of the Central Christian Church. Additional playground land was acquired, and 32 shade trees were planted around the perimeter of the property. Clean, new toilets were added. Around 1916, the name was changed back to honor John T. Brackenridge. By 1920, there were 17 total rooms, albeit some in the undesirable basement just as at many other Houston schools.[44]

The outdoor gym at Reagan/Brackenridge ES. HISD

In 1925, Brackenridge became a poster child for changing neighborhood demographics in a time of some-times virulent racism and segregation. Residents in that all-White portion of Fifth Ward around Brackenridge School became outraged when a developer bought the nearby Brady Estate with a plan to subdivide it for "Negro housing." Petitions were circulated to the press and the Houston board of realtors. Ultimately, the neighborhood attracted more and more African American residents. By 1955, HISD changed the campus to one for Black children, and transferred the John M. Langston name to the 50 year old building. Eventually, the original structure was demolished and replaced by a new one. Langston Elementary gave way to Langston Early Childhood Development Center in 1991, and the campus was closed for school purposes entirely in 2004.[45]

Outdoor gymnasiums

In the first decade of the 1900s, mothers' clubs around the city became enamored with outdoor gymnasi-ums and bought several for their children's schools. These monstrous contraptions were placed in various elementary school yards and were generally considered to be "a constant source of profit and pleasure to the pupils." The school principals, such as Helena Holley at Reagan Elementary, found other benefits: "Aside from the pleasure and physical exercise derived from these by the children, they have proven of inestimable value. The pugnacious propensity of the boy has been expended on trapeze and climbing pole instead of on his fellow student. As a consequence, fights have been few and far between, while the boy in the school room has been quieter and more attentive to his books."

Cost for each apparatus was about $225.00. A smaller model for a more cramped school yard still contained "two swinging trapezes, two pair of acting rings, two rows of swinging rings, four climbing poles, two hand-over-hand ladders, and two parallel bars." With uppermost perches well over 10 feet high, the outdoor gymnasium would no doubt be a modern insurance company's nightmare.[46]

BRAY'S BAYOU SCHOOL

German immigrant John Kuhlman moved to land south of Houston on Brays Bayou in 1839, and his brothers George and Henry soon followed. The family prospered, amassing land on both sides of the bayou. The Kuhlmans also supported a school for their own children and others in the neighborhood at least by 1855 and likely earlier. All three brothers served as trustees at various times over the next four decades, as did George Ramier whose name was attached to the school for a few years. Upon county school reorganization in the 1880s, Bray's Bayou became District 22. A road led from the little school just north of Brays Bayou and east of the Almeda Road back to the streetcar line that ran down Main Street to Bellaire Boulevard. Lester McGraw, a motorman on that car, met Miss Minnie Allen, a teacher at Bray's Bayou School, on that streetcar, and the two were married about 1910.[47]

A picnic in front of Brays Bayou School. HHRC

BRAYS BAYOU COLORED SCHOOL

It appears that there were two schools that bore the name of Bray's Bayou Colored, but the scant surviving records make determining details difficult. The one that was located south of that bayou near the Almeda Road appears as early as 1886 as part of District 22 along with the White Bray's Bayou School and later as part of District 24. This was a single room building on a 50 x 100 foot lot that was annexed into the Houston school system in 1913 when it was described as "not very clean." Sometime between 1921 and 1935, the Bray's Bayou Colored School name was relocated to the Riceville community much farther west, and south of the bayou on today's South Gessner Road. It was closed approximately 1966.[48]

BRINK SCHOOL

The one room Brink School seems to have originated in the heavily German community near Cypress between 1895 and August 1898 when Johan August Brink deeded a one acre tract to County Judge W.N. Shaw. The school plot was conveyed, along with a reversion clause in the event that the usage changed, to each successive county judge until it passed directly to County School District 6 in May of 1934. By that time, a second room had been added to the building that sat near the intersection of today's Barker-Cypress and FM 529.[49]

Brink School on bookmobile day. HCPL

Brink was consolidated with Cypress in 1934, but because of transportation issues, the students didn't move to Cypress until summer 1935. The room added in 1926 was dismantled at that time, and the original one room school was moved to the campus of the Cypress School at Telge and Cypress North Houston.[50]

BRISCOE E S

Briscoe Elementary honors Andrew Briscoe, Texas revolutionary and the first chief administrator of Harris, then Harrisburg County. Called Forest Hill School in its planning stages, for the street on which it was to sit, it opened on March 8, 1929 with only two teachers and 82 pupils. Soon all eight classrooms and the play-lunchroom at the single story building were in operation. In less than ten years, the faculty had grown to 12 teachers plus the principal, Mrs. Mabel R.T. Woods, and 485 students were enrolled.[51]

Mayfete at Briscoe ES in 1938. HHRC

In the mid-1930s, Briscoe was often noted for inventive student activities that included a Kindergarten Rhythm Band, a Harmonica Band, and an annual April 1st pet show. The May Fetes at Briscoe that decade were extravagant with costumes that appear relatively costly for the middle of the Great Depression including a plantation tableau complete with White children in blackface portraying smiling slaves.[52]

BROCK, RICHARD E S

See Washington, Booker T. Elementary School

BROOKLINE E S

Brookline Elementary School, opened on Telephone Road and Gould in 1914 to serve the very small community of that name along the Houston-Galveston Interurban line. It was initially part of the Harrisburg School District, remaining there until it was absorbed into the Houston city limits and HISD in April 1927. The campus moved away from the Brookline neighborhood in 1953 to a new building on Holmes Road that would become part of Loop 610 a few years later. Today, the Brookline name lives on at a 21st Century structure at 6301 South Loop East. The original 1914 structure stood until April 2024, first as the orange-painted brick HISD Media Center then as a mostly vacant building, when it fell victim to a catastrophic fire. HISD looked to sell the property entirely later that same year.[53]

Brookline ES building on Telephone Road. Left vacant and lost to fire. Laurie Feinswog photo

BROOK'S ACADEMY

Major Brooks lent his name to this private institution that opened on Liberty Street in February 1869 offering its 30 students instruction in "English, Music, Languages, Mathematics and Drawing, at the usual rates."[54]

BROWNING E S

Robert Browning Elementary School, named for the 19th century British poet, started life as Woodland School in County District 25. In 1918, it was listed as a brick house with one teacher under the name of the Brookesmith addition in which it stood, but two years later, as part of HISD, Woodland School was a new building of six rooms and 240 desks. Four classrooms were above the six foot basement, and two roomfuls of students studied in the low ceilinged area itself. The school district architect noted that "with new buildings springing up in every direction, it is evident that the buildings will be badly overcrowded in another year."[55]

The Woodland School experienced a tragedy early in its life when the sitting principal, Miss Bell Taylor, died in February 1918. She had taught in the county schools for a decade, and her funeral was attended by teachers, former students, and the Woodland Mothers Club. The campus at 607 Northwood finally got a new school building in 1927 as part of the school bond construction. That building made statewide news in 1953 when a series of four arson fires were started, each causing relatively minimal damage. It still stands today, supplemented by a one story addition.[56]

BRUBAKER SCHOOL

The Brubaker School served the subdivision of the same name in County District 29 in the Aldine area. Specifically, it sat near the intersection of Blue Bell Road and the part of East Montgomery that today is Airline Drive. It remained active at least into the early 1930s.[57]

BRUCE E S

Bruce Elementary School has one of the longest pedigrees in the City of Houston. It began as the Fifth Ward Colored School when tax-supported public education was brought in under the Reconstruction government in 1871 and was reorganized under the new Constitution of 1876. The city owned the property, a two story wood building with a single classroom on each floor, and desks that were considered "old-fashioned and inconvenient" even in 1879, two years after it opened. The plot of ground on which it sat was on the west side of Bremond between Liberty Road and Green Street, with the International & Great Northern train tracks running across the street at a time when tracks were largely at grade level and most every roadway had a crossing.[58]

John S. Tibbitt was the first principal, gone by winter of 1883 when a *Galveston Daily News* reporter wrote that the school lacked discipline and order and was "about the most unsatisfactory school in the entire system." Overcrowding followed, and calls for a new structure came as early as 1885, though they would be largely unheeded for another 35 years. Rooms were added, and the address changed to Bremond and Conti, two streets that have almost vanished after many years and vast changes to what was then a largely mixed-race residential neighborhood for railroad workers.

The leadership over the years at Fifth Ward Colored included two Jamaican-born educators, William B. Cogle and William Francis. B.H. Grimes held the job around 1907 at a time when each teacher had up to 75 pupils in class.[59]

The most famous principal arrived in 1909, the year a Mothers Club started and about the time the school was renamed in honor of Blanche Kelso Bruce, a man who had been the first African American to serve a full term in the U.S. Senate. This longtime principal at Bruce was Nat Q. Henderson, who became a true leader of Houston's Black community. Born in Columbus, Texas he was an early graduate of Prairie View A&M, but also studied at Fisk, Southern Cal, and Columbia. Prior to his career in Houston schools, Henderson had success in government and politics that included serving as Deputy Federal Revenue Collector and as a delegate to the Republican National Convention. He established a home for delinquent Black women and girls that became the county's Dorcas Home and was active in Gregg Street Presbyterian Church, multiple fraternal organizations, and many community causes for Black Houstonians from day care to libraries. Henderson was the father of six children, at least five of whom became teachers including Jocelyn Henderson, a teacher at Blackshear who continued to live with her parents for some time.[60]

Though the building at Bruce, known less than affectionately as "the Old Red Barn," was "old and dilapidated", Henderson saw that it was tidy and functional. Conti Street was graveled at the time he took over, but Bremond had no paving at all, yet the school undertook a "systematic effort to create rivalry in gardens and clean premises." A branch of the Colored Carnegie Library was opened at Bruce, and Principal Henderson sought to foster a "kindly feeling between White and colored children."[61]

A 6th grade class at Bruce ES in 1932. HHRC

Bruce students and faculty finally got a new eight room school building in April 1920, and the old wooden structure was sold by the city. The new school was located at 713 Bringhurst, although the address of 800 Cage also appeared. Within a year, two temporary rooms had been added to meet the endlessly growing need. Principal Henderson served until 1942, by which time he oversaw a faculty of 26 teachers plus a school nurse. The Bruce School playground opened in the summer of 1922. It was a safer spot for children than the one across from busy railroad tracks, until Interstate 10 was placed along the northside of the campus in the late 1950s.[62]

The location at Cage and Bringhurst finally closed in June 2007. By that time, it sat across the street from a superfund cleanup site. Today the Bruce Elementary name is still thriving in a new building at 510 Jensen specializing in music with an entire wing devoted to music pursuits.[63]

African American PTAs Called For

Having noticed the activity upon the part of the Parent-Teacher Associations at the local White public schools and the recognition accorded these organizations by the board of education and head of the local public educational system, The *Informer* is of the opinion that our colored public schools, particularly the ward or elementary schools, should have such organizations.

So many of the colored parents and patrons of the public schools of Houston think that the teachers of the race should take the initiative in all matters affecting the welfare of the children and the race, and thus they "pass the buck" on all such matters to the colored school principals and teachers, and then criticise (sic) and lambast said teachers when they do not take the lead in many matters arising in the local system that vitally and directly affect our children and our race.

This is no brief for colored principals who are more concerned about holding their jobs and making a hit with the school head than in seeing to it that the children on their school campuses do not have to wade or swim in water every time it rains, or that the school structures are ill heated, poorly ventilated and withal unfit for modern school use; yet if many of these men felt that the parents of the children and patrons of the schools were interested in them and the children, and were willing to manifest this interest in a concrete and tangible manner, they would doubtless be more inclined and encouraged to do more in this respect than they are now doing or have done in the past.

Some of the ward schools formerly had such associations, but it appears that most of our colored principals looked askance at the movement and did everything they could to discourage and destroy it; with the result that the good race women, who were enthusiastically and actively engaged in this work, finally threw up the sponge and abandoned the cause.

Any number of improvements were made at some of the ward schools through this organization a few years ago; these women even making it possible for the children to stand on bring-bats. Rocks, shell and gravel, instead of in mud, slush, and water, under some of the ward school buildings; they even bought rocks, dirt, and shell and filled in many of the holes, ponds, and sloughs in the school yards, when the school system was directly connected with the municipal government; while in some schools they made it possible for the children to have pianos and phonographs.

The colored parents and patrons of the public schools of Houston need to take more interest in their children's education and welfare; and this can best be done only in an organized way and through the instrumentality of the parent-teacher association.

The Houston Informer, November 14, 1925

BRUNNER COLORED SCHOOL

The town of Brunner maintained a school for African American students at the northeast corner of Butt and Asbury that was also known as the Cottage Grove Colored School from 1919 to 1925. On the modern street grid, that is about three or four blocks north of Washington and the first block west of TC Jester.[64]

BRUNNER H S

See West End Junior High

BRUNNER SCHOOL

Anton Brunner began developing his addition about a mile west of the Houston city limits in 1888. Centered near Washington and Shepherd Roads, it was an unincorporated working class suburb. By 1894, the community was busy enough to warrant a school, and County District 25 paid Duffy & Lane $635 to erect one on two lots at the southeast corner of Bethje and Butt. That was just south of the railroad tracks, near today's intersection of Durham, which overlayed Bethje and Shuler. It was a 26 x 40 foot wood frame building perched atop six foot brick piers. Miss Julia Dunman was the first year teacher, replaced the following term by Eugenia Dixon. By 1896, a mirrored addition and a second teacher were added.[65]

Brunner ISD changed the school's name to Alexander in 1896, as well. In March 1901, the residents of Brunner voted overwhelmingly to incorporate for school purposes only, and the Brunner ISD was created, running from Buffalo Bayou at Vick's Bridge north to White Oak Bayou. By 1905, the area was uptown enough to afford a fancy brick school, so a new building, albeit without electricity, was erected on the south side of Lillian Street (formerly Welch) where Thompson still dead ends today. It was once again called Brunner School.[66]

When the City of Houston extended its limits in 1913, Brunner ISD was folded into Houston schools. With a new Brunner High School having been completed just months earlier, the older and smaller brick building became known as the Thompson Street School, a name it carried for several decades. The first impression noted by city school officials was unfavorable, and it remained that way. Over the next decade, Thompson Street School was called "a much abused building" and "in very bad condition," though the small Mothers Club tried their best by putting in walkways and sprucing up the old wood house that shared the campus with the eight-room, two story school. Masonry cracks were patched, and in 1922, the city report called the building "hardly safe." It was closed and replaced by the new Cleveland Elementary nearby.[67]

BUNDICK SCHOOL

See Pitchman School

BURBANK E S

Construction of Burbank School on Tidwell began in 1926, the same year that its namesake, famed horticulturist Luther Burbank died. For a man who developed over 800 strains and varieties of plants during his long life, the consolidated elementary and high school that catered to a largely rural, agricultural area was a most fitting tribute. In fact, Burbank was the only campus in HISD to offer instruction in farming, catering to local boys who came to school of a morning with a "hoe and rake under (their) arm and books slung over (their) shoulder."[68]

The pastoral setting at Burbank ES. HISD

More than the instruction itself, many of the students had home projects that might be raising a calf, chickens, or a patch of cotton or corn. John Seward, an A&M grad, was their instructor. Several ag-related outbuildings shared the 16-acre campus with the sprawling single story school. Among the students were a large number of Italian Americans who operated nearby truck farms, and some children made a good amount of extra money taking their eggs, crops, or chickens to sell in town.

Expected to struggle to fill classrooms in the sparsely populated country with its unpaved roads, the school was full from the start. Houston had just annexed the county's Durkee School, so the thirteen room building was well attended. Two additions followed, doubling the size of the plant. There were over 1,000 pupils and 34 teachers by 1936. In 1949, a middle school of the same name opened not far away, relieving Burbank of its older charges.[69]

There are issues with hanging on to an old school such as retrofitting electrical outlets in a building that originally offered only one per classroom. Teachers remarked that if they wished to plug in an overhead projector, it meant unplugging the fan. The fans were needed, too, since the school was not air conditioned until the early 1980s. Still, over the years, Burbank Elementary has fostered an uncommon fondness among many of the teachers assigned there. One longtime P.E. teacher's ashes were scattered in the school's rose garden, the school library hosted a wedding between a teacher and the school secretary, and when HISD superintendent Kay Stripling retired, she came back to spend her last day at Burbank where she had once been the principal.[70]

BURBANK J H S

One of the few school names to appear on two campuses in HISD, the Burbank Middle School at 600 Berry opened in 1949, leaving the original as an elementary school only. The new two and a quarter million dollar campus, the most expensive in HISD at the time, opened above its planned capacity from day one. When sewer problems at nearby Fonville caused the temporary combination of the schools, it handled 2,980 students, "forcing some classes to meet in hallways and in a school bus."[71]

Field Trip Down the Ship Channel

Still another instance of service which the school system has rendered directly to the community may be found in the excursions down the Ship Channel to the Turning Basin, which the efficient business representative of the Board last year organized and conducted. In connection with a local firm of real estate men and with the paper known as the *School Mirror*, Mr. Peine last year took some 6,000 school children on boats down the Ship Channel to the Turning Basin. These were taken on successive Saturdays, by schools. Prizes were offered to those children writing the best essays on Houston as a Deep Water City, and similar subjects. While it is true that the project was in some sense a private advertising affair, it is nevertheless true, in my judgment, that nothing has ever been done to arouse the people of our city more fully to an interest in things that pertain to its vital welfare in the matter of commercial supremacy. It is not only educational to teach children about the resources of their own section, but it is patriotic, and is commercially valuable.

Superintendent Paul W. Horn

Houston City Schools Report 1909-10

BURKE SCHOOL

Burke School in County District 23, also written as Burk's on occasion, first appears in 1897 on the Richmond Road a quarter mile southwest of the GH&SA Railroad tracks. That would place the location not far from the present campus of St. Thomas University. In May 1907, the district trustees received permission to sell the Burke school house and property.[72]

BURKHART'S SCHOOL

Burkhart's School appears briefly in the late 1880s in County District 7 with the Cypress schools.[73]

Burnet ES. HISD

BURNET E S

David G. Burnet was the interim president of a rebellious Texas. In 1926, he was honored with an elementary school at 5403 Canal. At the time it opened, the school, with 19 classrooms and an auditorium/play/lunchroom, hosted a largely Anglo and Jewish population, but the area was already in the process of becoming more Hispanic as the ship channel neighborhood grew more industrialized. With that industrialization came increased street traffic along Canal. In 1936, the hazards were apparent when L.L. Pugh wrote that the "location of this building on a street of great traffic hazard necessitates the …constant surveillance of a policeman."[74]

BURNET SCHOOL, BAYTOWN

Pre-statehood politician David G. Burnet owned a home along the water in the Baytown area, so it was only natural that the GCCISD named a school after him. The elementary opened with seven rooms in 1930 on today's Bayway Drive, near the site of the old Wooster School. Burnet closed as a regular school in 1970.[75]

BURRUS E S

Independence Heights was a land promotion northwest of Houston for African Americans that started selling lots about 1908. Within a few years there were over 400 residents in what had become an incorporated town, and eventually there would be retail stores, restaurants, contractor businesses, and half a dozen churches. In 1911, the community got its own school, a two-room building that was moved from Sunset Heights to the 600 block of E. 39th Street where O.L. Hubbard, a future Independence Heights mayor, worked as principal. Another early top man at the small school was O.P. DeWalt who would later go on to head Houston's NAACP.[76]

The city of Independence Heights voted to dissolve and be annexed by Houston in 1929, but even before that, HISD had taken over the school. They found that in ten short years, the facilities had gone quickly downhill. One hundred plus pupils were jammed into the "old one-story wood building, practically useless." Other students were relegated to the top floor of a wooden store. The area benefitted from bond elections before the decade was through, and in 1928, a new brick school opened at 701 E. 33rd and Avenue B, named for James Burrus, a pioneering Black educator and philanthropist who died that year. Some 340 pupils entered the new school under Principal P.H. Holden.[77]

A class at recess at Burrus ES. HISD

A feeling of community stayed strong in Independence Heights for many decades, and hundreds of former residents recall attending Mrs. Susie Booker's kindergarten before entering Burrus, or elementary teacher Karmolete Walker who taught at Burrus for roughly 40 years with the mantra that "there was no such thing as a bad child."[78]

Schools C

CAGE E S

The record of historic building preservation in the Houston ISD is abominable, so it is considered by some to be a minor miracle when a building such as the old Cage Elementary at 1415 Telephone Road survives into the 21st Century. If the neighborhood in which it stands had been in more demand during the latter decades of the 20th, there is little doubt that it would not have.[1]

Originally, the school was part of County District 21, beginning life as the Kirby School about 1902 on the opposite side of the street and a little ways north. It honored W.A. Kirby, a school district trustee. By 1910, armed with $10,000 in bond money, the district took bids on two new two-story brick schools: Fullerton on Harrisburg, and this one on Telephone Road to be called Cage after philanthropist and school board president Rufus Cage who had donated the land on which both it and the original school were situated. There were four classrooms and an auditorium created by means of a sliding door. The Mothers Club provided a piano and a large American flag. There were library books, but the "majority of the pupils have read all of them." [2]

The area around Cage was sparsely populated agricultural prairie, and when Houston schools annexed District 21 in 1914, they closed the little school, divided it up into four rented apartments, and sent the 45 Cage students to nearby Eastwood Elementary. It took almost a decade, but the neighborhood, led by Mrs. H.C. Lane, the daughter of W.A. Kirby and by then a mother herself, succeeded in having the stucco building restored to school purposes. The student body had doubled in size, and the mothers outfitted a kitchen with a kerosene stove and cooked lunches themselves. By then, the city had paved Telephone Road right up to the school building. Beyond that it was "given the inverted penetration process" of being coated with oil.[3]

There were additions in the 1940s including a modern kitchen. The basement area was converted into classrooms with barely a six foot ceiling, but by 1983, a new Cage Elementary was opened on Leeland, and the old Telephone Road landmark was fenced off and used for warehousing school supplies. After that, it sat idle for years before HISD conveyed the property to the city in 2014 with the hope that it would be preserved and used as a community center just as it had been a century earlier.

HISD board members and civic leaders post during an inspection of Cage School in 2011. This group was pushing for preservation and community use. Mike Vance photo.

HISD in the Depression

As in many other aspects of hardship during the Great Depression, the Houston area fared slightly better than many parts of the nation. In the school arena, the best description might be stagnation.

By the close of the 1920s, the city of Houston had seen amazing growth rates for decades, driven first by railroads, then oil and an expanded Ship Channel. Since the 1860 census, each ten year span had seen a population gain in the city of at least 62%, and the growth spurt between 1920 and 1930 was Houston's biggest yet with an increase of an astounding 111%.[4]

In the final school year of the Roaring Twenties, HISD's enrollment was right at 57,000 pupils attending 101 schools, several of which were brand new thanks to a trio of successful bond elections. That represented a jump of twelve thousands students in the previous five years. Expenditure per pupil was roughly fifty-eight dollars.[5]

Though the city escaped the Depression without a single major bank failure, the job-creating powerhouse of the past slowed down a mite. The city still gained 31.5% in population between the 1930 and 1940 census counts, but much of the growth came later in the decade when New Deal programs had kicked in and the shadow of possible war was getting larger.[6]

Looking at the five-year snapshot from the 1929-30 school year until 1934-35, HISD saw a net gain of only about 200 students. The totals were roughly 43,200 White students and 14,000 African American. The year 1935 saw 2,154 Houstonians graduate from high school. Unfortunately for those in school at the time, one thing not standing pat was the budget. Three million dollars were spent for instruction of pupils in 1934-35, which meant a drop of six dollars per student.[7]

CARPENTER'S BAYOU SCHOOL

The Carpenter's Bayou School was operating before 1884 just north of the modern I-10 along the west bank of Old River. It was the only White school in County District 18 which also had an African American schoolhouse during the same years. The small school district petitioned to consolidate with District 14, serving the almost vanished town of San Jacinto, in 1906, and by 1910 was part of the Deer Park district. The original District 18 remained alive, and became Channelview ISD in 1938.[8]

CARPENTER'S BAYOU COLORED SCHOOL

County District 18 provided a small school for African American students beginning in the 1880s and lasting for several decades. It was noted by county officials to need a new building by 1907. Few detailed records survive.[9]

CARTER CAREER CENTER

See Wheatley High School

CARVER, GEORGE WASHINGTON SCHOOL

The better known story about the Acres Homes neighborhood is that it was marketed just prior to WWI by the Wright Land Company for African Americans as a "bit of genteel county with quick and easy access to the city." There were also multiple Black families living in that rural area prior to that time, well back into the 19th century. The White Oak Colored School, and its White counterpart, were both operating in County District 26 in the late 1880s when Steve Blanchette was teaching there at a salary of $33 a month. A school year lasted less than six months.[10]

The exact location of that first school was near Brunner, closer to the city limits. It also served the Black population of the nearby Smokyville community. As the land development in Acres Homes increased the out-lying population, White Oak Colored School moved farther out, opening a new building at West Montgomery and Willow around 1915 on a parcel donated by Wright Land. It opened with 23 students ranging from ages eight to twenty-one. While being a rural setting near the employment opportunities of the city might have been attractive to residents, it was the bane of the school trustees. The better pay, transportation, and housing available in Houston was a constant lure for teachers like Steve Blanchette, who was living in Freedmen's Town by 1900. Between 1919 and 1942, there were 31 different hires at White Oak Colored School. [11]

Gradually the little school expanded its academic offerings. Seventh grade was added in 1934, and three years later, the school was annexed into the Aldine ISD. Enrollment by then topped 160, and soon there were five teachers and a school term of nine months. In 1941, the campus moved to five acres at 7436 Wheatley Road, and two more grades were added. The new principal, A.B. Anderson, brought many changes including making the school a full eleven grade high school in 1943 and changing the name to honor scientist George Washington Carver. A lighted football field came in 1945, an Ag and Home Ec building three years after that, and by the start of the 1950s, students attended classes in double shifts. That overcrowding led to construction of a new high school campus at 2100 South Victory in 1954, and the elementary pupils stayed behind at what was renamed A.B. Anderson Elementary.[12]

CARVER, G W E S, BAYTOWN

Six-room Carver Elementary on Lee Drive, a spin-off of the Carver School that served Baytown's Black students of all ages, opened in 1946 and operated until 1995 when "oil was detected seeping from an underground oil pit on the playground." A new Carver Elementary campus opened in GCCISD in 2002.[13]

Sustainable Farming at City Schools

"Let me suggest that you teach the children to grow not only flowers, but corn, cabbage, carrots – any vegetable. Let them find where the vegetables come from. Teach them that beyond the mart of the corner grocery, the stuffy stalls of our city market and the hucksters' wagons, there are outlying districts of beauty whence the vegetables come."

Dr. Kline quoted in the *Houston Post* July 1, 1910

CARVER, G W H S, BAYTOWN

George Washington Carver High School in Baytown began as a school for African American students of all grades, starting first in an area church. By the 1930s, there were multiple buildings on a single campus with roughly 280 elementary pupils and 100 in the high school, which became accredited as a four year institution in 1940. Prior to that, Black students from GCCISD went to Houston high schools, and in turn, after Carver became accredited, about ten percent of those it educated were from surrounding towns such as La Porte. In 1948, a new Carver High opened, financed with a postwar bond issue and built on six acres donated by Humble Oil where many of the students' parents worked. It remained in operation as an all-Black high school until integration in 1967 when students were moved to either Baytown's Lee or Sterling Highs.[14]

CARVERDALE SCHOOL

The African American community of Independence Garden around North Gessner and Tanner Road started its first school in a borrowed farmhouse in 1925, moving to Macedonia Baptist Church on Darcy Lane a year later. While there, pupils started each Monday stacking pews and moving their desks back in place. There were only about 19 or 20 students at a time at Fairbanks Colored School, spread across grades one through seven, but in 1937, the Wright Land Company donated a tract on Clara Road, and the Fairbanks ISD sent its old White school building to become the first building dedicated for the district's Black students.[15]

Those who graduated went into Houston to continue at Harper Junior High then Booker T. Washington High School. Some parents converted a green panel truck into a bus, adding wooden benches and painting "school bus" on the side in whitewash that had to be repainted every time it rained. In 1951, the Rose Hill district consolidated their Black students, two more rooms were added, and the school became known as Carverdale. It continued to expand, eventually providing grades all the way through high school. Carverdale School closed in 1970.

CASCARA SCHOOL

See Sherman

Poor Attendance

"The census of last year give 5,550 children of schools age, but only 3,152 were registered as pupils in our schools. The remaining 2,398 children (1,291 White and 1,107 colored) were not in the public schools for a single day last year. Supposing that 500 were attending private school, a very liberal estimate, there were in our city 1,898 children who received no formal scholastic instruction whatever. In other words, nearly 35% of the children of Houston were not receiving that education which the State believes is necessary to her own welfare."

   Houston City Schools Report 1888-89

CEDAR BAYOU SCHOOL

The original Cedar Bayou Community was across the line in Liberty County prior to the Civil War, but when the name was born into a town in 1871, complete with a post office, it was on the Harris County side of the water at a place that was previously known as Shearn. The community's primary industry was brickmaking with as many as eleven kilns operating at one time. The Cedar Bayou School first opened in the new Methodist Church, but in 1876, the same year Texas schools reorganized under a new constitution and public schools law, the school moved to the new Masonic Lodge. That building still stands at 2850 Ferry Road. It would remain there as the main school in County District 15 until residents approved a bond, and a new brick building was opened in fall of 1910, though it lacked walkways, window shades, maps, dictionaries, and a library. Around this time, classes for the first two years of high school were added.[16]

Masonic Lodge building at Cedar Bayou. Mike Vance photo

Cedar Bayou formed an Independent School District in 1917, and just over a decade later, a new mission style building opened on the same campus near Crosby-Cedar Bayou Road and Cedar Bayou Ferry Road. More buildings were added to the Cedar Bayou campus through the 1930s and 40s including a cafeteria and gym. In 1938 there were 12 rooms in the elementary building and eight in the brand new high school building. After one failed attempt, voters in Cedar Bayou agreed to consolidate with Goose Creek ISD in March 1954, and high school students moved to Lee High in Baytown. The old campus continued as a junior high. The collection of old buildings was razed and a new Cedar Bayou Middle School was built in May 2002.[17]

CEDAR BAYOU COLORED SCHOOL

The community of Cedar Bayou at the eastern edge of Harris County had a school for African American students at least as early as 1886 when it received public money as part of District 15. It was north of the Masonic Lodge that housed the White school, and may have actually been across the county line, meaning the bayou itself. The schoolhouse was definitely east of the water by 1894, and there are numerous mentions of the two counties sharing tax revenue in this case. By 1907, the building needed "some new repairs." A Rosenwald school was built at that site for Cedar Bayou Colored in 1921, part of the nationwide philanthropic program for Black children that was financed by the part owner of Sears, Roebuck & Co in conjunction with Booker T. Washington's organization. The school, by then in a new building, was officially renamed for longtime teacher, Victoria Walker in 1953, and it continued for another 11 years under that name before being closed. Though the final building at the site of the Cedar Bayou School was demolished in the late 1980s, the Victoria Walker name lives on at a new campus on Seabird Lane in Baytown.[18]

CEDAR BAYOU H S

See Cedar Bayou School

CENTRAL H S

See Houston High

A 1911 class photo at the Chaneyville White School shows the neighboring houses. HHRC.

CHANEYVILLE SCHOOL

See Abbott

CHANEYVILLE COLORED SCHOOL

See Harper

Maggie Johnson Hicks and Yearly Teacher Contracts

For both city and county schools, teachers, from newbies to the most seasoned veterans, were notified yearly as to whether or not there was an offer for their employment during the upcoming school term. Only the superintendent and top district staff might count on the luxury of a multi-year pact.

On the last day of May 1919, Maggie Johnson, a 21-year-old Houston native, received a pre-printed postcard at the Chaneyville house on Court Street that she shared with her parents. Her father, Walter Alexander Johnson who went by Alex, was a foreman in the press room at one of the nearby cottonseed oil mills, and Maggie had attended the African American school in the neighborhood before going on to Colored High School.[19]

The postcard informed her that she had been elected to a supernumerary teaching position with the Houston Public Schools at a salary of $25 a month, the standard pay scale for a second-year Black teacher in that role. She had two weeks to notify her acceptance which she could do by returning the stub attached to the postcard. As a supernumerary, she was subject to assignment at whatever school needed her. Soon after, she became a regular classroom teacher for the city, including at Harper School near her home.

If the yearly uncertainty was an imposition for Maggie Johnson, there was no evidence. She married postal worker Charles W. Hicks, Jr. and continued her education, attending Prairie View and Houston Negro Junior College from which she earned a bachelor's degree and later a master's after it had grown into Texas Southern University. She also received certification in dramatics, storytelling, and folk dancing and continued leading educational workshops until the 1960s.[20]

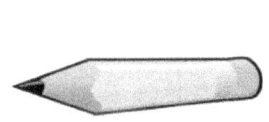

CHANNEL VIEW SCHOOL

The community of Channel View, previously farm and grazing land on the north side of the Ship Channel, began to coalesce about the time that Carpenter's Bayou School was abandoning Common District 18. It was the discovery of oil in that part of the county, and an influx of blue collar workers to service that industry, that brought the beginning of a community. A school was in operation by 1916, and ten years later, there were 31 students. Channelview got a post office in 1933, though growth remained rather slow for a few more years. Two new small schools opened around the time that the district became an ISD in summer of 1938.[21]

CHAPMANSVILLE SCHOOL

Under the Reconstruction era public school law, a Mrs. Lang taught about 30 students at this co-educational school in the neighborhood north of the Hardy Yards, a large Southern Pacific Railroad facility.[22]

CHASE SCHOOL

Nothing but a reference to this name is found in HISD records.

CHERRYHURST SCHOOL

See Woodrow Wilson

CHEW SCHOOL

See Atherton

CHRIST CHURCH EPISCOPAL SCHOOL

Christ Church Cathedral, the oldest congregation in Houston still located on its original site, opened its first church building in 1845 and operated a pre-school and kindergarten for much of its existence. In 1896, the school was located at the back of the courtyard that faces Texas Avenue. Many wealthy Houstonians went there including Howard Hughes, Jr. and his first wife, Ella Rice. In 1903 it was known as Gray Grammar School of Christ Church with W.L. Cook as headmaster.[23]

CHRIST THE KING SCHOOL

The Dominican Sisters of St. Agnes opened Christ the King School on North Main in 1930, two years after the parish was established to serve working class Czech and Polish families in the area of Houston Heights. Christ the King closed the school in 1981 but reopened it in 1996 for children at Pre-K and kindergarten levels.[24]

CHRISTEN'S SCHOOL

This school was named for John Peter Christen, Sr. and operated in the Cypress area and District 7 at least from the mid-1880s until the mid-1890s. Christen, and his son who shared the same name, operated a sawmill and later a cotton gin. The elder Christen was also Justice of the Peace for about 30 years, and one of the two men served briefly as a teacher in the district.[25]

CITY SCHOOL

Houston's first powerful mayor was Francis Moore, Jr. in the late 1830s, and one of his desires was to establish public schools after the model of his native Massachusetts. Though the original 1836 Borden map of Houston set aside a School House Square bounded by Texas, Prairie, Fannin, and San Jacinto, the two-story schoolhouse was built by the city with help from the Odd Fellows Lodge on Travis Street midway between Texas and Prairie. It was a spot that would later be occupied by the Chronicle Building for over a century. The trouble was that no one recalled that the same plot had been promised to the Methodists for a church. Once the school was built and operating, the Methodists came calling, and a compromise gave them half the property.[26]

The City School opened its door on February 11, 1839 with 104 pupils under the guidance of Rev. Richard Salmon of New York and his assistant Austin Bodman. Salmon had been ordained as an Episcopal priest in New York and served parishioners upstate until he hatched the plan to bring a colony of them to Texas. He arrived at Velasco in October 1836 at the age of 39. Though his initial plans disintegrated, he was the first minister of his faith to preach regularly in the new Republic. He first spent time in Brazoria, serving as chaplain of the Senate at Columbia and officiating at Stephen F. Austin's funeral. Salmon was consumptive and had great batches of down time due to his illness, but it was he who was chosen to lead the new Houston City School.[27]

The course load was mightily ambitious for a school with only two instructors and listed: Spelling, Reading, Writing, Arithmetic, English Grammar, Geography, Chronology, History, Rhetoric, Declamation, Botany, Latin, Greek, Geometry, Trigonometry, Surveying, Algebra, Mixed Mathematics, Natural Philosophy, Moral Philosophy, Metaphysics, Book-keeping, and Music, if particularly requested by parents.[28]

Actual attendance settled in at around 50 students after the first weeks. The inaugural term closed in July, and the next one opened with a new principal, a post that seemed to need filling each year. The second school year began in September 1839, but closed a few weeks later due to the city's worst outbreak of yellow fever, remaining shuttered for some two months until reopening on December 9th. That outbreak of "yellow jack" killed a full ten percent of the young city's population.[29]

The school was overseen by City Council and a small group of trustees. Classes were not free. There was a tuition of three dollars a month, but parents could apply for a certificate that qualified them as indigent and eligible for a waiver of all costs. The city set aside $2,000 for the purpose in 1845, but only $655 was spent. Overall, the town leaders appeared to lose interest in the expense of operating a school. Many of the wealthiest citizens continued to send their children to boarding school in the northeast. In the end, the Methodists built a permanent church on their portion of the property, and the schoolhouse was eventually sold for $105 around the time Texas officially joined the United States in early 1846.[30]

CLAWSON SCHOOL

This small one room school served a rural area in the northeast part of the county in the last years of the 19th century. It sat at the southeast corner of FM 1492 and Clawson Lane. There were only about 15 students when the schoolhouse was closed and pupils folded into Crosby school in 1934.[31]

CLEVELAND, WILLIAM D E S

At the start of the 1920s, the West End and former community of Brunner was served by Thompson Elementary which was held in great disdain as an unsafe, dilapidated, inviable building. The answer to HISDs needs was Cleveland Elementary at 400 Jackson Hill, a few blocks south of Washington Avenue. It was named not for the former U.S. President but for William D. Cleveland, a merchant, civic booster, and Cotton Exchange executive who had died in 1912.[32]

The two-story schoolhouse opened in 1926 at a total cost of over $135,000 and was lauded as a beautiful edifice. An early principal at Cleveland was Helen DeChaumes, daughter of an 1830s Houston French immigrant family and sister and housemate to both Henrietta, another HISD teacher, and Hortense, who was principal at Alexander Hamiton Junior High. Near the end of its school life, Cleveland was briefly considered as a home for the new HSPVA in the early 1970s, but was not chosen. It closed its doors in 1977.[33]

Janitors

Almost as soon as there were urban school buildings in Houston, there were janitors. The buildings had to be kept clean and in working order. As larger buildings appeared, janitors began to live on site, and were expected to act as night watchmen, as well. Most commonly, there was a simple room fitted out in the building's half-basement for accommodations.

The jobs as janitors at city schools were open to women, mostly African Americans. For the school year starting in 1888, First Ward Colored and Fourth Ward North Colored (which became Sixth Ward) had female janitors - Anna Blanks and Lucy Halsy respectively. By 1914, there were at least nine females working as janitors, several of them African American women.[34]

City school officials found the employment of women encouraging, writing the following: "We notice that there is a woman assistant to the janitor at a number of the different school buildings. We think this a good idea, and recommend that it be extended to include all buildings. In order to facilitate this, we commend the plan of having janitor's quarters wherever possible. This is being done in many buildings, and should be done especially at all of the new buildings. This would make it possible to secure the services of a man and wife who can stay in the building at all hours, and can be of service in many ways not possible if the janitor's home is elsewhere than at the building."

Like virtually everything else at the time, pay for janitors differed by race. In the early 1890s, salaries ranged from $50 to 25 a month in White schools, and from $35 to 10 a month in Black schools. To be somewhat fair, the three janitors drawing only $10 worked at one or two-room schools in First Ward, San Felipe, and Fourth Ward North. Rueben Mays at Colored High School was the highest paid janitor at an African American school. The highest custodial salary in the district belonged to Michael Curtin, an Irish immigrant who was a married father of six children. In 1900, Curtin was 75-years-old and still working as a school janitor.[35]

Though the pay was unequal, the opportunity to work in a given school was less restricted. Using the year 1914 as an example, there were seven Black janitors working in White schools, all of them women.[36]

In 1916, the school district began asking their janitors to wear "a simple uniform for house service." Enforcement for the first year was lax, but "the idea will be more rigidly enforced during the coming year and before the term is well started each man and woman in this department will be properly and neatly dressed."[37]

By 1920, the idea of live-in janitors was still going strong. The district was working hard to make at least some of the accommodations more attractive. At Travis Elementary in Woodland Heights "the janitors dwelling at this school has been overhauled, repainted, an additional room added, sanitary sewerage and water has been provided, making it a comfortable dwelling."[38]

CLINTON PARK E S

HISD opened a small school at 158 Mississippi Street in 1941 to serve the Clinton Park housing project on the east side of downtown. The first person in charge was Robert C. Chatham, son of Hempstead watermelon farmers, whose brother, Theodore, was also an HISD principal. The first year at Clinton Park, the operation was so small that Chatham was called "head teacher" instead of principal. A new building was constructed in 1958, and the school finally closed in May 2005.[39]

CLINTON SCHOOL

See Galena Park

CLINTON COLORED SCHOOL

See Fidelity

CLOPPER INSTITUTE

See Houston High

CLOVERLEAF ES

Cloverleaf Elementary at 1035 Frankie Street opened in 1943 as part of the Galena Park ISD. The area was booming due to WWII workers in Ship Channel industries. By 1949, children were attending Cloverleaf in shifts, and the district continued adding school buildings through the early 1950s to deal with the crowding.[40]

CLOW SCHOOL

An undated article from the *Spring Times* newspaper lists an African American Clow School off Steubner Airline that was brought into Spring ISD upon its formation in 1935. There was at least one Black family by that name living there prior to 1910, and a street by that name still exits.[41]

COLORED H S

See Washington, Booker T HS

Colored HS as it looked shortly after opening. The tower was later removed and it was renamed to honor Booker T. Washington. HISD

COLYER SCHOOL

The Colyer School at 1506 Caroline was a college preparatory school run by Mr. & Mrs. Nathaniel Colyer. It was established in September 1909 and operated at least through 1915.[42]

CONCORD SCHOOL

Concord School was a Black school at least during the mid-1880s until the late-1890s in District 23 which ran west and southwest of Houston. Extant records did not reveal a location or much other information. Henry Turpin taught there for several years splitting his time with other African American schools, indicating that Concord might not have offered a long and complete term.[43]

CONDIT E S

The first official school in Bellaire opened in a brown one-room building at Cedar and Third with a bare minimum of 20 students in Fall of 1911, not quite three years after the founding of the town by Iowa developer and railroad man William Wright Baldwin. After purchasing an almost 9,500 acre ranch from the William Marsh Rice estate, Baldwin subdivided it into agricultural tracts dubbed Westmoreland Farms and built not only the new town but an electric trolley and a boulevard to connect his holdings to the south end of Houston's Main Street about four miles to the east. He also lured Missouri horticulturist Edward Teas to set up shop east of the fledgling community. Growth was steady enough that the older grades soon moved to a rented room above Munger's general store on Fifth St. In 1914, Bellaire residents constructed a larger raised building near the southeast corner of Rice Avenue and Laurel where a school remains to this day.[44]

The trolley car was the lifeblood of Bellaire. Passengers with pink and yellow transfer tickets, which were part of the nickel fare, left Main Street and Eagle (near Wheeler Avenue) on the half hour. The return to town left Bellaire's stop on the hour. After the students at the new Rice Institute left the car south of Houston, the Bellaire school children who lived on the Westmoreland Farms hopped on or off the car. In the earliest years, they were overseen by conductor "Dad" Thetford who not only punched their tickets but corrected bad behavior. If the children were "careless with their tickets he punishes by making them get out and walk."[45]

In the 1920s, the Bellaire School, led by its principal Mrs. O.W. Wilcox, began an extensive program of student government that gained even some national attention. The first through seventh graders, numbering 40 when the plan started and growing to 200 pupils, almost all had a role in the daily operation of the school. Aside from the usual tasks of ringing bells, filling ink wells, cleaning erasers, monitoring halls and restrooms, and cleaning the school yard, the Bellaire students wrote official school correspondence, acted as press representatives, handled school announcements, performed janitorial tasks, administered quizzes when a teacher was out sick, and even chauffeured the principal's car to run small errands in the little town.[46]

The student council meted out almost all punishments, and every student was called for jury duty. The accused child had the right to appeal to the teacher, who acted "as the supreme court for the school. If the case comes before the supreme court, the council must produce witnesses and prove their case or the child is excused." The sentences handed out usually consisted of extra school work or loss of a privilege. It was enough to spur pupils to avoid absences. The attendance for the school stood at 95% "even when the children have to wear boots and walk in water to their knees." There were runners and bicycle riders who went to the nearby street car platform to hurry along students who were running late.[47]

Demolition at Condit ES in 1959. Houston Post photo.
HHRC

Even the health officers were fellow students who inspected the "hair, nails, teeth and elbows of all children in the room." The pupils took a Health Crusaders oath to have health, strength, and honor and be a "faithful soldier in the children's army of peace." In practical terms that meant washing hands before every meal, carrying a clean handkerchief, playing outdoors for at least half an hour, drinking two glasses of milk and three glasses of water a day "but no tea or coffee", being in bed for eleven or more hours, taking a bath on the days of the week that are marked on their card and pledging that "I tried hard to keep fingers and pencils out of my mouth and nose."[48]

In June 1927, residents of Bellaire petitioned the HISD to leave County District 23 and join the big city district. After the Houston authorities reported that the Bellaire buildings were in poor shape, a four room addition was added to the school with recessed lockers in lieu of a cloak room. Teacher salaries were also brought up to HISD standards. By the end of the decade, there were 15 teachers at Bellaire School serving over 600 students. Also about this time, the school was renamed to honor Alfred J. Condit, Bellaire businessman, advocate of education and good drainage, and the man who had served as William Baldwin's right hand in the community until his death.[49]

In 1959, the 45-year-old raised schoolhouse with the high steps was demolished and replaced with a new twelve room wing, though the late 1920s addition remained. In 2016, that construction in turn gave way to a more modern replacement. While Condit Elementary underwent its additions and remodels, Little Brown, the original 1911 school, with a small addition, survived just shy of a century. Converted to a private residence, it was finally destroyed by a fire on January 6, 2010.[50]

CONVENT OF THE GOOD SHEPHERD

Opening in 1914 at 1410 Richmond Road between Graustark and Loretto was the Convent of the Good Shepherd, an institution designed to help underprivileged, incorrigible juvenile delinquent girls. It was also known as St. Euphrasia School. The staff of eight sisters and three lay teachers served as many as 90 to 100 girls at a time, schooling them in home economics, music, and, if they remained long enough, furnishing an accredited high school course. Sisters preferred the girls stay at least two years, until they were capable of rejoining society. As one sister stated: "It is an institution which is reclaiming those who have been so unfortunate as to become victims of this evil."[51]

COOLEY E S

The first dedicated schoolhouse in Houston Heights opened on six lots at the southwest corner of Rutland and 17th in 1894, three years after construction began on the planned community. It was named for Daniel Denton Cooley, who along with his wife, Helen, led efforts to create the one-room brick building with green shutters. It had an unfinished upstairs that was not completed until several months later. Two outhouses were located in back. The first teacher, handling all eight grades, was Miss J. Deady from Harrisburg, daughter of the man for whom a Houston middle school is named. She had already been teaching at a room above an Ashland Street store prior to Cooley School's opening.[52]

It grew along with the town of Houston Heights. A year before its first expansion in 1906, some classes had to be transferred to rooms over a nearby drugstore and in a Methodist church. It became so crowded at one point that pupils were put on a half day schedule. The building grew to a 12 room school by 1912, 22 rooms by 1936, and sprouted temporary buildings even after that. Beginning as part of County District 25, Cooley then came under the control of Heights city school board and finally became part of HISD in 1918 when the area was annexed to Houston. The old building known so well to Heights residents was destroyed by fire on a cold February night in 1961, but was rebuilt and continued as an elementary school until 1980. The final years for Cooley were as home of the HISD alternative certification program until 2010 when the property was sold for development.[53]

Cooley ES. Houston Post photo. HHRC

E. E. Oberholtzer

His name was a bit unwieldy. Edison Ellsworth Oberholtzer. His legacy in Houston, however, was anything but. An Indiana native, Oberholtzer devoted his life to education. Starting at age 18 and armed with courses taken at Westfield College and Indiana State Normal School, he taught in small schools around his home state, quickly moving up to administrative posts in Terre Haute, Evansville, and Clinton, Indiana. In 1913, Oberholtzer took a bigger job, moving to the oil boomtown of Tulsa to oversee the school system there. He stayed ten years, during which he also earned a master's degree from the University of Chicago.[54]

His hiring in Houston came when the fledgling independent school district was in great need of clarity and command. Though formed in March 1923, HISD had been ruled illegal because four of the trustees were holdovers from the old city-run system. It took almost a year to untangle the mess and elect a new board. Their first superintendent hire was the 43-year-old Oberholtzer, and he was praised for having guided the rapidly growing Tulsa system, a reality certainly facing Houston. Above all, city boosters thought they were getting a "high-enthusiasm... man who believes in his mission."[55]

One of his first tasks in Houston was to remake the school system with an aggressive campaign of new buildings and curriculum reform. The approach he instituted was based on the progressive "child-centered" programs that were popular in educational academics, and it earned widespread praise from "the nation's foremost educators." Oberholtzer directed the creation of two segregated junior colleges as part of the HISD system in 1927, and those schools would eventually go on to become the University of Houston and Texas Southern University. The goal was not just to offer an accessible option for higher education to the citizenry, including students turned away from the city's Rice Institute, but also to provide for further training of HISD teachers whose pay he tied to their training.[56]

Oberholtzer was respected nationwide. In 1934, the NEA membership elected him president of their super-intendence department. At the time he described himself as "Liberal but not radical."[57]

Though later historians have criticized Oberholtzer for giving more power to administrators over teachers and for continuing a harshly segregated system, he did put more money into African American education than had previously been done in Houston's public schools. It was enough to earn high praise from Ira. B. Bryant when he released his history of Houston's Black schools in 1935, writing: "The present Negro schools of that city are monuments of Dr. Oberholtzer's attitude toward adequate educational facilities toward Negro children."[58]

E.E. Oberholtzer. University of Houston Special Collections

In 1945, after 22 years as superintendent of HISD, E.E. Oberholtzer resigned to take over as full-time president of the University of Houston, a school that he viewed as his creation. He had been instrumental not only in the founding but in securing a donation of 105 swampy acres from Ben Taub on which the new campus was placed, and many millions from oilman Hugh Roy Cullen who became the school's greatest benefactor. He served for five years as university president, then became president emeritus until his death in 1954. A building on the UH Central Campus bears his name. Oberholtzer is buried next to his wife, Myrtle, at Forest Park Mausoleum in Houston. [59]

COOP E S

The school named for Ethel R. Coop, a 14 year member of the HISD Board, was built at 10130 Aldine-Westfield in 1950.

COOPER HILL SCHOOL

Cooper Hill Schoolhouse in District 31 served an area near the community of Steubner, appearing in records from at least 1886 until after 1922. It sat on Hufsmith Road near Hufsmith Cemetery, seemingly just west of the intersection with Steubner-Airline. In 1894, it received the money scheduled to go to the Steubner School. A.H. Steubner was a trustee at Cooper Hill for several years around that time, and served as secretary at a meeting of Steubner Democrats there.[60]

COTTAGE GROVE HS

See Stevenson E S

COTTAGE GROVE COLORED SCHOOL

See Brunner Colored

COURTNEY SCHOOL

Courtney, an original school under the 1876 authorization, was, with French School, the heart of County District 3. It remained in operation until at least 1895.[61]

CRAWFORD E S

Mabel Wesley, the first principal of this school at 1510 Clark Street which opened in 1916, suggested that it be named for Joseph H. Crawford, a former teacher at Colored High School and professor of science at Prairie View A&M. The new six-room building was the replacement for a much maligned Hollywood School after that edifice burned. It had eight rooms within two years of opening, all under the supervision of the well-respected Mabel Wesley. Still, it was not enough to meet the neighborhood need. The city report of 1921-22 said that in addition to the two-story brick building, described as in good condition, there were "four temporary rooms in yard, and one improvised room in building." to meet the needs of between 700 and 800 students. Crawford campus closed for good about 2012.[62]

Crawford ES prior to occupation. HISD

Mabel Wesley

Mabel Wesley was one of the most accomplished educators in Houston, and it just so happened that her achievements came when being a woman, especially an African American woman, was a most definite handicap to career advancement.

Her birthdate was listed by her son as unknown, and records differ on whether she drew her first breath in Houston or in Montgomery County. Census records from her childhood and her obituary show that she was born around 1862 in the midst of the Civil War, a time when it was almost a certainty that she and her family were enslaved. She was the oldest child of Letitia Gordon and Fred Green, who by the 1870s and 80s were living in Houston's Fifth Ward where Fred was working as a laborer at the nearby railroad yards.[63]

Mabel Green Wesley was among the first students at Gregory Institute. By about 1880, she was a teacher, having secured a job at Hine's, a Black school in thriving County District 25 that ran mostly north and northwest of the city. Her salary by 1889 was thirty dollars a month. She also taught during the same time period at Hart's School, another one room county schoolhouse off Wallisville Road and at Lily White to the west of Houston. Her own education continued at the summer normal offered for African American teachers.[64]

During the early years of her teaching career, Mabel Green married Harry Wesley, a roustabout for the railroad. Their first child, Harry, Jr. was born in September 1885, followed by Freeman, and finally by Carter in 1892. The marriage did not last. By 1900, the couple was living apart. Over the next 15 years, both Mabel and Harry listed themselves as widowed, until Harry, Sr.'s death in 1915.[65]

At least two tax collection suits were filed against Mabel Wesley during the period between her separation from Harry and his death. Whether they were connected to marital finances is unknown. They appear to have been dismissed. Also unknown is any monetary connection to the fact that Mabel Wesley was listed as the janitor at Hollywood school for several years in addition to her teaching duties. She was not alone. G.B.M. Turner, the principal at Chaneyville Colored School, was also named as the janitor. It was common for teachers at one-room schools to be responsible for cleaning, but the specific listing as janitor is a step beyond. Plus, Hollywood was not a single room. What extra pay, if any, was gained by the double duty is not recorded.[66]

Professionally, Mabel Wesley left the employee of Harris County schools to begin teaching in the city system. In 1904, she was the junior teacher at Hollywood School, overseeing first and second grade. The principal there was E.O. Smith who handled third and fourth, the only other grades offered. Her younger sister, Rachel, was teaching at nearby Chaneyville Colored that year.[67]

Mabel Wesley briefly accompanied Smith to Booker T. Washington School in First Ward, but had returned to Hollywood as principal by the 1909-10 school year with a second teacher under her charge. She started, at her own expense, the first sewing class for the female students. After multiple reports on overcrowding at Hollywood School, the city finally replaced it in 1916 with Crawford, a six-room brick building on Clark Road, and Mrs. Wesley became the principal there. The school expanded over the years, eventually gaining a faculty of almost two dozen and making it the largest school in the state headed by a woman.[68]

Though she had to give up her classroom duties, Mabel Wesley remained an expert in primary grade education. She headed the Primary Section for the Colored Teachers' Texas Association for nearly 25 years. She studied at Prairie View A&M in her off time and received her bachelor's degree in 1930 at the age of 68.

The family remained close to her. Her youngest son, Carter, lived with her for a time as an adult, as did her grandson Horace and her sister, Rachel, after her own divorce. The family home for most of the early 20th century was at 3200 Washington Avenue near the Brown Chapel Methodist Church. It was one of the churches with which she was active and involved, though her "faithful membership" was at Trinity A.M.E, the site of her funeral in May 1941. At the time of her death, Mabel Wesley was still the principal at Crawford Elementary.[69]

Today an HISD school in Acres Homes bears her name.

CROCKETT E S

Houston city schools enjoyed a flurry of new construction and remodeling at the start of the 1910s, and one of those new buildings was Crockett Elementary which opened at the corner of Crockett and Henderson streets in First Ward in 1912. It honored the famed Alamo martyr. Trumpeted as welcome relief for nearby Hawthorne, Crockett opened with 12 classrooms, an auditorium lunch room, facilities for manual training and domestic science, and a club room. It was said to be a "model of convenience" with attractive wall and woodwork, spacious grounds, and harmonious color schemes for children in grades one through seven.[70]

Crockett ES students and their "store." HISD

The first principal at the school was W.W. Higgins, one time superintendent of Harris County Schools. He remained at the school for 16 years and oversaw much growth. By 1920, the school had 25 rooms, many of them shacks that covered the rest of the school's block. The First Ward neighborhood rode peaks and valleys in popularity over the decades, and the original Crockett School was demolished and replaced with a new building in 1980.[71]

CROCKETT ES CHANNELVIEW

A five-room elementary named for David Crockett opened on nine acres of ground in Channelview ISD about 1938.[72]

CROOMS PARK COLORED SCHOOL

This school name appears only one year, in 1912, located one block west of Reinerman Street between Pine and Buffalo Bayou.

CROSBY SCHOOL

Crosby got its first retail business the year the Civil War ended, and with the coming of the railroad, it was a transportation hub for much of East Harris County. Its first school was tuition-based, situated behind a home at 307 Live Oak, and for many years, the sole public school in County District 17 was south of the town on the property of Rueben White. The community of Crosby did not get its first public school building for grades one through five until 1894 when a one-room frame structure opened at 602 Kernohan. It served the community until 1910 when residents passed a $10,000 bond to build a new two-story edifice in the 700 block of Runneberg.[73]

It was the first brick building in town, and residents considered it "one of the most magnificent buildings in the county." With six classrooms and cloak rooms and an auditorium, Principal Tom Blackstone felt sure that "a future of no mean worth awaits Crosby and her people." He did want more than the three-acre grounds in order to more "fully enjoy baseball. We have boys that put them over center, and come across the plate with a home run." By 1912, the school went to ninth grade, and tenth grade came a decade later. By that time, Crosby was an ISD with just over 500 total students. The elementary was up to ten classrooms by the end of the 1930s.[74]

The first school bus at Crosby. Crosby Historical Society

CROSBY COLORED SCHOOL
See Barrett

CROSBY H S
High School age students in Crosby got their own building, across Runneberg Street from the 1910 "brick school," in 1925, the same year that the 11th grade was added. At the time, the town's entire student population was less than 200. Each room had a separate coal burning stove, and for the first two years, lights were provided by a stand-alone system since the schools were not on the power grid. Additional rooms were added along with a cafeteria and gymnasium in the late 1930s. The class of 1941 was the first to complete 12 grades, and the 39 graduates that year donated a row of live oaks planted along Runneberg Street.[75]

Football was played at Buffalo Field behind the school which had no lights and no bleachers. Fans sat on the ground or stood until grandstands were built years later. It was a popular pastime for the bulk of the town in spite of the seating arrangements, and large numbers of them ponied up the $5.50 cost for season tickets in the late 1940s. After integration of Crosby schools, the mascot was changed from the Buffaloes to the Cougars. The high school moved to a new location on today's FM 2100, and in 2016 a new building was opened and the previous one renovated for use as a middle school.[76]

CROSS TIMBERS SCHOOL

Houstonians know Crosstimbers as a street name, but its origin is as a small community on the railroad northeast of downtown. The school was one of several in what was the crowded District 25. In 1886, the building was rented, but soon there was a frame building owned by the district. After it was sold in the summer of 1895, a new building was erected in its place. It sat on brick piers six feet off the ground, measured 26' x 40' with four big windows on each side and one more on either side of the front door. There were two large closets, heart pine flooring, a shingle roof, and galvanized gutters that led to a 2,000 gallon cypress cistern. The contractor received $145 for building it, and when it was completed, it got two coats of white paint and fresh green shutters. Cross Timbers (two words) continued to have its own school house at least as late as WWI.[77]

CROSS TIMBERS COLORED SCHOOL

The community of Cross Timbers also had an African American school building, though records are scant, showing up only in the lone surviving district minutes book for years between 1894 and 1896.[78]

CULMORE SCHOOL

Blanche Culmore ran a school at 2118 German Street, later to be renamed Canal, for almost the entire first decade of the 20th century. She shows up again in the city directory on McKinney only for the year 1923.[79]

CYPRESS E S

Cypress Elementary School was the more modern campus that rose from the ashes of the 1942 fire that destroyed much of the amalgam of wooden buildings that had been assembled at the southwest corner of Telge and Cypress-North Houston over the years. All the young students marched out safely, but they were forced to attend classes in the nearby high school until the first four rooms of a new school were constructed, a process that moved slowly during WWII. More rooms were added in 1951, and the elementary was renamed for George Lamkin on May 23, 1955.[80]

CYPRESS H S

See Cypress-Fairbanks High School

CYPRESS SCHOOL

The immediate area around the town of Cypress, at today's Hempstead Highway and Spring-Cypress Road, had settlers all the way back to 1833, but the town itself was started by William Robinson Baker, the Houstonian who owned a major share of the railroad that came through in 1856. He bought the land, built a depot, and platted a town before selling it a few years later for a nice profit. It was known as Cypress City or Cypress Top in the mid to late 1800s. Cypress City was listed among those Harris County communities in an 1861 school census along with Little Cypress and Big Cypress, and there was a Cypress School among the 1876 original public schools ledger. The name Cypress School, however, is used often in reference for what became known as Big Cypress, and occasionally for Little Cypress, as well, so differentiating between them is sometimes difficult. The exact location of any separate school within the confines of Cypress City is unknown.[81]

CYPRESS COLORED SCHOOL

There was a school for African American students in the Cypress area, County District 6, though the name seems to have been listed as both Cypress Colored and Big Cypress Colored at varying times. As with many other rural county districts, remaining records are few, though the school definitely existed by 1886 and likely earlier since the 1870 census enumerates several Black and mulatto families in the immediate area. The men were working as farm hands or railroad laborers, and some of the women as domestic servants. As the 20th century progressed, the Black schools of the area sometimes inherited outdated White school buildings. A 1940 survey described the Cypress Negro School as being valued at about $1,000 with well water and no electric lights for the 41 students in grades one through seven. There was one teacher.[82]

CYPRESS - FAIRBANKS H S

Not surprisingly, Cypress-Fairbanks High School grew out of the consolidated Cypress and Fairbanks school districts, a combination that is largely credited to Superintendents E.A. Millsap of Cypress and J.F. Bane of Fairbanks. At their urging, elections were held in 1939 and residents of each ISD voted to merge, though the issue carried in Fairbanks by a margin of only 90 to 87. With a $200,000 bond approved, 100 acres of land was purchased for $75 an acre the following year, and in 1941 construction began on a modern brick building. It was especially welcome to Fairbanks high school age students who were being bussed to Houston.[83]

The site was adjacent to the previous Cypress Rural High School Number 5, a wood-framed building that had opened just a few years prior in 1937. At the time it opened, providing a separate building for Cypress high schoolers for the first time, it was considered modern itself with a music room and a gymnasium/auditorium. Given to the elementary students when the new brick building opened, this structure is the one that burned in 1942.

Cy-Fair HS in the 21st century. Wikimedia Commons

The Cy-Fair area was still quite rural in the 1940s. Residents didn't often make the hour or two drive into downtown Houston. Recreation was more often found at the F&M Jersey Ranch ice cream parlor, the Hot Wells swimming pool, or music at Tin Hall for those who didn't object to dancing and beer. The Cy-Fair Rodeo, organized by principal Forrest Arnold in 1944, became a big area draw on Friday nights, and combined with extensive agricultural operations earned the high school the nickname "Little A&M".[84]

Many additions have been made, but the original 1941 building still stands at Cy-Fair High along US 290.

Schools D - E

DAIRY SCHOOL

See Alief

DAIRY COLORED SCHOOL

Most African Americans in the Dairy area at the end of the 19th century worked on the farm of Della Kay Ren, and it was near there, at the intersection of todays' Renn Road and Eldridge, that the Dairy Colored School opened in 1896. Resident Dave Outley, father of 12 of the children who attended the school, served as spokesperson for the Black community with the District 10 school board. Today the Prairie Grove Cemetery is on the site, holding the mostly unmarked graves of many of those residents.[1]

DAVIS H S

Jeff Davis High School was one of three senior highs that grew out of HISD's 1920s bond elections, specifically the first one from June 1924. The district spent just shy of $50,000 for the site across Quitman Street from the decade old Marshall Junior High and set aside about $207,000 for the building, but that was not the end. The school opened in 1926 with 510 students, but that same year, with funds from the next bond issue, another parcel of land and another $58,000 went into the campus. When all was finished by the end of the decade, Davis High had 41 classrooms, offices, a gym, swimming pool, auditorium, two laboratories, a lunchroom, and an auditorium.[2]

An alumni group was formed only a year after the school opened, funding a scholarship, various programs and awards, and money to assist with student entertainments. There were plenty more eligible members to come. By 1932, enrollment had topped 1,000. Multiple Davis graduates have made a national mark including singer Kenny Rogers, longtime Congressman Gene Green, and basketball Hall of Famer Slater Martin.[3]

Davis HS shortly after opening. HISD

When the Confederate-related school name controversy erupted in 2015, many Houstonians felt that a campus honoring the leader of a treasonous and rebellious would-be nation was by far the most inappropriate of the lot, but that was weighed against the personal history of thousands of northside citizens who had proudly graduated wearing the purple and white of the Panthers. Ironically, there had been a loud controversy in 1925 when seven new and four existing HISD schools got new monikers. Davis had gone on the drawing board as North Side High School, the very name that it carries today. Though there were bitter battles, the selection of Jefferson Davis drew some protest, but not as much as several others. Briefly, there was a counter-proposal to name the school for Judah P. Benjamin, a Jewish pro-slavery U.S. Senator who went on to hold all three of the top cabinet positions in the Confederacy before fleeing permanently for Europe at the end of the Civil War. In the end, only the Davis name was seriously considered, and when the cornerstone was laid in spring 1925, it was dedicated by the Confederate Veterans and Auxiliary of Dick Dowling Camp.[4]

A Football Cat Fight

As far as the Sam Houston Tigers were concerned, their game at Rice Field on October 17, 1930 was in hand. They had a comfortable lead on Jeff Davis, and the fourth quarter was winding down. The Panther fans, however, were unruly. Fights were breaking out along the Davis sideline that involved over 100 people, to the point that the gridiron action was temporarily halted so police could restore order. That was not happening. "Within a few minutes... other fights were in progress on the Sam Houston side of the field. The two policemen on the field were unable to cope with the situation." Student "cadets and civilians mixed it furiously in one combat" to the point that bones were broken, and several cases were sent off to nearby hospitals.[5]

The game of high school football had just recently suffered a setback when the Houston school board voted down a proposal to allow night games. It was a recipe for trouble, and having unchaperoned boys and girls out at night was just a flat bad idea the board said. After the Tigers/Panthers main event on a Friday afternoon, some voices around the Bayou City were calling for an end to football games altogether, the most un-Texan sacrilege to ever pass Lone Star lips.[6]

In the end, the board sided with people like local insurance agent E.J. Stidston who had been at the game in question and took the time to write both HISD Board President K.C. Barkley and Superintendent Oberholtzer. The board was convinced the trouble started courtesy of "the menace of hoodlums who are ever-present and who attach themselves to every school student body." The answer was uniformed off-duty policemen who for $5 a game could do a much better job than well-meaning student cadets, even if the cadets were the cheaper option. Pulling a paddy wagon up to the edge of the grounds might help, too. After all, given the fact that there were multiple high school football games each week, things were not that bad. "I think there has been a minimum number of riots," Barkley said.[7]

So HISD football survived. By the fall of 1933, HISD trustees had changed their tune, and high schools were even enjoying some Friday night lights. As E.E. Oberholtzer pointed out, it was less of a burden on class schedules and it "attracts a larger crowd and brings in greater revenue."[8]

DE ALCALA SCHOOL

Little is known about this private school that was listed as "Spanish" for a two year period in the early 1920s. There were two addresses shown simultaneously: 107 Main and 1911 Gentry, the latter clearly a house on the Northside.[9]

DE ZAVALA E S

The school named for Texas Revolutionary patriot and Yucatan native Lorenzo de Zavala has an instructive history as to how Mexican immigrants and their offspring were treated around Harris County. Unlike HISD, where segregation of Hispanic students was a somewhat ad hoc and uneven affair as opposed to the official policy of strictly separate schools that existed for African Americans, other districts were more official. One of those was the Harrisburg ISD which dedicated Magnolia Park School Number 2 in 1920 at the northeast corner of 75th and Avenue H. The two-room white stucco building very quickly became known as "the Mexican School." Whether that name was ever actually adopted by the district is unclear, but that is the name that appeared in the city directories of the 1920s. The many Mexican-origin pupils had previously been attending school with other European-descended children in the district, but school officials felt that was not working out.[10]

The feeling of the White Harrisburg school officials and parents was far from unique. Corpus Christi had established a Mexican School as early as 1896 and was followed by other south Texas cities such as Harlingen and Kingsville. It fit perfectly with a push for Americanization that reached a peak in the early 1910s. HISD was very proud of its work to help immigrants assimilate, and administrators felt that it was extremely important. Immigration was booming in that decade, and when the U.S. entered WWI it was discovered that about a half million draftees were unable to understand orders given in English. Though Americanization was aimed primarily at people such as the many thousands of Italians and Eastern Europeans who were coming to the Northeast United States, the Mexican exodus into Texas was happening at exactly the same time. More than 30 states enacted laws that required school teachers and administrators to teach only in English. The Texas version was passed by the legislature in 1918.[11]

In November 1926, the Harrisburg school district became part of HISD, and, for several years, the segregation policy of the school being exclusively for children of Mexican parentage was continued. For over 20 years, there had been Mexican American students in nearly a dozen other HISD White schools. Separation there developed in some of them by custom, with those whom administrations found to lack language skills in English being placed in their own classes. Other HISD White schools were not segregated at all. There were also many situations were children zoned to another city elementary were "encouraged" to attend one of the majority "Mexican" schools such as Rusk or Jones elementaries instead, but again, not in every case. Across Harris County, only elementary schools, as opposed to secondary schools, focused on separate instruction for Mexican-origin children. Almost all campuses told children, many of whom spoke only Spanish at home, to use only English at school, often with threat of punishment.[12]

The rationale was the same as that voiced by Harrisburg ISD in the beginning - that the separate facilities provided these "children an opportunity to acquire an English speaking vocabulary sufficient to enable them to compete in class work with American children." Since the widespread immigration to escape the revolution in northern Mexico had started around 1910, many of the children attending the Mexican School were no doubt Americans, as well.[13]

When Harrisburg ISD opened the school, Principal Velma Woods enrolled 75 pupils on day one. The following day there were only 20, and on the third day, just three. Mexican civic leaders had been very successful at convincing parents that the segregation was discriminatory. The Mexican Consul asked to meet with Harrisburg school superintendent Hanner and board president Burchfield about what might be an international problem. The community meeting took place at the Mutualista Benito Juarez Hall on Navigation, and after discussion, amity was restored and the students returned to "the Mexican School." Attendance grew so that another teacher was hired later that year. Two rooms were added in 1925 and six more, along with showers for students who did not have them at home. In 1928 the school was officially named in honor of De Zavala. Major upgrades and rebuilding occurred in 2001-02, and the campus still serves the Magnolia Park area.[14]

DE ZAVALA SCHOOL, BAYTOWN

Goose Creek CISD opened a segregated school for its Mexican immigrant and Mexican American students in Humble Oil's "Mexican community hall" in 1923, and a few years later, a three-room building was constructed on Magnolia Street near the Missouri Pacific tracks in Old Baytown from proceeds of the bond election of 1927. The 500 or so Mexican-heritage residents were centered in the Airhart subdivision, and many worked for Humble. When the new school opened for classes in 1928, none of the three teachers were fluent in Spanish, and many of the students had never been to school before. There were 72 pupils in First Grade but only 17 in grades five through seven combined. As in other "Mexican" schools, the campus was English only, but by the late 1930s, a Mexican American teacher had instituted a boys' band and a girls' tipica orchestra, celebrating at least the musical side of the students' heritage. Later renamed to honor Lorenzo de Zavala, the original building closed in 1968 then spent a few more years as home to a Head Start program. A new De Zavala Elementary opened in GCCISD in 1992.[15]

DE ZAVALA SCHOOL, CHANNELVIEW

Channelview opened a four room, brick De Zavala School in the middle 1930s on an acre of property. It is not far from the 1830s homestead of Lorenzo de Zavala and his family.

DEADY J H S

James Swan Deady was Mr. Harrisburg in many ways. In the final decades of that town's life as a separate municipality, he served as mayor, J.P., and school board president, so it was not surprising that a southeast Houston junior high that opened at 2500 Broadway in 1928 was named in his honor. It was one of the rare times that a building was named for a still-living person since Deady did not die until 1942. Using funds from the third of the 1920s bond issues, the property, equipment, and building cost almost $278,000. Though Loop 610 has long since intruded on the area around the campus, students still climb the steps and walk through the triple blue front doors. In 2025, the campus is a magnet for energy, medicine, and aerospace technology.[16]

The new Deady JHS. HISD

Guns and Houston School Children

Just as in most every other large town in the United States in the late 19th and early 20th century, the carrying of firearms around the Bayou City was highly regulated. Even Houston police officers did not normally carry guns for several decades in the late 1800s.With the availability of those weapons much lower than today, the incidence of gun tragedies involving schoolchildren was also lower, but they did happen.[17]

Many were the same tragedies we still see thanks to irresponsible adults. In mid-June 1904, an eleven-year-old local girl accidentally shot her thirteen-year-old brother while the two had been left home alone.[18]

That same spring, seven-year-old Ammon Hubble was playing along the banks of Buffalo Bayou when he was "shot below the eye by a stray bullet." His initial story to police was that he was "shot by a negro," though he had not actually seen such a perpetrator. A *Post* reporter expressed open skepticism, writing "why he made that statement is a mystery." After battling for about four weeks, the young Hubble boy succumbed to his wounds on May 17, 1904, but not before giving the name Harold Jones to the authorities. An arrest was made.[19]

Motives for some child shootings mirrored those of grown-ups, including plain old-fashioned jealousy. In October 1933, a twelve-year-old boy who lived near Shepherd and Westheimer shattered the hip of 14-year-old E.W. Sayers with a bullet through a living room window after the older boy sashayed past his home with a girl the youngster had been eyeing. The unnamed twelve-year-old grabbed a .22 rifle from his garage and followed the couple to a neighbor's home where he fired the malicious shot. Police woke the shooter from a sound slumber two hours later, and were given a confession that officers described as being "without emotion."[20]

"I was jealous of him," the spurned youngster said. "He was beating my time with a girl."[21]

Robbery also came into play. At the end of a party at Jack Yates High School on Elgin in March 1934, the teachers, including Ella Walls Montgomery, were counting the money raised by the ten-cent ticket charge when an armed hijacker broke into the room waving a gun and demanding that they hand over the loot. He grabbed Montgomery's purse, but it had only $2.35 of her own money since she had hidden the dance proceeds. In the midst of the hub-bub, school janitor E.V. Pitts, who "had a special police commission to carry a gun," emerged and fired a shot from behind a partially opened door. The would-be robber returned four shots, all of which went wild, before dropping Mrs. Montgomery's purse and running for the door.[22]

DEEPWATER SCHOOL

Though a current school in Deer Park ISD carries the Deepwater name, the original one room school in County District 40 dates back to the mid-1890s. Located between Pasadena and Deer Park on the south side of Buffalo Bayou, the community on the Galveston, Houston and Northern Railroad had about 200 residents. That translated to a White student population of 40 shortly after the turn of the century. As Deer Park grew and developed its own schools, the Deepwater school, about three miles east of Deer Park, was converted to an institution for Mexican American students, mostly children of strawberry farmers, in grades one through three. The older Hispanic grade schoolers attended San Jacinto Elementary with everyone else.[23]

"Deepwater Mexican School." HCPL

DEEPWATER COLORED SCHOOL

Records of the Deepwater Colored School are scant, but notes in the late 1890s reference a White school as if there was a Black school, as well. By 1905, there were 25 African American pupils at a one-room, one-teacher school. Around this time, the old White schoolhouse was handed down to the Black children. Some students may have ridden the ferry from Penn City across the bayou. A study of Deer Park ISD just prior to WWII notes that there was no Black school in DPISD at that time.[24]

DEER PARK H S

In the 1940s, Deer Park housed all students from grades one through twelve in the same building. It and a gymnasium were the lone structures on the 24-acre campus that also served as the de facto community center for the small town that was dominated by the Shell refinery. The multi-colored brick school building held 16 classrooms, a library, an auditorium-gymnasium, a clinic, a teacher's lounge, a school kitchen, and two offices. In the sparsely populated district, two busses logged 126 miles a day bringing students to and from classes.[25]

The core of the building had opened in 1931 covering students through seventh grade. Deer Park high schoolers had to travel to La Porte or Pasadena. Eighth and ninth grades were added in 1937, along with more rooms, and it became a four year high school two years later. It remained the only scholastic game in town until San Jacinto Elementary opened on 8th Street in 1949.[26]

DEER PARK SCHOOL

County District 14 was originally the home to the schools in the small, and now lost, community of San Jacinto, but by 1908 there were classes being held in the Marsh home in the fledgling town of Deer Park under the tutelage of Miss Myrtle B. Goode. Previously children of the community rode with the mail carrier via ferry across the bayou to Lynchburg. A proper school building by the La Porte Road opened two years later with about 20 children. [27]

A commute to school at Deer park. Courtesy Shell Refinery

By 1920, the school and the post office were discontinued, and once again, the mail carrier and the ferry took students to Lynchburg when the weather permitted. Deer Park dropped to fewer than a dozen buildings including the abandoned schoolhouse. It was saved in November 1928 when the first engineers and workers from the St. Louis area to begin constructing a new Shell refinery. They used the empty schoolhouse as an office.

Growth was so rapid that workers lived in a tent city that included a makeshift school for the children of Shell employees. The lone rooming house was notorious for shootings, knifings, and bootlegging until the G-men shut it down. The final threat to Deer Park schools was a narrowly won referendum that prevented the district from being absorbed by La Porte. In 1931, the new brick school opened on Ivy Street, and the old wooden structure was moved from the Shell property to become the Baptist Church.[28]

DODSON E S

Dodson Elementary was one of the examples of a segregated school constructed for White children that switched to an African American campus with changing neighborhood demographics. It happened a number of times in HISD, and included the school that opened as James Bowie in May 1922. It was a one-story Spanish style building with a basement on a substantial piece of property at 1808 Sampson.[29]

In 1945, the aging Luckie School was closed, and Bowie was converted to a campus for Black pupils with the name being changed to honor the longtime principal at Luckie, Julius N. Dodson. It grew to be the second largest Black elementary in Third Ward for a time, and in its last years served as a Montessori magnet program. The original Bowie schoolhouse gave way to a modern building with only the old Spanish style front door pediments remaining. The Dodson Elementary campus closed in 2014 and the students were transferred to Blackshear Elementary while the Energy Institute High School was relocated to the site on Sampson.[30]

DOGAN E S

Grant Park Elementary, a segregated elementary school for African American students was opened at 4202 Liberty Road in 1949 and later renamed in honor of Matthew W. Dogan, the longtime President of Wiley College. Mildred Kilpatrick was the first teacher at Grant Park. A new building was erected on the site in the 2000s.[31]

DORCAS HOME/ SCHOOL

The Dorcas Home started small. Initially it was a private philanthropic effort led by longtime Houston educator Nat Q. Henderson to provide education and a home for delinquent African American girls. Public spirited Black Houstonians footed the bill. In 1917, there was only room for seven young ladies who were placed there by the Juvenile Court. They were under the charge of Jennie Bell who was serving without salary. The county did provide a detention facility for these girls, most of whom were there in answer to morals charges, but the Dorcas Home sought to be an educational and rehabilitative haven. Though the small farm was bare-bones, the residents maintained a truck garden using well water and supplied vegetables to the homes for White delinquent boys and girls before those facilities moved to Bellaire.[32]

By 1920, there were calls for the city and county to increase their contributions to the operation, funds that totaled $100 a month, and a year later they were looking for a new home for the facility which had lost its main building to fire some years prior. The first site contracted was at the community of Little York, and 116 residents there signed a petition in opposition to the home. It finally settled on fourteen acres of land with several existing houses one mile north of Sunset Heights, near present day 34th Street, that was purchased for $4,000. The

Dorcas Home continued to struggle for funding, and in 1930, the oversight grand jury opined that it "should be abolished or converted into a 'decent place in which humans can live.'"[33]

DOUGHTIE'S SCHOOL

Likely named for landowner L.O. Doughtie, this was a one-teacher school in County District 2 along with Oak Grove. It appears in the records from the mid-1880s until the mid to late 1890s.[34]

DOUGLASS E S

One of the longest tenured Black school names in Houston sadly ceased to exist in 2005. Though the last of its four buildings lives on at Sauer and Trulley in Third Ward, the most famous African American of the 19th century is no longer honored by a local place of education.

It began its run of 126 consecutive years as the Third Ward Colored School, opening on October 1, 1877 when the city started public schools authorized by the new Constitution of the previous year. Situated on the north side of Walker between Hamilton and Chartres, it was taught that first year by Mrs. L.C. Fisher with Hannah Dibble, daughter of the prominent Methodist minister Elias Dibble, acting as her assistant. About 80 students of grades one through four attended. Crowding soon became a problem at the two room schoolhouse, and within a few years, first and second graders only attended half a day.[35]

By June 1885, the school board had determined that a bigger space was needed for the Black children of Third Ward. The old school house was sold as a residence to James F. Lucas for $1500. Its replacement was a new four room frame building at the northwest corner of Jackson and Calhoun that boasted 204 seats. By 1887, its enrollment was 267. The principal for the next several years was Charles B. Atherton who would become a fixture in Houston's early African American education scene.[36]

By 1895, the Third Ward Colored School had been renamed for Frederick Douglass, a man who escaped from slavery to become a leading abolitionist, lecturer, and advocate for civil rights.[37]

Once again, the growing Black population in the southern portion of Third Ward strained Douglass School to bursting. Now catering to grades one through six, enrollment neared 350, remaining crowded in spite of additional rooms being added. Respite came in the form of the donation of a "block of land on McGowan Avenue, east of Dowling St." by realtor William A. Wilson for a new Douglass School in an addition he was developing. It would replace the Jackson Street campus which, like several other local schools, was still operating without electricity.[38]

The new $10,000 building in the 2900 block of McGowan, the site of today's Blue Triangle Community Center, opened in 1908 with seven classrooms. School principal W.S. Francis, a native Jamaican like Atherton, made the move to the new building. He stayed for twenty years, roughly half of his total service time in Houston schools, before moving on to Langston and then Gregory School, earning respect from the community in spite of being described as living a reclusive life.[39]

The 1908 Douglass ES building. HISD

The Mothers Club at Douglass, started the same year as the new building, was the largest at any African American school in town. They pushed for improvements such as paving the basement area and building brick walkways. One upgrade that took a few years to achieve was the addition of flush toilets and city water which did not extend to the immediate area at the time of the school's opening.[40]

After hearing numerous complaints, Mrs. Presley K. Ewing, head of Houston's Mothers Clubs, encouraged Douglass School parents to circulate a petition which she in turn forwarded to the city health officer, Dr. C.C. Green.

"The colored people whose children attend Douglass School have come to me repeatedly, asking if I could not help them get city water in the school, as their children will not drink the well water," Mrs. Ewing wrote in her straightforward style. "They claim the well water at times is slimy, that it is not pleasant to drink, and though I am a layman myself, it seems to me in this section well water would be unhealthy, and I can not help believing all the colored people claim. It seems to me that good, pure water for the school would be less expensive to the city than a possible typhoid epidemic. Typhoid sometimes spreads beyond the confines in which it is contracted. And it seems, too, that common humanity demands pure drinking water for these children." Hoping you will pursue this request. Sincerely, Mrs. Preston K. Ewing."[41]

The school grew to accommodate seventh grade, as well. By 1920, there were 19 rooms and 650 desks. Four annex buildings were placed in the middle of the block and five sheds lined the rear of the property along Bremond. When HISD had an influx of cash from three 1920s bond elections, the Douglass School moved to a fourth location. That building at 3000 Trulley proved to be the longest tenured for the Douglass School name, introducing many thousands of Third Ward children to the classroom and lasting until it was sold by HISD in 2005. The building lives happily on today as the private Yellowstone Academy.

Black Teachers Scandal of 1904

In 1903, a "normal" was held in Conroe for African American teachers, and an examination for teaching certificates was given by J. P. Jones, the principal of First Ward Colored School in Houston. Of the 23 prospective teachers from the Bayou City, only one passed the examination. The poor results caught the attention of Jones and others, including State Superintendent Arthur Lefevre.

Some of the would-be teachers retook the exam in September of that year and passed. One was a woman who got a job in a Harris County school, and her boss, County Superintendent L.L. Pugh, soon became another educational leader who suspected something rotten in the certification process. When the following exam was given, there were three times the usual number of applicants, and among those who failed were several who were outraged, flatly refusing to believe the results.[42]

Principal Jones went to a study group of prospective teachers in late 1903 and found that copies of a certification exam were available. He testified before the Houston school board that he "suspected" that they were the real McCoy. Reports of his testimony was vague, and no names were given, but the teacher who had the test claimed that he got it from another local teacher who in turn got it from a colleague in Orange.

Pugh's investigation into the county teachers was more stringent, perhaps because as their boss, he had the leeway to demand answers. Under his strident questioning of those who had doubted their own test failure, one woman flatly admitted that she had paid $25 for a copy of the test, and another said $40. Another woman reported that the teacher who sold her the quiz had hidden himself beneath the Taylor School building and encouraged her to take frequent bathroom breaks during which she would walk past him for answers. The problem that emerged for several of the teachers was that the person selling the exam had gotten several answers wrong themselves.

The Houston School Board relieved five teachers of their duty, and the county targeted roughly a dozen more for revocation of certificates that were fraudulently obtained. Pugh even got an attorney general's opinion that he could withhold the pay of those he deemed guilty. Due to the investigative efforts of Pugh and Lefevre, dozens of African American teachers were fired or arrested around Texas.

Though the names of the fired teachers in the City of Houston were not immediately released in the newspapers, the identities of their replacements were. Among those coming into open positions were J.N.

Dodson, who would render service to HISD that would get a campus named after him, and Pinkie Yates, the daughter of Reverend Jack Yates.

One of the possible casualties of the firings was James D. Ryan, a teacher at Colored High School. His dismissal came after the other teachers but was described as "dismissing another colored teacher from the service of the city." By the Summer Normal of 1906, Ryan was teaching geometry to the teachers and back as the mathematics instructor at the high school again. In 1912, Ryan took over from Charles Atherton as principal at the school, became the first principal at Yates High School, and today, an HISD middle school campus is named in his honor.[43]

The new Houston School Superintendent Paul Horn was not so subtle. When the uproar was slightly fresher, Horn penned his first annual report and had this to say about the scandal: "The investigation among the colored teachers during the past year seems to have had a healthful effect, and as one of their own number stated: 'It is a step in the right direction; for if the teachers do not have a high moral plane in which to conduct themselves, they cannot expect to have their pupils occupy any such plane.' These investigations and remarks, of course, apply in no way to the large number of colored teachers who have so faithfully and honorably served their people in this city for a number of years."[44]

DOW E S

Justin E. Dow, Dartmouth College class of 1854, was promoted from principal of Houston High School to Houston School Superintendent in 1885, and he died in that office just two years later on his way to the Southern Pacific Depot to catch a train. Within months, the new Washington Street School was renamed in his honor.[45]

The T-shaped wood frame building had opened in January 1888, and the students and teachers, over 170 strong, "marched in a body" from the two-room Fourth Ward School at State and Trinity to the new six-room edifice. Joining them there were other children from the San Felipe Street School and some from Taylor School. Their new digs sat high above the street level and were heated by stoves that burned wood or coal.[46]

Like every other school in the growing town of Houston, Dow filled up. In March 1894, it shed 150 of its 362 students to the new Hawthorne School, an almost identical design that was nearby on Houston Avenue. Ten years later, Dow, now expanded to eleven rooms, held 553 seats and the city was renting a two-room Dow Annex that accommodated 74 more. Improvements continued at the school. In 1909-10, new toilets were placed in the space underneath the building, replacing the original outhouses. The same year, four new rooms were added, but still it was not enough.[47]

The year 1910 also brought a bond election for Houston schools, one that passed by a 16 to 1 margin, and a large portion of the money was earmarked for brick replacements for Dow, Longfellow, and Taylor. Grounds were purchased for the new Dow which would move off the Washington Avenue thoroughfare into the Sixth Ward neighborhood immediately to the south. Principal E.A. Cochran and sixteen teachers moved to the new school, a veritable palace with a total price tag that surpassed $100,000. The property at Washington and Ash was kept by HISD and the old building served as the location of the district's business office, finally being sold in February 1962.[48]

Dow School just prior to opening in 1913. The building has been restored and is in use. HISD

The new brick Dow building on Kane Street opened in 1913 with 16 rooms and would eventually grow to 28, including four temporary shacks. Superintendent Horn noted an immediate need for more classrooms there, and he had already gathered bids prior to the grand opening. Late to the party, Dow did not organize a Mothers Club until it moved into the new "fire-proof" building, but they raised funds quickly and spent them on a gas stove, kitchen utensils, and a piano. One of the trumpeted features in the new building was a "special room for greatly retarded pupils." The thirty students, both girls and boys, spent the majority of their instruction time building and tending their own individual garden plot on the grounds, then doing school work related to it.[49]

Like many other schools, Dow was soon crowded, answering first with temporary buildings then with an addition in 1926. The "new" Dow served the Sixth Ward for almost 80 years before it was targeted for closure at the start of 1991 by Superintendent Joan Raymond. Many neighbors saw it as "an act of abandonment" and the loss of the "anchor of the neighborhood." The void was filled in 1993 when the school building was leased for a dollar a year to MECA, Multicultural Education and Counseling Through the Arts, a non-profit that has produced many talented artists and musicians.[50]

Houston Schools in WWI

When the Germans began torpedoing neutral American shipping in 1916, followed by the Zimmerman Letter in which Germany promised to give Texas back to Mexico, anti-German sentiment in the heavily German-populated state began to turn dramatically. German societies and communities that had been thriving for decades suddenly changed names or began holding meetings in English rather than the language of their forebears.

In Houston, the German Cemetery became Washington Cemetery, named after the road that fronted it. German Street in the East End became Canal, no doubt foisting unplanned stationary costs onto a few businesses. Citizens had been requesting a name change for some weeks. Several people wanted the new name of Mattes to honor the Illinois Guard officer killed in the Camp Logan Riot the previous summer, but after some objections, Canal Street won out.[51]

The city's German institutions that did survive the backlash, popular clubs such as the Turnverein, Sons of Hermann, and the Saengerbund, saw their members and children of members join the American Army to fight in Europe.

Support for the war was not universal. There was opposition to the war, especially in certain nooks of academia. Two major Texas universities experienced anti-war crises. A University of Texas professor of international history named Lindley Keasby was dismissed from his job for being an outspoken pacifist. Closer to home, male students at Rice staged a full blown insurrection after the unilateral decision to turn the college into a military school overnight, complete with crack-of-dawn drills, mandatory uniforms for all students, and frequent confinement to dorm rooms. The protests eventually led to the disappearance of some hated rules and addition of a student dean at Rice.[52]

Less than a year after the war ended, Rice Institute professor Dr. Lyford Edwards took great heat from the Houston press over comments supporting Soviet leader Vladimir Lenin. The outcry escalated to a fever pitch and included a scathing demand from the city's Mayor Ammerman for Edwards' dismissal. Ultimately, following an interview with the Canadian-born professor, Rice trustees declared his views totally at odds with the Institute. They demanded and got his resignation.[53]

By and large, however, once American men began donning military uniforms, the outpouring of patriotism was solid and loud, including in the local public schools. The purchase of Liberty Bonds and Thrift Stamps became every American family's duty. War gardens were started at the majority of schools, both White and Black, and children were encouraged to help create gardens at home. School domestic science kitchens were used for public demonstrations of canning and making preserves, and school lunchrooms observed both meatless and wheatless days in deference to the war effort.[54]

The Red Cross, ubiquitous in military camps at home and abroad, was also evident in many local schools through Junior Red Cross auxiliary chapters. Girls, teachers, and mothers met to roll and wrap cotton gauze and muslin bandages. Girls in the high school sewing classes made surgical dressings under the guidance of certified instructors. The same girls also made "hundreds of garments for the orphans of Belgium and France." Students at Almeda School in the southern part of the county went the city children one better. They planted cotton on an acre of ground next to their building, raising and picking it themselves and donating the full bale to the Red Cross.[55]

The war work was not confined solely to the White schools, either. Another Junior Red Cross project "was the making of twelve large hospital rugs for the American Red Cross House Committee. The order came from the Headquarters of the Southwestern Division in St. Louis. Eleven of the rugs were woven by the ungraded children at the Rusk and Dow Schools. The material was prepared by the Fourth and Fifth Grades of other Ward Schools. The other large oval hand-braided rug was made by the colored children of the Langston and Crawford Schools under the direction of Laura E. Payne."

Manual training classes began to crank out all sorts of items in spite of budget cuts and the higher wartime cost of certain supplies. Students in the shop classes made furniture including tables, book cases, and filing cabinets for the facilities at the nearby Camp Logan and other Texas army installations. They also cranked out 300 sets of checkers to keep the soldiers occupied.[56]

To support war efforts being made by their fellow students, Houston manual training students constructed 200 garden rakes, 10 wheeled plows, a dozen hoes, and sections of fencing for school war gardens. The boys also made items to be sold, such as play tables and chairs, magazine and book racks, stools, vases, and candle holders, with proceeds going to the Junior Red Cross. The shop teachers themselves took on some of the more difficult tasks, turning out three gate folding hospital tables and three library tables destined for nearby army camps.[57]

Some of the Houston and Harris County teachers went off to join the military or were drafted. The districts were quick to remind those who did stay that they were invaluable resources, sometimes going a bit over the top in doing so. "Every American school teacher who was worthwhile has during the past year considered himself not merely as a teacher of the three E's, but rather as a Captain of the Reserves," the city administration told them. "While General Pershing and others have been keeping the young men in the trenches fit and in order, the American schoolmaster has at home been entrusted with the far greater task of bringing up the reserves—the millions of American boys now in the public schools who may perhaps have to serve in the trenches before the war is won, and the millions of American girls who may have to give their brains and enthusiasm and energy to the same task."[58]

In order to keep the patriotic fires stoked, the federal government conducted a campaign to educate students about the "causes and objects of the war, together with general war information." One hundred forty area men pledged to speak for ten minutes at least one night per month in order to reach all the city schools and the 116 Harris County schools, as well.[59]

One particularly touching effort took place on April 5, 1918 when the City of Houston school children observed Rose Day, sending forty car loads of fresh roses to Camp Logan where the soldiers training there could enjoy a bit of beauty before their impending deployment to the front in France.[60]

A local WWI legend involves Jennie Eichler, a young German woman who briefly taught a popular pre-school nicknamed Miss Eichler's University. *Post* writer Marguerite Johnston wrote that Miss Eichler vanished during WWI due to hostility toward Germans. Mrs. E.O. Lovett told Johnston in the 1950s that Eichler was hidden in a house in Houston for two years during the war. Evidence does not seem to back up such a dire situation, and the mysterious story is likely overblown. Jennie Eichler's footprint in Houston was not a lengthy one. She first appeared in the city directory in 1913, and other than an ad for the reopening of her pre-school in October 1916, she does not appear to stick around long after. Whether that was because of any threat on the life of a popular young woman teacher is not known.[61]

In the months following the Armistice of November 1918, there was much talk about the American spirit, tying it to the values imbued in good old American schoolrooms such as existed in Harris County. City officials crowed thusly: "If there is any one single fact that our great war has demonstrated, it is the fact that the American public schools have made good. The war has shown that they were worth every cent of money that has been expended upon them. The American boy, trained in the American public schools, was put into direct personal conflict with the German soldier, trained under the much vaunted German educational and military system. Every one knows what the result was."[62]

The county and city schools were not above using that patriotism to make a pitch for votes in favor of a new school tax. A two-year-long effort to win a 50 cent per $100 levy coincided with the war years. For his part city superintendent Horn wrote: "Surely the present would be no time for the Houston public to refuse to spend upon their schools whatever money may be needed to maintain them."[63]

Houston has much more of a lasting legacy from WWI than most of its modern citizens realize. Hundreds of live oak trees line the streets through Hermann Park where they were placed to honor lost Houston soldiers. Memorial Park owes its name and its very existence to the war, created as another honor to the military, this one for the Illinois National Guard soldiers who had trained at Camp Logan on the site of the park. And dozens of Houston street names honor local boys who died either in combat or while in uniform during the Spanish Flu pandemic of 1918. Among the more recognizable names are Bissonnet, Banks, Riesner, D'Amico, Dismuke, Pecore, Patterson, Westcott, Dunlavy, Jensen, and Waugh.[64]

DOWDELL SCHOOL

This was a small room in the Dowdell Building on McGowen that housed one teacher beginning in September 1897 to relieve the overcrowding at Fannin Street School. The *Post* reported that "pupils who attend the Dowdell school will be designated by the principal of the Fannin street school; hence all pupils in that district should report tomorrow morning at the Fannin street school, and none should go to the Dowdell building until sent there by the principal of the Fannin street school."[65]

DUDLEY SCHOOL

See Betsy Ross ES

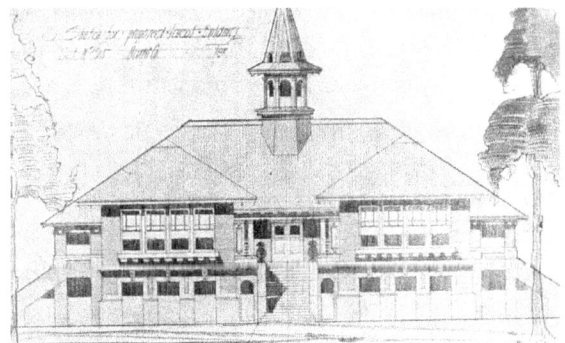

Architectural drawing of proposed Dudley School.
HISD

DUNBAR, PAUL L SCHOOL

Dunbar Elementary opened as a six-room building at the corner of Clark and Liberty in 1909 to alleviate what seemed like perpetual overcrowding in the Fifth Ward schools, both Black and White. It was named for Paul Laurence Dunbar, an internationally recognized African American poet, playwright, and novelist who had died of tuberculosis only three years prior.[66]

The first principal at Dunbar was the remarkable Buchanan H. Grimes. Enslaved in Texas prior to the Civil War, Grimes' family moved to Houston when freedom came, as did many other Blacks from nearby rural areas. His first job in Houston schools was as a janitor at the White high school, but when he was given the chance to take the teacher's exam, he "scored the highest mark." Grimes began teaching in 1884, but, like some other Black teachers, still supplemented his income with janitorial duties. He taught at Green Pond, Bruce, Gregory, Second Ward, and Sixth Ward before becoming principal at Fifth Ward Colored, then the brand new Dunbar, all without benefit of a high school or college degree. Two of his daughters, Wessie and Jessie, were also Houston teachers.[67]

The Dunbar school itself was soon experiencing the same overcrowding that spawned it in the first place. By 1922, there were six additional shacks standing in the school yard, all were "old and in bad condition," and the 572 students were stretching the facilities close to bursting. The Dunbar name was moved to the site of the old Longfellow School in 1961 and remained for 20 years before closure.[68]

Nicodemus

This story appeared in Superintendent Paul Horn's 1909-10 school report:

"Readers of our local papers are familiar with the name of Nicodemus—or used to be. He was not exactly a headliner, but his name was formerly good for a few inches of space in the police columns almost any day. By the time he was twelve years old he was a professional jail-bird. He was a petty thief, housebreaker and general juvenile offender. Incidentally, he didn't know a from b. He was too young to send to the penitentiary, and too bad to leave out of it. Our juvenile court law had gone just far enough to make it impossible to do anything with him. He had been arrested repeatedly, jailed, and turned loose again. The officers were hopefully awaiting the time when he would be old enough to send to the penitentiary.

"While matters were in this condition, it came about one day that the teachers of the Booker T. Washington School became interested in Nicodemus. They asked why he did not go to school. He told them that he had once tried to enter one of our colored schools, and had been refused admittance on account of his general record as an undesirable. They told him that the Booker T. Washington would be glad to take him— and to keep him, so long as he behaved himself. Nicodemus decided that the experiment might be worth trying; at any rate, he didn't see how it could make matters much worse with him. The result was that he secured a primer and entered the low first grade along with the little tots who were just starting. They knew as much as he did—about books, at any rate.

"He not only started, but he stuck. It caused a mild sensation among colored circles when it was learned that Nicodemus had been in school a month, and had not burned the school house down or stolen it. The man for whom he did odd jobs, in return for which he was given a place to sleep, was one of the first to notice the change, and to comment upon it. The Superintendent heard of it, and began to take a little friendly interest in Nicodemus, He sent word that when the boy could read every lesson in the book, he would give him another. That book was soon called for, and was delivered, with the word that when this was finished there would be another one sent. Soon after, the Superintendent heard him read the last lesson in this book, and gave him another, with the inscription: "To Nicodemus. As a reward for good conduct."

"This inscription seemed to please Nicodemus though the idea was rather a novel one to him. It was probably about the first time he had ever been told that his conduct was good. He spoke of these books as "The ones the boss man gave me."

"When Nicodemus was forced on account of sickness to be absent a day from school, he anxiously sent word as to the cause, lest, his teacher might think he had gone back to his old ways. In one year's time he has been transformed from an incorrigible thief and jail-bird to an industrious, hard-working Negro boy... He has even dug up another name, which he says is his right one. He refuses to be known any longer as Nicodemus. I do not give his new name, because it is not right that he should be embarrassed by his past."

A follow-up appeared in the 1910-11 report and read in part:

"For the benefit of any who may still be interested, it may be stated that Nicodemus was forced to drop out of school in the latter part of last year in order to work to secure some clothes and other necessities of life. He still insists that he intends to return to school as early as possible and to complete his education. He is a hard-working, sober, reliable Negro boy, in whom one would never recognize the jail-bird and habitual thief who used to be known as Nicodemus. The transformation which the school worked in him alone would be worth in actual dollars and cents to the State as much as is spent on all our colored schools in a year."

DUNMAN SCHOOL

Joseph Dunman was an early settler to Austin's Colony, prior to the Texas Revolution. It was Dunman who carried a pleading letter from William Barret Travis all the way to the towns of Liberty and Anahuac, pleading for reinforcements to come to the Alamo. For his service to the Republic, Dunman was rewarded with a land grant, the first patent for which dates to 1844 in an area along the south bank of the San Jacinto River's West Fork, at the top of the James Strange Survey. The settlement named for him is listed in 1854-55 school census showing a small group of potential school children there, but the one room schoolhouse known as Joe Dunman's was located on a 160 acre grant south of modern Humble that was secured by Joseph W. Dunman, the son of the earlier settler. The school the younger Dunman sponsored was opened on his property between that 1870 grant and its use as a polling place in May 1873.[69]

Though a privately owned and tuition supported school at first, Dunman's became part of the county school system. In 1883, a school community was organized, and the small building on Atascocita Road reported a student count of 13. Soon, it was being referenced as Dunman's Prairie School in County District 28. That assignment was short lived, since in 1888, the district was split into Humble to the north and Dunman's Prairie to the south with the latter becoming District 35 and supporting an enrollment of 41 pupils by the mid-1890s.[70]

Joseph W. Dunman died in March 1903, and when the school year ended, County District 35 closed the school on his property and built a new one farther southwest down the Atascocita Road, renaming it Singleton in honor of Reed Singleton, a member of the district school board and the brother of Joe Dunman's son-in-law.[71]

DUNMAN COLORED SCHOOL

This school for African Americans was located in county district 28, south of the modern town of Humble. A listing under this name appears in the county treasurer's ledgers in 1886-87 with teacher C.H. Smith. Three years later, the only Black school in that district is Narrow Gauge.[72]

DUNMAN SCHOOL, SOUTH

Dunman's was a small school at Dunman's Landing near Cedar Bayou in District 17. A Nancy Dunman was matriarch of a family living in the Lynchburg area prior to and during the Civil War. Any connection to the Humble Dunman family is unknown. The school operated for a time in the late 19th century.[73]

DURDIN SCHOOL

Durdin was one of the original 1876 county schools in today's Humble area. Town namesake Pleasant Humble and G.L. Durdin were two of the trustees. This may have been a forerunner to Higgs School.[74]

DURKEE E S

In the years just prior to the start of the 20th century, J.E. Durkee was developing a community named Little York in honor of his home state. The people who were buying his large plots of land were almost exclusively Italian immigrants, to the point that by 1903, when District 25 was building a school in the neighborhood, it was called simply "The Italian School." A four-room brick building, named officially for Durkee, opened in November 1911 on the site of the present day Fonville Middle School, and principal Kate Napier reported that all but two of the 74 children that first year were of Italian heritage. From 1931 to 1947, the school was closed, but reopened when the area's population increased. Durkee moved to a new campus farther south on Nordling in 1954, and additions were made to the school four years later.[75]

DUVERNOY'S SCHOOL

French-born Gustav Duvernoy fled Germany, where he had been a college student, as a political refugee following the democratic revolutions of 1848 and 1849. By 1854, he had settled in Galveston where he taught music, coming to Houston when Union soldiers occupied the island. Soon he would join those soldiers fighting Indians at a frontier cavalry post before opening his own private school in the Bayou City. Around 1878, Duvernoy went to work for the Houston public schools as one of the first three instructors at the high school, specializing in foreign languages and all things musical.[76]

Professor Duvernoy spent 39 years teaching at the Houston High School and also served as the registrar. At the age of 87, illness forced him to miss the last few weeks of the school year in 1917, and he died a few weeks later at his home at 1910 Jackson Street. The top educational leaders in the city acted as honorary pallbearers and the Saengerbund singers, with whom he had sung for decades, performed at his funeral mass at Annunciation. Superintendent Paul Horn called him "a magnificent influence over the schools and was beloved by everyone."[77]

Gustav Duvernoy. HISD

Language Electives

Teaching a foreign language has been a goal of English and American educational systems for centuries. For much of that time, a classical education meant the mandatory inclusion of lessons in Greek and Latin, and perhaps French, as well. While some pupils no doubt went on to become classics scholars themselves, the much more common result was a legion of farmers from Kentucky or Kansas who could recite "Mica, mica parva stella" well into middle age.

In more recent centuries, many students prefer to study languages with which they already had a passing acquaintance. It might mean an easier grade. Though it may be hard to fathom today, in 19th century Texas that language was not Spanish from nearby Mexico. There were almost no early listings for Spanish classes beyond T. Leger's ad in spring of 1839.[78]

Gustav Duvernoy was the learned man in charge of languages at the Houston High School in the early years of the institution. In 1889, he reported that 48 ½% of the Houston students in fourth grade and above were learning German. At the start of that decade, French and German had both been included in the high school's general course of study. There were six German teachers in the district by the turn of the century, and a supervisor of a German Department. It was the policy of city schools that foreign language teachers be natives of that tongue.[79]

Nudged by the urging of many local citizens, Spanish was added as an elective for the first time in 1900 along with typewriting and stenography. Fifteen years later, the list of high school electives showed that 258 pupils took stenography and type-writing and another 53 were taking bookkeeping, but it was the language elective that remained king. With the influx of Mexican immigrants seeking a life safe from that country's revolution, Spanish outpaced German with 365 students compared to 287. Latin was still top dog, though, with 1,379 students.[80]

DYERSDALE SCHOOL

The small village of Dyersdale northeast of Houston had its own school in the 1910s that sat on seven lots in the middle of the community. Part of County District 48, it eventually was absorbed by East Houston about 1920.[81]

EAST HOUSTON SCHOOL

The East Houston School, which in 1921 sat just north of the T&NO tracks and Liberty Road and east of the HB&T track curve, started as part of County District 34 but in 1910 a new separate District 48 was created to accommodate it. Four years later, Mount Houston and Dyersdale had also become part of the district.[82]

Though Dyersdale was gone, consolidated with East Houston about 1920, the East and Mount Houston district had a single, new brick school serving some 340 White children of the area by the mid-1930s with grades one through seven. It offered seven classrooms, and an auditorium that held 200. There was a cafeteria and electric lights, but other features were more rural such as well water, pit toilets, and wood or coal stoves. The consolidated East and Mount Houston was still operating in 1954 when R.W. Akrdige transferred from Cedar Bayou to take over as superintendent.[83]

The East Houston School building is still utilized. Mike Vance photo

EAST & MOUNT HOUSTON COLORED SCHOOL

This school was part of County District 48 with East Houston and Mount Houston. For several decades, there was a one-room frame building for the Black students in the district from grades one through seven. In 1939, the total enrollment was only 12 pupils with a single teacher.[84]

EAST ROSEHILL

This name surfaces on a 1916 USGS Rosehill quadrant map. Nothing further is known.

EASTWOOD SCHOOL

See Lantrip

ECKERT SCHOOL

A single mention of a school using this name refers to a "barbeque and public speaking" being held there on November 10, 1910.

EDISON J H S

The school at 6901 Avenue I in the East End began life as Magnolia Park Junior High in the Harrisburg ISD. In 1925, it became Park Junior High, then in 1932 was renamed for Thomas Edison. The new choice, hoping to end confusion with Park Place Elementary School, came via a vote by parents, students, and faculty. The inventor waxed the second place finisher, President James Monroe, by a tally of 876 to 74.[85]

The school had opened with about 300 pupils, but added roughly 100 students a year from the outset, nearing a mixed Anglo and Mexican American scholastic population of 1,000 by 1930. After becoming a part of HISD only a year after its opening, the fruits of a school bond election brought the junior high campus eight more classrooms, an indoor swimming pool, gymnasium, and a revamped lunchroom. The faculty swelled to 33 plus a dean, secretary, and librarian.[86]

The new Edison JHS. HISD

EDMUNDSON SCHOOL

Edmundson School served students of the first three grades in an area east of Dowling and south of McKinney that represented the southeastern most extent of the city limits in 1913. It sat at the corner of Velasco and

Calhoun, described at its opening as "a very attractive little building, well kept, with yard, toilets and all in good condition."[87]

The name came from a well-to-do area resident, wholesale hay dealer William L. Edmundson, or from the nearby street that bore his name. A Mothers Club was organized the first year, beautifying grounds, and installing drinking fountains and yard benches. Two additional grades were added within as many years, and soon calls for a new building at Edmundson surfaced. Ultimately, its students, numbering around 150 in 1921, were zoned to other new schools.[88]

EIGHTH AVENUE E S

Development of Houston Heights began in 1890 as a planned community with residential, commercial, and industrial areas, and the plan included segregated housing for African American employees at the industrial plants and factories. Educational facilities were eventually opened for the children of those Black workers, and the school that served the southern portion of the Heights was Eighth Avenue which opened in 1907 on a lot donated by that municipality. Jennie D. Smith was the first teacher.[89]

The school initially sat near 8th and Railroad (now Nicholson), but quickly moved to a small block at 727 Waverly, just south of 8th. The wooden building was a single room with an outbuilding on the back alley. The school grew, however, and by the time the Heights was annexed by Houston in 1918, there were three teachers for 93 students. There were calls over the years to give "suitable" names to 8th Avenue and 23rd Avenue, the two Black schools in the Heights, but they never came to fruition. Principal Libbe Boutte was in the limelight briefly when correspondence from Union National Bank arrived with the suffix "nig" after her name. The *Informer* made that front page news and urged Black businessmen to launch more enterprises dedicated to their race.[90]

A new brick school was completed in 1958, lasting until 2004 when Eighth Avenue Elementary closed for good. By summer of 2006, the lot has been razed in preparation for townhomes.[91]

ELENA SCHOOL

See Highlands

ELIOT E S

At a time when much of the area near the Houston Ship Channel lay outside the city limits, multiple county schools were built. One that opened in 1915, the year the of the much-ballyhooed visit of the Saltilla as the first ocean-going cargo ship to call at the newly deepened port, was the two-room brick building called Harbor School. It was located on the west side of Port Street, a block north of Laredo, in Denver Harbor Addition, which would place it in Nieto Park today. The school began as part of County District 25 but was annexed into HISD in 1920. The Port Houston School was rolled into Harbor in 1922, and as more port and railroad workers moved into the area, two temporary shacks were placed in the yard. By 1926, the district made a new modern school for the area one of the first two buildings constructed with money from the first bond issue.[92]

Lunchroom staff at Eliot ES in 1951. Mike Vance Collection

The red brick, U-shaped school was named for Charles Eliot who served as Harvard president for 40 years and wielded great influence on advances in education. The original 1926 school remains, but additions and upgrades to Eliot have come in the 1970s, 80s, 90s and 2000s.[93]

ELLIS LEAGUE SCHOOL

Ellis School Road remains an exit on Interstate 10 east of Houston, and the road runs east from the south side of the town of Highlands. The County District 15 school for which the road is named sat very near the Baytown Fairgrounds, just a bit north of the modern freeway.[94]

The schoolhouse at Ellis League. HHRC

ELYSIAN STREET SCHOOL

See Anson Jones

EMANCIPATION SCHOOL

This name is noted next to South Houston in County District 24 in the treasurer's ledger of 1893-94.

EMANCIPATION PARK SCHOOL

See Blackshear ES

ERIN SCHOOL

Erin School in County District 45 served a small community of that name that sat along the west side of Mykawa Road and the Santa Fe Railroad about five blocks south of Almeda-Genoa Road. [95]

ETTA SCHOOL

See Harlow

EUREKA SCHOOL

Eureka was one of the schools operating prior to 1876 when trustees registered it under the new public school law, and it remained in operation at least until 1883 when it had eleven pupils. It was located for the workers at Eureka Mills, a textile operation started on the Houston & Texas Central Railroad in 1866 and located five miles northwest of Houston. Eureka even had a federal post office from 1872 until 1879.[96]

EVANGEL LUTHERAN

The German Evangelical Church with its 65-foot spire sat on the west side of Louisiana between Preston and Prairie in the 1880s and 90s, and the one-room church school, taught by Fred Doepke, was directly behind it. Just north of the school, at the corner with Preston, sat the Germania Hotel and its barroom.[97]

Schools F

FAIRBANKS SCHOOL

See Bane ES

FAIRBANKS H S

See Cy-Fair HS

FANNIN E S

For much of its early life, Fannin School was known as being the "Silk Stocking" institution thanks to the many fine and fancy homes being built in the South End around and after the turn of the century. It opened as Fannin Street School, first in 1890 in a building that had previously been a shirt factory, then, three years later, in six rooms of a rented building at the northwest corner of Fannin and McGowen. The word Street was dropped from the name when it moved to a beautiful new triangular shaped, twelve-room brick building on a full city block at the southwest corner of Louisiana and Tuam in 1899. As the South End prospered, Fannin became overcrowded. An annex room was rented across Louisiana Street. Rooms were added twice, and part of the basement was converted to class space. In spite of the handicaps, Fannin sent more of its pupils on to the High School than any other elementary, with over 10 percent of its 842 students continuing their education in 1911.[1]

Fannin ES, Houston's "silk stocking" school. HISD

For a brief interlude, Fannin was home to the bell off the Harriet Lane, the most visible prize from the Confederate victory at the Battle of Galveston at the start of 1863. The bell summoned students to class, but when the new building experienced a bad fire on December 3, 1900, the hired salvager took the relic as a souvenir. When this was discovered, the contractor refused to hand over his prize, and it took over two years of litigation before the bell was returned to city hands and placed at the new Sam Houston Park to signal opening and closing of the gates.[2]

The old building at Fannin aged, but continued to serve. The principal for almost all of the first three decades at the big building on Louisiana was Charles A. Jameson who had moved to Houston from Springfield, Missouri in the late 1890s and died in 1929, still holding the helm at Fannin. The school closed after a large fire in 1971, but a few of the lovely oak trees that sat on the back side of the campus still remained in the 2010s.[3]

The Advent of School Lunches

The beginning of lunches served by the public schools in Houston goes hand in hand with the formation of the first Mother's Club, and it began as a story of the city's haves and have nots. The catalyst was an incident that took place at Fannin Elementary School, an institution at Louisiana and Tuam that was referred to as the "silk stocking" school of the city because of the many high end homes nearby.

In the 19th century, as America became more urban, and both the male workers and their school-aged children left home for the entire day, it was common practice to pack a lunch. Though some of the more well-to-do might use fancy baskets or paper sacks, the common carrier was a metal lunch pail. Factory or mine workers might have a multi-piece bucket that could even be warmed, but for schoolchildren, a lunchbox was often a used tobacco or coffee bin with a handle bolted onto it, and milk was brought in all sorts of rinsed out bottles.[4]

The contents of a school lunch pail varied, of course, but a standard mix would have been a piece of bread, a hunk of cheese and perhaps a few strawberries or pecans. In poorer areas, the pickings might be slimmer, and some children no doubt came to school with no lunch at all. City school superintendent Paul Horn opined that "it is a very difficult matter in the average household for the mother to send the children to school in the morning with a lunch which will be really palatable and nutritious for the child. Nobody is particularly fond of eating cold lunches."

Available alternatives were a complete patchwork. In Houston, by 1906, school principals at Allen, Hawthorne, Sherman, and Jones elementaries had worked a deal to allow outside parties to come onto school property to sell low cost food to the students. At Longfellow Elementary on the east edge of downtown, children were allowed to go to the restaurant next door and buy hot lunches. At the city's lone high school, pupils were on their own.[5]

Another variant of the solution, at least for those kids with some pocket change, was what happened every noontime at Fannin Elementary. Vendors with carts pulled up outside, and sometimes inside the gates and sold the kind of non-nourishing things that school children craved: candy, pickles, "pink ice cream, impossible 'hamburgers,' sausages of questionable origin and other alleged eatables." Everyone seemed fine with, or at least resigned to, the system until a notable number of children got sick from eating chili con carne from one such vendor.[6]

The food poisoning unified the Fannin School mothers. The terms "sanitary" or "hygienic" lunches became a rallying cry. They determined to take matters into their own hands and furnish "wholesome nourishment" to the children at cost. On their first day of serving, they planned for 200 lunches, but 300 children showed up. Though it left the lunchroom looking "like the track of a devastating hurricane," the ladies, under the supervision of Mrs. A. Mendes, fed everyone. Fare for the grade schoolers that first day was hot soups, roast beef and bread, hot chocolate, tea, and coffee. In spite of their not-for-profit intentions, they managed to pay all of their expenses, including the original investment in equipment, and still have $300 left over. That sum became part of the $1,000 they donated to equip rooms from manual training and domestic science. And active Mother's Club was born, the first in Houston.[7]

*A Fannin School class in 1925. By this time, the children were well
accustomed to safer food options. Mike Vance Collection*

Fannin principal Charles A. Jameson, who would stay at the school until his death in 1929, welcomed
the arrangement. The Mother's Club was still supervising the serving of hot lunches at the school nine
years later and had expended a total of $7,695.00 on that and other school improvement projects including
regular upgrades to a school kitchen.[8]

Some in Houston felt that the free-enterprise system worked just fine, but Superintendent Horn
disagreed. "It seems to me that the subject of the food eaten by the children during the noon hour is
an eminently proper one for school authorities to consider," he wrote in 1907. "It seems to me to be
a short-sighted policy which would provide the best and most expensive teaching for a child, and yet
would overlook a condition which might render that teaching partially ineffective. It matters not that
some children may actually prefer indigestible food stuff, and that some parents may be perfectly willing
to allow that preference to be gratified... It is our duty to so arrange matters that every child in our schools
who prefers to have a wholesome and nutritious bowl of soup at the noon hour rather than to make a
hasty meal on bologna sausage and pickles should at least have the opportunity to do so."

By the fall of 1916, the Houston City Schools had a dietician on the payroll, Christina Wardlow, who
reported that hers was a "trying" job due to fluctuating food costs, but they had been successful by offering
a menu with few choices and striving to have no leftovers. Yet, it was still a completely patchwork system.
The school district was only directly serving lunches in three schools: South End Junior High, North Side
Junior High, and Rusk Elementary. The following year, Travis Elementary became the fourth school on
the program. Adding to the problems in 1917-18 were wartime restrictions that called for a meatless day
and a wheatless day.[9]

Rusk School was the biggest problem in those early days. They had been offering penny lunches, and
still some students could not afford them. When the price of a glass of milk forced then to charge an
additional penny there, many of the poor Second Ward children had to do without. The meals at Rusk
were prepared by Mrs. Bliss' Domestic Science classes, but as diligent and generous as she was, the effort
was not widely appreciated. In 1917, the Council of Jewish Women began donating ten dollars a month
to the Rusk school lunch program, money which was "a great help."[10]

The Domestic Science students at other schools including Brackenridge were also in charge of furnishing the lunches of their classmates. At Dow, the PTA equipped a lunchroom in 1914, and at Longfellow, Fullerton, Fannin, and Taylor, the Mothers' Clubs still handled the feeding. In at least three schools - Rusk, Longfellow, and South End Junior High - the boys in the manual training classes constructed 30 to 40 lunch tables for the school. By 1917, at least three African American schools - Colored High and Douglass and Washington Elementaries - were also using Home Ec students to at least partially feed their classmates.[11]

During the 1919-20 school year, the Houston Parent-Teachers Association sponsored a malnutrition study. After examining roughly 6,000 students across the city, nurses and home welfare experts found an average of 50% of Houston students to be malnourished and underweight. The two highest percentages came from two of the wealthiest schools - Eastwood and Montrose. After a program was developed, reports sent home to 5,300 parents and physician referrals given, the overall percentage of the malnourished kids dropped to 21%. Long-term recommendations included supervised lunchrooms and a longer lunch period. There was one caveat: Judging by the report, the examinations were done only in the White schools.[12]

By 1920, the city school system was committed to the idea of having students eat at school, but it was not yet a total necessity. When the emergency appropriation to build a replacement for the burned Houston High School came up short, the lunchroom was temporarily omitted along with the gymnasium and the swimming pools. Things improved. Between 1924 and 1930, HISD built a total of 39 combination play-lunchrooms as either new construction or school additions.[13]

Their foray into a district department to provide food for the children began in February 1925 when six lunchrooms were taken over by the board to "test the policy of giving good, wholesome food at cost, plus the necessary operating expenses, including the upkeep on the equipment." The efforts were supervised at first by the Home Economics Department, but proved so successful in such a short time, that a separate Lunch Room Department was formed for the following school year.[14]

The department grew like South Texas weeds. When the report on the 1929-30 school year was issued, a total of 81 lunchrooms were in operation handing over tens of thousands of meals a day across the counters. The only schools still without a facility were "a few one and two-teachers school on the outer fringes of the district." The next school year opened with 225 lunchroom department employees.[15]

Money-wise, the volume of business was just north of $425,000. Some schools operated at a loss and some made a profit, but not all lunches were paid. Roughly 22,000 lunches were given to students free of charge, asking for the performance of "small odd jobs in the lunchroom in payment for their food." As the Depression deepened, the free meals kept coming, sometimes through the generosity of anonymous benefactors supplementing the public school, state, and federal funds expended. The free lunches continued even during the summer, and by the time the school year ended in June 1933, the district announced that they had given away over 315,000 lunches.[16]

A full blown, lawsuit-pocked controversy erupted in October 1929 when the HISD board unanimously voted to restrict lunch options for pupils to meals either brought from home, eaten at home, or purchased in the school cafeteria. It took only two days for a suit to be filed in a local court claiming that the ban on leaving to buy lunch elsewhere was a gross violation of constitutional rights. A second lawsuit, one that included both parents and food merchants, followed before the week was out. The daughter of P.K. Bishop was suspended for flaunting the rule against leaving campus to purchase lunch, and that meant another court case. During the chaotic months, students testified in court, a hot dog vendor outside Marshall Junior High was tossed in jail, cafeteria doors were locked and guarded and students sang mock jail songs. Ultimately, appeals courts and the Texas Supreme Court weighted in, all backing HISD's right to control and monitor its young charges.[17]

Improvements to the school cafeterias kept coming, A half decade later, supervisor Clare Kimble reported of HISD lunch rooms that all department workers "had health certificates and that there was constant supervision to ensure sanitation." Prices ranged from a dime for a plate lunch to three cents for milk, two cents for a bread and butter sandwich, and a penny for candy. The biggest thing lacking in her assessment was anything resembling a vow of deliciousness. The best she could muster along those lines was this: "Our food is prepared in a manner most digestible with least loss of nutritional elements, yet appetizing." Sounds yummy.[18]

Not that it was planned overall, and certainly not at the upper middle class Fannin School of the early 1900s, but some historians credited school lunches as a major tool in Americanizing the many immigrants to the United States. Whether they learned nutritional value from their school meals or not is doubtful, but like it or not, the foreign children ate things like salmon croquettes and beef stew. Reports said that as a group it was the Italians who were most resistant to American fare. Compared to what they likely got at home, who could blame them.[19]

FARMER SCHOOL

John Farmer School, in County District 25, operated in the late-1890s. It merged with McDonald School to form Berry about 1910.[20]

FAUNA SCHOOL

The community of Fauna was located on the T&NO Railroad at what is now the southern end of Sheldon Reservoir. It had its own post office from 1903 until approximately 1930. The school there operated from an undetermined number of years.

FIDELITY SCHOOL

County District 16 operated multiple small schools for African American students in the 1880s and 90s including Clinton Colored School and both a Green's Bayou Colored and Upper Green's Bayou Colored. By 1907, there were two remaining in the district. The one-teacher Clinton Colored School, known briefly in the 1920s as Morgan School, outlived the other two. It was described by Mrs. Freddie Sandle, who began commuting by boat from Harrisburg to teach there in 1923, as a "shanty" located at E Street and Main. When the White school got a new building in the 1930s, their old one was moved to Bolden Street and Fidelity Road and renamed the Fidelity School. Mrs. Sandle, who remained at the school for 38 years, became principal of a growing staff. By the time a new Fidelity Manor Elementary was built in 1956, there were 14 rooms in the old building. The new school had 25 classrooms, and a new segregated Fidelity Manor High School on Sixteenth Street was opened a year prior. Galena Park ISD absorbed the all-Black Fidelity Manor schools in 1970 when the district was integrated, a fact lamented by many of the Fidelity graduates as a loss of identity.[21]

The decorative front door of Field ES. Laurie Feinswog photo

FIELD E S

Eugene Field Elementary School at 703 E. 17th between Beverly and Studewood opened in 1929 with money from the final bond issue of the 1920s. It has sported a salmon pink stucco exterior and a multi-hued tile roof since the beginning. An addition in 1935 brought Field up to 16 classrooms, and the entire E-shaped structure was renovated in 1985.[22]

School Zones and the Advent of Automobiles

The first cars began to show up on Houston streets about the start of the 20th century. As more and more of them competed with horses and carts, eventually forcing the equine transportation from the roads, safety trouble appeared, and traffic laws followed. The city introduced one-way streets downtown in 1920, and, one year later, policemen in specially built stands manually operated traffic signals at seven busy intersections in the business district. The three-color, fully-automated lights were in wide use before the end of the decade.[23]

Many of the efforts were soon aimed at curbing accidents that had cost school children their lives. The South Texas Motor League sponsored an essay writing contest in Houston high schools to promote a "general awakening of the idea of safety first in street crossings, auto driving" and "to stop, look and listen when danger is near." Signs were placed, but the deaths grew more numerous.[24]

Eleven-year-old Lovenia Cox was struck and killed outside Burnet Elementary on Canal Street. Two students were badly injured in accidents at Sam Houston High, and in January 1930, five-year-old Norma Lee Lewis, described as having the happiest week of her life because she was finally old enough to start at Eugene Field School, was fatally run over by a city garbage truck that did not see her.[25]

Houston leaders continued to explore ideas. "A 'marker' built on the order of downtown traffic control lights, having one red light and below it a highly polished aluminum disk which revolves, may be used to designate the eight mile per hour zone near schools," suggested Houston City Manager Claude Belk in 1924. The signs which had been in place were not heeded often enough, and "putting new signs up will have little or no effect."[26]

By the end of the 1920s, traffic signals had been specifically installed at over two dozen problem intersections near schools and at least fifteen, all White elementaries, also had policemen stationed there. When Officer R.Q. Wells, who watched the children at Austin Elementary on St. Emanuel St., died unexpectedly, he was heartily mourned. As the stock market crash made money tight, other ideas were explored including paying school janitors a little extra to serve as crossing guards. An ordinance to prevent cars from parking curbside near schools was proposed. Low wire fences around school yards were also suggested. Eventually, all of those safety measures were augmented by adult crossing guards and student safety patrols.[27]

FIFTH WARD COLORED SCHOOL

See Bruce ES

FIFTH WARD SCHOOL

See Jones, Anson

FINCH'S SCHOOL

Finch's was a late 19th century school for White children in the crowded County District 25. It was perhaps named for F.E. Finch who drew pay for teaching there in 1890.[28]

FIRST WARD COLORED SCHOOL

See Washington, Booker T. Elementary

FIRST WARD SCHOOL

See Hawthorne

FIRST HOUSTON PRIVATE SCHOOLS

At the end of October 1857, the *Telegraph* reported that "There were as many as a dozen schools in operation each year." Still only about a quarter of the school age children in the city were enrolled in any of the private, tuition-based institutions. It had been the case since Houston's founding, and keeping track of every school in the ever-changing pre-Civil War landscape is almost impossible today. From the first late-1830s schools of Mrs. Andrews and Mrs. Hamilton, the places of learning were located either in a teacher's home or in a rented room, often on the second floor, of one of the fledgling town's retail buildings. Many took only girls as pupils, but Mr. Mylard and Mr. Thompson offered a day school for young men and boys in 1839 with "every exertion for the advancement of the pupil plus attention to their moral deportment." The cost was five to eight dollars a month, much higher than private school tuition would become in subsequent decades. These same men also taught "arithmetic, surveying and mathematics" from 7 to 10 in the evening for five dollars a month.[29]

Among those teaching in the mid-1840s were W.J. Thurber, Miss Avery, Miss Madden, Rev. Reid, and the Misses Humphrey. Mrs. M.J. Longley, prominent churchwoman, opened a free school in the vestibule of the Presbyterian Church, underwriting many costs herself, and pupils attended "in such numbers that they overflowed into the church auditorium." Multiple articles from *Texas Presbyterian* indicate that Mrs. Longley might have taught at the first free city school. It is known that by 1848, she and Mr. John W. Lawrence were running a tuition-based private school styled the Select Male and Female School. Mrs. Longley was also offering board for students "at moderate terms."[30]

By the time the *Telegraph* commented on the proliferation of private school options in the late 1850s, there were schools both new and established. Among them were: separate high school male and female departments operated at the old Episcopal Church by Professor and Miss Ruter, a young ladies' school run by Miss Julia Maher, a "school for daughters" with Mrs. Stiles on Prairie Street near the bayou, Mr. and Mrs. W. P. Cunningham's school for boys and girls near the Catholic Church, Miss Van Alstyne's school for girls on Carolina Street, Mrs. Green's on Prairie Street opposite Judge Shearn's residence, Mrs. H. L. Cotton's female school on Congress Street, and Miss K. Payne teaching music at her residence as well as schools taught by A. Keech, Jr., John B. Kellogg, and W.C. Painter. Still with all of these private schools, only two hundred of the seven hundred Houston children between 6 and 16 were enrolled. [31]

Japanese Letter

The following letter was written by a young Japanese boy who had been attending one of our night schools during the few months he had been in America. It is addressed to one of his teachers in the night school, and is written in an elegant handwriting, such as would be a credit to any American:

"Dear Teacher Mr. Gibbson:

"Thanks a thousand times for your kind teaching, and I am glad that I have got a great many new knowledge by your bright teach. But am so sorry that I cannot attend any more in your school, because I have made up my mind so suddenly to leave here for New York and I left Houston this morning for Galveston. Hoping that you will be well always and please present my best, regards to all of your students,

"Your pupil,

"S. Takagi."

Houston City Schools Report 1910-11

FONDREN E S

Humble Oil founder Walter W. Fondren has his name two HISD campuses. The more famous is the middle school in southwest Houston, but the first was the elementary school that opened at 12405 Carlsbad in 1949.[32]

FOREST HILLS E S

See Briscoe

FOSTER E S

Marcellus E. Foster left the *Houston Post* to establish the *Houston Chronicle* in 1901, and subsequently became editor at the *Houston Press* daily. His journalistic crusades sometimes went against the popular grain such as when he strongly opposed the Klan and the brutal, overcrowded Texas prison system. A school carrying his name was opened at 3919 Ward in 1949, seven years after Foster died.[33]

FOURTH WARD COLORED SCHOOL

See Gregory

FOURTH WARD NORTH SCHOOL

See Dow

FOURTH WARD NORTH COLORED SCHOOL

Houston originally had four wards, quarters of the city that radiated from the center of the intersection of Congress and Main. In 1866, those Second Ward residents north of the bayou finally got the Fifth, a ward structure of their own. Population is what split the Fourth Ward. Though Sixth Ward was officially chartered on the first day of 1877, more than a decade later the name of Fourth Ward North was still hanging strong, certainly within the school system. The White students there had a two room school at State and Trinity at least into the early 1880s, but the Black students, along with their neighbors in First Ward, went across downtown for classes.[34]

In January 1888, the Washington Street School, soon to be called Dow, opened in the neighborhood for Whites, and at the same time the Fourth Ward North Colored School began showing up in school listings at the same corner of State and Trinity, also as a two room school. Though evidence points that way, it is impossible to say for certain if it was the precise city schoolhouse that was given over to African American students.[35]

FOURTH WARD SCHOOL

When the city organized schools under the revised school law of 1876, most adhered to the theory of one White and one Black school per ward, but the Fourth Ward had more than one school for White children, at least for the first year or so. One was the school listed in this book as Mrs. Noble's, but there was also the school of Mrs. M. H. Wynne with 21 children and Mrs. Kate DePelchin who had 31.[36]

FOUTS SCHOOL

Fouts was a small school building located at present day 612 Kernohan in downtown Crosby for an unknown number of years in the first half of the 20th century.

FRANKLIN E S

Franklin Elementary got its start as Magnolia Park School in the district of the same name. It opened at 71st and Canal in 1913. After it was absorbed into HISD, the neighborhood residents were offered an opportunity of picking a new name and overwhelming chose to honor Benjamin Franklin. Enrollment at the school grew to be the largest in Houston by the early 1930s, with over 1,350 pupils and 40 teachers in the 24-room building plus temporary shacks next door. R.C. Roebuck was principal at the time, getting the job at age 22 when he was the youngest in the city at that position. Franklin, which was remodeled in 1928, was also home to a 670-member parent-teacher organization, the largest in Texas then. The old Franklin was replaced with a new structure at the end of the 1970s.[37]

The Silver Nitrate Cure

Two especially interesting instances may be mentioned of work done last year in the matter of personal health in our schools. One of these has reference to the fact that 162 boys were given the nitrate of silver cure as a means of breaking up the cigarette habit. One of the illustrations in this volume shows a typical case. In the first picture, the boy is seen smoking a cigarette. The second shows our school physician in the act of applying the nitrate of silver solution to the boy's tongue. The third shows the same boy after the treatment, endeavoring to smoke a cigarette. The wry look on his face shows that he is not enjoying the process.

The silver cure for cigarette smoking, like the gold cure for drunkenness, may not work in every individual case. All we can do for the boy is to put him in such condition that the indulgence of the bad habit will for quite a while cause him considerable bodily discomfiture. This will compel him to quit for so long a time that he will get the poison out of his system, and will lose the desire for the harmful stimulation. If, at the end of this time, he desires to continue his freedom, he can do so. If, on the other hand, he desires to go back to the fetters of his bad habit, he can do that also. However, if the cure was permanent in only half the cases treated, and if eighty-one boys of Houston ceased to be cigarette fiends on account of the treatment given by our school physician, that alone will be worth more to our city than was spent on that official's salary for the entire year.

Houston City Schools Report 1913

FREEDMEN'S BUREAU SCHOOLS

While several of the eastern slave-holding states had laws prohibiting the teaching of slaves to read or write, Texas did not. That fact did not mean education was readily available for the state's Blacks, though. There was some, but not universal resistance to the idea, and one Union official in Liberty following the Civil War opined that "Whites did not (even) educate their own children." It was not until the occupying Union Army and its Bureau of Refugees, Freedmen and Abandoned Lands took charge of administering the state in the latter half of 1865 that schooling opportunities, along with aid in housing, food, and legal matters, popped up on a widespread basis. Under the command of General Edgar M. Gregory and initially supervised by Lt. Edwin Wheelock, Freedmen Bureau schools opened in partnership with the American Missionary Association in the most populated areas of the Lone Star State. By June 1866 there were about 4,500 African American students at 100 Bureau schools in Texas.[38]

In Houston, the Freedmen's Bureau schools started in three Black churches: Antioch Baptist, then near the west end of Rusk, Trinity Methodist at Travis and Texas, and Mount Zion Baptist on German Street in Second Ward. Originally, there was a tuition charge of $1.50 which kept a damper on attendance by some families transitioning from slavery. When General Joseph Kiddoo replaced General Gregory in April 1866, some free schools emerged, but when General Charles Griffin took over in early 1867, all tuition-free options disappeared again, though the cost was lowered.[39]

PRIMARY SCHOOL FOR FREEDMEN, IN CHARGE OF Mrs. GREEN, AT VICKSBURG, MISSISSIPPI.—See Page 499.]

The schools proved very popular among freedmen, with only a shortage of teachers and buildings holding down enrollment. There were some African American teachers at first including William Debrew in Houston, but most of the earliest teachers were White women who were shunned by local families in part because of the depth of the courtesies they showed their Black charges, including house visits. In some boarding houses, it was reported that Yankee women and Southern women were asked to eat at opposite ends of the table. Still, the Houston Freedmen's Bureau schools were said to be "large and flourishing beyond... expectations." Lt. Wheelock thought that "These schools are felt among the freedmen as a moral power. With increased intelligence, self-respect is quickened, conscience awakened, and the restraints of decorum and morality observed." The Ku Klux Klan, active in other locales, did not appear as powerful opposition to education in Houston. On the other hand, former interim President of the Republic of Texas David G. Burnet railed against the Bureau and eventually succeeded in getting Gen. Gregory replaced.[40]

Congress did away with the bulk of the Freedmen's Bureau duties in 1868, extending only the responsibility for education for one more year. Houston let a contract for the Gregory Institute in 1869, and there was a seamless transition with four other Black schools operating in town by 1870. Part of that was due to community support for the idea such as it was expressed in the *Telegraph* that year: "Above all, let everything be done for their education. Help them build churches and school houses, go among them and bring their children into Sunday schools, encourage our own citizens to become teachers in their day schools and show an interest in their welfare in every way."[41]

FRENCH SCHOOL

The French School, in County District 3, was in existence prior to 1876 when it was registered as one of the original institutions in Harris County to operate under the new Texas Constitution's public school provisions. Many of the children who originally attended the schoolhouse were from French immigrants including the Pillot, Boudreaux, and Deschaumes families who had settled near Willow Creek almost immediately after the Texas Revolution. In the early years, teachers came and went to the one-room school that sat at what is now the southeast corner of Spring-Steubner and Rhodes Road. There were three different instructors during the 1889-90 school year. In 1911, Theo and Mary Hildebrandt sold the schoolhouse and an acre of land to Harris County with a reversion clause if it ever ceased being used for school purposes. French was one of the Klein area schools consolidated into Rural High School No. 1 in 1928. The building was moved next to the new high school and used as a residence for the principal and superintendent.[42]

A class at French School. Klein ISD

FRIENDSHIP SCHOOL

Friendship School served the African American Black Hope and Elia Carson subdivisions near Crosby which were established prior to WWI. Students above fifth grade were merged into the Barrett School in 1940, with the younger students going to Barrett in 1947.[43]

FUCHS SCHOOL

Fuchs School on Grant Road west of Perry was deeded for school purposes by J.N. West to the Harris County Judge in 1877. The building was passed from one county judge to another until Henry Fuchs deeded the acre of land to the county 20 years later while reserving the right to open a gate and graze his livestock on the school grounds. Fuchs was consolidated with the Cypress schools in 1934, and the building was moved to the combined campus on Telge Road where Lamkin Elementary now stands.[44]

A girl at Fuchs School takes a reading break on bookmobile day. HCPL

FULLER SCHOOL

Fuller School was a one-room school house in County District 14 in the early part of the 20th century.[45]

FULLERTON E S

One of the few happy preservation stories among historic Harris County schools belongs to Fullerton at 5803 Harrisburg at Norwood. Today the 1908 school that began in County District 21 has a wonderfully restored exterior and tasteful additions to what is now the Open Door Mission for Men. Real estate man Herbert E. Fuller who donated the land over a century ago would be proud.[46]

On the edge of Houston in the Harrisburg district, Fullerton was one of the larger county schools. Principal Mabel Tharp reported 143 students in 1910, the year the Mothers Club organized. It was an active organization, fitting out a kitchen, building a stage, buying lights, and paying Mothers Club members to cook and clean. By the time the Houston Schools had taken it over in October 1913, enrollment topped 300. The principal by that time, moving from county to city schools, was H.L. Mills who would soon become the longtime business manager of HISD, lasting into the anti-segregation and anti-communist brouhahas of the 1950s.[47]

The girl's basketball team at Fullerton School. Mike Vance Collection

The Eastwood and Oak Lawn Park Civic Clubs supported the school, and city bought six adjacent lots for playground use. The school remained in use until June 1962, and was used as storage by HISD for several years before becoming home to the mission.[48]

Testing for Graduation from County Schools

Texan Billy Joe Shaver, in a famous progressive county song from the 1970s, sang about "an eighth grade education," and for most Americans of the 19th and early 20th century, that was indeed their highest educational achievement. It was even more the norm in rural areas. For a time in Harris County, before the creation of a 12th grade in 1940, many local students got only a seventh grade education. To move along to one of the handful of two or four years high schools in the county, or just to get a seventh grade diploma and begin one's adult life, there were tests to pass.

By 1912, the tests were held twice a year under the auspices of each school's principal or teacher in charge. The questions were prepared by the County School Board, and an average of 80% on all subjects was required to pass. There were multiple independent school districts in the county by that year, located in Brunner, Spring, La Porte, Pasadena, and Houston Heights. Additionally, the City of Houston's schools held, by a wide margin, more pupils than all others combined. That left over 7,500 students under the jurisdiction of the Harris County Common Schools.[49]

Of that number 149 county students took the test to obtain seventh grade diplomas. Sixty-seven passed and 82 failed. Of those who succeeded, there were 22 boys and 45 girls. County Superintendent Pugh noted that it was fewer failures than the previous year "but too many to be satisfactory." The smaller independent districts in the county took the same exams.[50]

The success rate improved quickly, though the graduates remained mostly White. Only eight African Americans, three boys and five girls, earned seventh grade diplomas from the county in 1912-13, and the only high school option that awaited them was Colored High School in Houston.

By the following school year, though only 103 seventh graders sat for the graduation exam, there "were 85 promotions and only 18 failures." Pugh determined that the results showed "greater efficiency on the part of the teacher." A list of the graduates showed a heavy sprinkling of German and other Northern European surnames mixed in among the Anglo ones.[51]

Harris County even held graduation exercises beginning in 1908 as a "means of encouraging boys and girls to finish the work of county schools and go to high school."[52]

Schools G

GAILLARD'S LANDING SCHOOL

Residents in the area known as Gaillard's Landing, in the current Goose Creek CISD, attended a one-room school prior to 1876, perhaps as much as a decade earlier. The area was named for wealthy landowner Thomas Benjamin Gaillard, a Mississippian who had settled his family on the east side of Goose Creek in 1867. The eponymous landing was on Tabb's Bay, and from that dock, Thomas Gaillard ran a steamship business that supplemented his agricultural income. He donated land and had a public school erected. Three of the Gaillard daughters, Linna, Katie, and Minnie, taught at the family schoolhouse and, later, the Goose Creek School.[1]

GALENA PARK E S

The town of Clinton on the north shore of the Ship Channel was home to a one-room, wooden White school from about 1917 at 401 North Main in what is now Galena Park. The original building was moved to Fidelity for use by African American students at the start of the 1930s when Galena Park also organized as an ISD, and the White elementary students attended a new brick building. That school received numerous additions in subsequent years, the most recent in 2007.[2]

The 1929 basketball squad at Galena Park HS. HHRC

GALENA PARK H S

In 1928, Clinton High, along with the town itself, changed its name to Galena Park after the Galena Oil Company that dominated that section of the Ship Channel. A permanent home for the high school opened on the north side of 3rd Street, two blocks east of Main, a year later. Prior to that time, older students from the area rode a ferry to Harrisburg to attend high school. The GPHS Yellowjackets moved into their current location at 1000 Keene Street in March of 1950, and the 1929 building, used for decades by the junior high, was finally demolished in 1992.[3]

GALENA PARK J H S

The middle school now located at 400 Keene in Galena Park came into existence as Galena Park Junior High in 1950 when the high school moved away from its location on Third Street. The junior high itself moved into a new structure in 1992, taking the old cornerstone and time capsule with it.[4]

GARDEN OAKS E S

Developer Edward Lillo Crain bought 750 acres northwest of Houston Heights and started building Garden Oaks in 1937, advertised as a cheaper alternative to River Oaks. The neighborhood proved so popular that within two years, HISD was scrambling to move the children of the area out of a dozen temporary buildings scattered about campuses to the south. The new elementary opened in 1940 in the 900 block of Sue Barnett at Garden Oaks Boulevard. The old school was demolished and replaced on the same large wooded campus in 1981, leaving a portion of only one original building.[5]

GARDEN VILLAS E S

The Garden Villas development on the prairie southeast of Houston started on part of the old Allen Ranch in 1924, and the first school by that name appeared in 1928. The city directory listed it as being on the south side of Avenue B, two blocks west of Telephone Road. It was initially part of County District 45, and that entity opened the current campus at the corner of Santa Fe and Prentiss in 1931. Four years later the neighborhood school was annexed by popular vote on July 19, 1935.[6]

An old portion of Garden Villas ES flanked by the new in the 2010s. Laurie Feinswog photo

GARDENS E S

This elementary school at 1105 E Harris in Pasadena ISD opened in 1944.

GARDENTOWN SCHOOL

Gardentown was a small and seemingly short lived community located in County District 19, northeast of the present town of Webster. In 1891, the Gardentown School was one of three in the district, used as a voting place as well as for education. Two years later, the schools patrons asked the commissioners court to move the building and school operations into the town of Webster, which had only recently dropped the suffix "ville" from its name. By the 1894-95 school year, Gardentown's name had disappeared from the ledgers.[7]

GENOA E S

When the Genoa School began at the end of the 19th century, it was part of County District 43. It served a "progressive and flourishing little town" on the GH&H Railroad. The frame schoolhouse sat roughly where Genoa Elementary sat in 2025, south of the Almeda-Genoa Road and just west of Highway 3. In 1913, the people of the town voted a bond of $7,000 to construct a new brick building, and it was that structure that was merged into the Pasadena ISD in 1935. For a time, the campus was called O.P Thompson after a longtime member of the District 43 school board.[8]

GENOA MEXICAN SCHOOL

The Genoa Mexican School, also called the Allen-Genoa School in some listings, was a segregated institution located at the end of a dirt road about a mile from the White school in Genoa. The school was incorporated into Pasadena ISD when the Genoa district was absorbed in 1935. It was closed, and the Mexican American students were permitted at the other campus near the end of WWII.[9]

A class at the Genoa Mexican School. Courtesy David Contreras

Mexican Immigrants in Schools

For an area that was once Mexico, there were not a large number of people of Mexican descent in Houston during the first several decades of the city's existence. In 1880, 75 Mexican dockworkers were brought in as strikebreakers to replace Black workers at the wharves, but when the strike ended, they were shipped out of town. The census of

1900 showed only about 500 Mexican-born people in Houston, working jobs such as tamale vendors, barbers, and tailors. There was at least one firm, run by Martin Jimenez on Congress Ave, advertising that they furnished Mexican laborers for farms and railroads. The first Deis y Seis celebration took place in 1907, organized by Prof J.J. Mercado who taught Spanish in public schools.[10]

It was the Revolution which began late in 1910 that led to the big relocation of Mexicans to the area. Many of the working class people who came didn't necessarily plan to stay, but they did. The first settlement area was in El Segundo Barrio, the Second Ward area immediately east of downtown. Late in 1911, the *Galveston Daily News* wrote that there was a row of homemade shacks along the banks of the bayou made from tin, sheet iron, barrel staves, boxes, or any other material at hand. A longtime resident said the land was owned by the city and that no restrictions were placed upon them. By the 1920s, some of the later immigrants were already calling the Second Ward residents Tejanos and saying that they were different since many were born here, not in Mexico.[11]

Most of the newly arrived Mexicans lived in what had originally been large single-family homes that had been subdivided into rooming houses or apartments.

Rusk School, with a new building from 1912, became the predominantly Mexican public school in Houston. When it was built, the school system bragged about all of the various nationalities schooled there. They also had night school for adults. The Rusk Settlement House next door worked closely with the new immigrants just as it had with the Jewish Europeans a decade before. It taught hygiene, offered day care, and trained young Mexican women in craft skills. There was even a free clinic operated there. There were special class times for young boys working as newsboys and messengers during the day. By the 1920s there was also a free dental clinic. It was not a segregated school. A 1936 report said that about 85% of the almost 900 students were of Mexican origin.[12]

Other Mexican neighborhoods sprung up around railroad yards in First and Sixth Ward and in Northside (Fifth Ward) since such a large number of the immigrants worked for the railroads as laborers. There was an isolated group of Mexican workers in the Heights who worked at the Oriental Textile Mill and lived in worker housing set up on the street behind the plant. There were even some boxcar living arrangements set up by the railroads since city directories show Latino-surnamed people living at SP Place and I&GN Place, not real Houston street names. Magnolia Park was another area where many of the new Mexican Americans lived and worked at the nearby Ship Channel. One neighborhood specifically was around Ave K, Ave L, and 77th Street which was new land created by sand dredged to make the Turning Basin and the new wharves. The spot was called El Arenal, The Sands.[13]

At the time, Magnolia Park was in Harrisburg ISD. They made plans to bring in Spanish-speaking teachers and set them up in a separate school. Many Anglo residents objected, but De Zavala ES opened anyway in 1920. Immaculate Heart of Mary Church opened for Mexican Americans in 1926 on 75th St.[14]

The Mexican business district was along Congress, in the 1700 to 2100 blocks, behind today's Minute Maid Park. There were all sorts of businesses owned by and catering to Mexican Americans. By the 1930s, that included the Azteca Theatre showing movies in Spanish at 1809 Congress. Some Anglo-owned business extended Jim

Crow policies from Blacks to Mexicans, though the law was clear that Mexican immigrants were White. By the 1930s, the League of United Latin American Citizens adamantly resisted the various attempts to classify Mexican immigrants as "colored."[15]

Much of the discrimination was done by custom rather than anything codified, and those with lighter skin tone faced less resistance. Though the laws were unchanged, those with brown skin were generally excluded from things such as jury duty. Overall, the immigrants within the city of Houston fared better than those in surrounding small towns including Wharton and Rosenberg where the discrimination was more defined.[16]

Many close-in neighborhoods became predominantly Mexican and Mexican American when Anglos moved to new suburbs like Montrose in the later 1910s. Slums grew up by the 1920s. El Alacran, Shrimpf's Alley in Frost Town near Rusk School was a slum by the middle of that decade.[17]

Services followed eventually. The Mexican Clinic opened in 1924, first on Franklin and then moving to Canal offering all sorts of free medical care, including pre-natal care to people regardless of race or color. It was run by the Catholic Women of Houston. In 1919, Sociedad Mutualista Mexicana Benito Juarez was started in Magnolia to stress Mexican ideals and values and offer support to working class people in their adopted new homeland. Mexico Bello started in Northside in 1924 for social and recreation purposes. *El Tecolote* newspaper and others were born to keep the immigrant community informed.[18]

Though some elementary schools in the new Houston ISD were predominantly Hispanic by custom, and in a handful of cases, by coercion, the junior highs and high school never were. East End and Northside schools like Deady, Edison, and Jackson junior highs and Milby, Austin, and Davis high schools were the first to develop significant Mexican-descended populations. Though the percentage of those immigrant students who completed the then 11 years of public schooling was notably lower than their Anglo counterparts, there were Mexican American graduates from Houston schools by the end of the 1920s. Even some Mexican American civil rights leaders, such as John J. Herrera who had Lyndon B. Johnson as a teacher at Houston HS, stressed that Houston public schools provided their foundation.[19]

GENOSKY SCHOOL

See Janosky.

GEORGI SCHOOL

Oft times a rural school was named for the land owner who hosted, and many times, built the frame school buildings on their property. In the case of Henry Paul Georgi, known as Paul, it was named not only for the land owner and board member, but for the man who taught there, as well. Georgi was an immigrant from Germany who arrived in the U.S. in 1870, prior to his 20th birthday. By 1884, he was listed as a school trustee in the heavily German District 12 in the far northwest part of the county, and two years later, he was teaching at the district's only schoolhouse for $50 a month. Even after Paul Georgi's retirement from the classroom and his subsequent death in 1901, the name lived on in the school house.[20]

For much of its early life, the school sat on the east side of what is now Bauer Road, known as Georgi Road in the late 1800s, just north of Hopfe Road which was named for one of Paul Georgi's closest neighbors. Mistakes over the Georgi name are common, as well, with those not from the area trying to "correct" the mistake and recording it as Georgia School.

Children at Georgi School. Courtesy Kleb Woods, Harris County Pct. 3.

One of the interesting, but far from unique, things about the Georgi School was that the building was moved around the small county district, pulled by mules and rolled across the prairie on logs. It remained in use as a school until at least 1928 when the district was absorbed into County District 1. In 2010, history researchers in northwest Harris County believed that the final Georgi School building was still in existence and sitting just off FM 2920, used as a hay barn.[21]

GEORGI COLORED SCHOOL

Located in County District 12, this school for African Americans is listed in the mid-1880s. By the start of the following decade, funding, and presumably students, had transferred to Hockley Colored School. There appears to have been a rebirth of the school since it is listed in 1907 with a four month term, but it is unclear how long that lasted.[22]

GERMAN CATHOLIC SCHOOL

The first Catholic church in Houston was St. Vincent that opened on Franklin near Caroline in 1842 with priests and sisters who were largely French, but there were also many Irish and German Catholics in the congregation and, eventually, many Irish sisters joined the clergy. When the new Annunciation Parish opened, many congregants moved the few blocks south to that grand sanctuary, but a predominantly German-speaking group of Catholics remained at St. Vincent for a decade. Though the last official sacraments on record took place in 1878, the associated school remained.[23]

Initially, this school utilized space in the church and monastery complex for two classrooms, one for boys on the south side of Franklin and one for girls on the north side. Though the Sisters of the Incarnate Word and Blessed Sacrament were associated with the first school on this site, teachers appear to have been lay people by 1880 when Samuel Archinard is listed as principal with Mrs. L.E. Archinard and Mrs. E.C Baldry as assistants. Other names, all men, are listed as teachers subsequently, though by 1887, the note "no teacher at present" appeared in the city directory.[24]

The final listing mentioning the German Catholic School came in 1889-90 as the fledgling St. Joseph Hospital began to grow, soon taking over all of the former St. Vincent Church buildings.

GERMAN ENGLISH SCHOOL

Another of the German schools in the city that catered both to immigrant and American-born families was the German-English School at the corner of Milam and McKinney. Opened as a private school, it entered the brief public school system of 1871, and upon that system's collapse, it emerged as a private school again, this time with teachers that included Kezia Depelchin. Along with bi-lingual lessons, this and other German schools stressed gymnastics and music, including a brass band. The building in which it was housed was an "old one story brick house" that dated to before the Civil War.[25]

GERMAN LUTHERAN SCHOOL

Of the many German schools offered for Houston children in the 19th century, the German Lutheran School conducted by Rev. Caspar Braun, formerly of Württemberg, was the best known and longest tenured. The school was located on the south side of Texas Avenue, immediately east of the large, wooden German Lutheran Church which sat at the corner of Milam. It was also known as the German Evangelical Lutheran Church at times. Church sermons were performed in German, but the school offered English and German instruction. Classes began in 1853, and remained popular for many years. When the first public schools started in 1871, Braun's school boasted about 100 pupils and one assistant teacher and operated under the public school law.[26]

Braun did not believe in sparing the rod, and recalcitrant boys were sent to an attic room to await the day's dismissal when they "were brought down to taste the pastor's wild peach tree switch." When he died in 1879, other reverend/teachers filled the void at the school, also known as the German-English School, for many more years.[27]

GERMAN SELECT SCHOOL

This is one of several German schools in the city, listed at the north end of Chenevert in 1877 with classes for boys and girls taught by Prof. F. Duerer.[28]

GIRL'S INDUSTRIAL SCHOOL

See Harris County School for Girls.

GLEASON'S RANCH SCHOOL

Gleason's Ranch was a late 19th century African American schoolhouse in District 20 along with the Harrisburg schools.[29]

GLEN COVE SCHOOL

Glen Cove was a small school for Black students in what is today considered the Third Ward, not far northwest of the current TDECU Stadium. It began as a county school in District 24, first receiving funds in December 1892. It is possible that the schoolhouse was moved at some point from one small lot on Napoleon Street to another, but by 1919, it is on the east side of the street, just south of Elgin.[30]

Free Textbooks and Uniformity

When the first one room subscription schoolhouses popped up in Austin's Colony and soon after became widely scattered in parts of the Republic of Texas, students came to school not with an assigned reader, but with any book the family owned. Martin McHenry Kenney attended a couple of frontier school houses during the Republic period, both near his family home between present day Brenham and Bellville. "The pupils brought such books as they happened to have," he wrote. "One young man had Robinson Crusoe for his reading book...

several had Weem's Life of Washington... one boy had an illustrated edition of Goldsmith's Natural History, and there were a variety of other books, nearly all by famous authors."[31]

As the Civil War approached, Houston merchants such as E.H. Cushing and J.S. Taft advertised new shipments of school texts, seeking to sell them to the parents of children attending the various private schools in the city. It was a system akin to buying college textbooks assigned by each professor, though noticeably less expensive.

Private enterprise ruled in Texas for many decades, long after statewide plans took hold elsewhere. In 1896, State Superintendent James M. Carlisle wrote about textbook uniformity, a subject which he said was still being debated. Though Texas had never adopted the idea, Carlisle quoted lengthy and strong testimonials from his counterparts in states including California, Iowa, New Jersey, Rhode Island, and Nebraska. He cited cost savings for everyone involved when the state, or even large districts, could buy their books in bulk numbers. This would be especially important for the poorest families, he noted.[32]

The powers that be moved slowly. The legislature passed an updated uniform textbook law in 1907, at the same time creating a state textbook board to make the decisions on what those books would be. There was much wrangling over whether the governor or a combination of the State Superintendent of Instruction and the President of the University of Texas would select members of the textbook board. Whatever the board's choices, it would remain up to the families of the students to make the purchases.[33]

It was still not a popular decision with everyone. Houston school superintendent Paul W. Horn wrote this in the 1907-08 city schools report: "At the beginning of the next year our schools will be called upon to pass through the ordeal of a sweeping change in text books. This is due to the fact that when the recent uniform text book law for the State of Texas was adopted, the cities, though nominally exempt, are exempt only under conditions which it is practically impossible to fulfill. Under these conditions it seems to me that the only thing left for us to do is to 'take our medicine,' and take it as gracefully as we can. I am free to state, however, as I have frequently stated before, that I think the inclusion of the cities within the operation of the uniform text book law is a mistake. It is impossible to find any book which will be the best book for all schools, just as it would be impossible to find a given tool which would be the best tool for all classes of work... If Houston were managing her own educational affairs in regard to text books, as she was under the former text book law, the necessity for these changes would not be upon us."[34]

Six years later, the schools of Houston took the final step, or at least part of it. City voters approved an amendment to the city charter in 1913, and moved its policy ahead of the state's. It was not without its opponents. Mr. E.T. Barden wrote the editor of the Post: "If we furnish a child its books, let the city be logical and furnish shoes, hats, dress, etc. There is no justification for such a change."[35]

Starting in September 1914, Houston school pupils in the first four grades, 9,728 of them to be exact, were furnished with free textbooks. A year later, grades five through seven were phased in, as well. Finally in

September 1916, students at the city's high schools joined their younger counterparts in receiving the use of free textbooks.[36]

The initial outlay for grades one through four was just shy of $10,000, but Superintendent Horn noted that "as the life of the great majority of the books will be more than one year, it is evident that the real cost will be far less than one dollar per year for all the pupils of the first four grades." If any parent wanted his or her child to furnish their own copy of a given textbook, that was permitted. Few took the city up on that offer.[37]

When the City of Houston went into the textbook business, they quickly found a couple of logistical needs came along with it. Forty thousand pounds of books were hard to store, and that was just for the first four grades. The district was expecting twice that number the following year when grades five through seven joined the program. The first solution was to commandeer two rooms on the main floor of the Houston High School building along with some hallway space, but a warehouse was soon to follow. As the city report noted that first year: "The unpacking, checking and marking and distribution of these books is by no means a trivial matter."[38]

In the pre-antibiotics era, communicable diseases were always a primary concern. Superintendent Horn's office talked with other school districts around the United States which had been using free text books for many years, as well as their own Director of School Hygiene. The resulting plan meant that "all text books that have been in use during the year have been, during the vacation season, fumigated with all possible care. All text books known to have been exposed to contagious diseases were at once destroyed without being allowed to be returned to the schools. During the summer the books have been carefully cleaned as well as fumigated. While in use by the children the books are covered with paper or cloth covers which are destroyed at the end of the term."[39]

Book fumigation at the high school. HISD

The final piece of the free textbook puzzle was how to pay for it all. In 1916, the legislature authorized a county school property tax that joined already existing state and school district property taxes. Two years later, they would raise the state tax so that the three entities could charge up to a combined $1.85 per $100 valuation. Texans still wanted a more solid funding for schools. On November 5, 1918, some 69.2% of participating Texas voters approved a law that raised the cap on state property taxes and allowed for the state to use tax money to meet educational needs. The first of these was free textbooks for the public schools. By 1920, the state had exempted all independent and common school districts from any tax limitation whatsoever.[40]

In 1935, with the Great Depression still upon the citizenry, the Texas Senate and House almost unanimously passed an amendment that would have extended the free textbook rule to students at private schools. The voters of Texas didn't see it as nearly such a good idea as the legislature had. Some 52.1% of them cast ballots against the amendment.[41]

GOLDEN ACRES E S

Golden Acres Elementary opened in the Pasadena ISD at 5232 Sycamore in 1938.[42]

GOLFCREST E S

The school named for the former Golfcrest Country Club and the subsequent surrounding residential neighborhoods that it serves in south Houston opened at 7414 Fairway in September 1949, albeit with unfinished drives and almost no furniture its first day. The golf course had been developed by Earl Gammage, Sr. and opened in 1927, serving as the initial catalyst to the development around it.[43]

GOOSE CREEK SCHOOL

The oldest schoolhouse in the modern day Baytown area was first called Cedar Bayou in the records, but its lineage belongs with Goose Creek School. Voting precinct records suggest that there was a bit of a turf war over which name to use for the community. The school first operated in a one-room log building at the Methodist Church in the 1840s, near today's Exxon Docks. A small community called Louisville that covered as many as 12 loose blocks of businesses and residences was located at that area but failed to grow into the town envisioned by its founders. The schoolhouse was possibly destroyed by a hurricane in 1854, but the institution continued, being listed in 1861 as the Civil War finally put an end to the indifferent public school law.[44]

The "Oil Field School" between 1913 and 1917. Bay Area Historical
Society

The community, by then firmly known as Goose Creek, had one of the original schools registered under the 1876 law. As shown, it was there earlier, though whether there was a gap in service is unclear. The widow of Anson Jones, the last President of the Republic of Texas, donated an acre and a half of land for the school that sat at the modern Baytown intersection of West Main, South Main, and Alexander Drive. By the 1880s, the school was part of District 15 with nearby Cedar Bayou. The building was moved a half mile north in 1884 and continued to serve a relatively sleepy community, potentially with a short gap in operation, until oil was discovered. By 1908, the drilling boom brought droves of workers, many moving from Humble with their families. A private school with tuition of $1.25 per month was opened in a tent near the Goose Creek Field in fall of 1912 taught by a graduate of Houston High School, Alice Mae Bullard. A one-room public school building that also served as a church and community center opened a year later, remaining until it was judged too dangerous and noisy to hold classes in the middle of an active oil field. In late 1917, the Goose Creek School opened in a large wood frame building at Commerce and Sterling that had seen previous service as a Blacksmith shop and boarding house. Known as the Barn, it was divided into six rooms. It still could not stay apace of the boom in oil field workers, and the district rented buildings such as an old store, and a former blacksmith's shop was donated by Gulf Oil. When Goose Creek ISD was formed from the nascent Cedar Bayou ISD, the Barn was subdivided again, into a total of 12 rooms for grades one through eight. Bond issues and contributions from oil companies quickly brought a flurry of new school buildings in the 1920s.[45]

Children at the rented Derrick Store in Goose Creek between 1919 and 1923. Bay Area Historical Society

GOOSE CREEK COLORED SCHOOL

A school reform law in 1884 required the election of a separate board of school trustees, usually three members, for African American schools in each county district. In other words, the trustees, like the students, had to be segregated. Goose Creek first shows a record of having a school for Black children in 1897, but the number of pupils may have been fewer than 10. The colored school closed about 1904 when trustee Ephraim Taylor sold the land on which the tiny building sat, and Black children in Goose Creek seem to have gone without a local schoolhouse until 1917 when rented space in the Anderson Store was utilized with Tillie Brown as the teacher. There may have been some sort of home school instruction in the interim. The district formerly acquired a Black school again in 1921.[46]

GOOSE CREEK H S

One of the early priorities after the formation of Goose Creek ISD in 1919 was the establishment of a high school. Classes were held first in an old YMCA building at Jones and Pearce Streets with the first graduates receiving their diplomas in 1923, a year after a bond issue set aside money for a dedicated high school building. That building was constructed on Pruett near the Southern Pacific tracks. Teachers in GCCISD in the early 1920s were paid between $75 and $125 a month, had to be at least 20 years old, and the women could not have "bobbed" hair. In 1928, when Lee High School opened in Baytown, the Goose Creek High School building became the Horace Mann Junior High.[47]

GRACIE'S SCHOOL HOUSE

Gracie's School was a voting place near Galveston Bay in the general area of today's Webster in the late 1870s.[48]

GRADY, HENRY W SCHOOL

The site of Neiman Marcus in the Galleria, at the southwest corner of Westheimer and Post Oak, was home to the Post Oak School in County District 23 for many decades. The area was home to many Italian and Mexican American truck farmers, and by the early 1900s, their children made up a majority of the students. It was the site of a large outbreak of ptomaine among students, parents, and faculty in 1910 when an ice cream social served tainted goods. Post Oak School was taken into HISD in 1927, and two years later the old building was upgraded, a new structure added, and additional land purchased. At the same time, it was renamed for Henry W. Grady, an influential 19th century Georgia newspaper editor who advocated strongly for an industrialized post-Civil War South and the continuation of White supremacy. In 1950, the campus moved to ten acres at 5215 San Felipe at Sage that had been donated by Tanglewood developer William Farrington. After operating for almost 30 years, it closed due to low enrollment, served as an administrative facility for some time, then reopened as a middle school in 1992. A new modern building replaced the mid-century one in the 2010s, and the school's website lists it as Tanglewood Middle School.[49]

GRANT SCHOOL

Grant was a one-room school in County District 8 in the northwest part of the county during the early years of the 20th century.[50]

GRANT PARK E S

See Dogan

GREEN POND SCHOOL

Baker's Colored School, near the San Felipe Road just west of Houston, appears as early as 1885, a year that it was used as an African American voting place. The following year, the name of the school is noted as having changed to Green Pond, but whether or not the school in District 23 moved farther west from the city limits is unclear. The community of Green Pond was a small neighborhood of recently freed slaves that centered not only around the school but also Nazarene Baptist Church that traces its roots to 1875. The African American College Park Memorial Cemetery sprawls just to the east. The term of school was likely short, and when teachers including B.H. Grimes and F.O. Yates taught there in the late 19th century, it was only for grades one up through three or four. Green Pond joined the city school system in 1913 thanks to annexation, and was replaced with a new wood frame building after the old one was destroyed by the 1915 hurricane. The 50' x 50' "box house" at Blackshear Street (today's Alpha) and Gross was an improvement, but as late as 1924, it remained without electricity and plumbing.[51]

GREEN'S BAYOU SCHOOL

There was a Green's Bayou stop on the Texas & New Orleans Railroad that ran northeast from Houston in the late 19th century continuing on through Sheldon and Crosby. School District 16 that served the area was in place by 1884, but the exact location of the schools therein is unknown. By the late-1890s, though the district continued to carry the name Green's Bayou, and Green's Bayou Colored schoolhouse continued to operate, the voting place for the district was at Clinton.[52]

GREEN'S BAYOU COLORED SCHOOL

In the late 19th century, County District 16 contained multiple schools with Green's Bayou in the name. In addition to Green's Bayou Colored School which shows up as early as 1886, there were Green's Bayou School, Little Green's Bayou Colored, and North Green's Bayou. The precise location for these schools is unknown, but the African American schoolhouses served both farm children and those of workers on the rail line. The Clinton schools became the primary locations in District 16.[53]

GREGORY INSTITUTE

The most storied name in African American education in Houston belongs to the Gregory Institute, named after a Union general involved in the Reconstruction efforts in the area. It began as a small operation at what is today an unknown location under the Freedmen's Bureau in the late 1860s, but it achieved its place of prominence thanks to shared efforts of a coalition of interested parties - local donors among the city's White business elite, "Radical Republican" state legislators, and the federal authorities on hand in Houston. With approval from Austin and the backing of local Black leaders Richard Allen and Rev. Elias Dibble, a four-room, two-story brick building was constructed at the western terminus of Jefferson Street, between what is now Smith and Louisiana, in 1870. The contractor was C. Bering.[54]

Like all the Freedmen's Bureau schools, the first teachers at Gregory Institute were White northerners, sent under the auspices of the American Missionary Association. Whether it was the miscegenation part or the Yankee part, many Houstonians complained loudly about the arrangement. Even before the city took over operation of many of the private schools in 1876, eliminating tuition at the Gregory Institute and elsewhere, the situation had changed to a White principal overseeing Black teachers.[55]

For all of the fuss about separating the races, Gregory was still a source of great pride to many who felt it was a symbol of the city's progressive and enlightened attitude. Harris County had notably more Blacks in school than anywhere else in the state, and the Institute was their flagship. A "skirt of timber" where children could play was near the 55' x 32' building. The cost including furniture had been a full $8,000, and featured "elegant seats and desks for 230 pupils" along with charts, blackboards, and globes. On the January day that it opened, a local scribe told of "a handsome two-story building, finely finished, with beautiful green blinds, desks of the most approved style of modern school architecture; two large recitation rooms, one above and one below, with smaller rooms for classes on both floors."[56]

The student body was varied, especially in the first years. Adults with a passion to get an education were often seen in classrooms with children. Newspapermen described the newly freed populace learning reading, writing, arithmetic and history as being of "every hue... from White... to Cimmerian Blackness." The initial plan was for the primary school to be downstairs and the high school above, but in practice, there were rarely any high school students. Newly emerged from the oppression of slavery, there was considerable catching up to be done among the Black citizens of Texas. By 1884, the principal, H.C. Hardy, was teaching all of the fifth, sixth, and seventh grade African American students in the city. Four years later, there was enough of an increase for an assistant to have taken over the fifth grade duties.[57]

Professor Hardy was a Jamaican with an island/English accent, an orderly manner, and a desire for the same order in his pupils. Among his first jobs in the United States was a three year stint at a combined plantation school in Louisiana, the building for which had been constructed by the newly freed slaves themselves. Among his Louisiana charges was young Joe Vance Lewis who also later moved to Houston. Lewis became one of the first Black attorneys in the Bayou City.[58]

The high school side of Gregory Institute continued to lag lamentably. By 1891, the city reported that there were "only 2 colored 8th graders in entire city, both girls at Gregory." Rapid growth in the Black communities in Second, Third, and Fifth Wards also let those ward schools overtake Gregory in enrollment, and it coincided with the planned opening of the new Colored High School in Fourth Ward. That occurrence was sped along in mid-April of 1893 when students at Gregory Institute suddenly got the sensation that the building was collapsing around them. There was a stampede for the exits, and one pupil was badly injured jumping from a second floor window. The students were moved to the not-quite-finished high school building on Frederick.[59]

By that summer, the school superintendent reported that "Gregory is gone and replaced by Colored High School." The old Gregory site at the end of Jefferson was sold, but the overcrowding situation only got worse. One year later, there were 561 students, from first grade and up, all crowded into the new six-room high school building. Six more rooms were soon rented, and other classes were being held in the hallways. In 1903, Fourth Ward finally got some relief when an eight-room frame elementary school opened at the corner of Cleveland and Wilson in Freedmen's Town, and the Gregory School name was revived. The principal there was W.E. Miller.[60]

A 1905 class posing at the new wood frame Gregory School. HHRC

In spite of efforts of the faculty and the Mothers Club, two problems showed themselves from the start. More temporary rooms had to be added, and the grounds flooded so horribly when it rained that the *Informer* took to calling it Lake Gregory and said that it was suitable for fishing and duck hunting. It became a major focus of the HISD bond elections in the 1920s, and finally, in 1926, a new 20-room brick school opened on the same block, facing Victor Street. The old wooden temporary buildings were used as a cafeteria and additional space, since the main 1903 school had been destroyed by fire a year earlier. Other outbuildings appeared over the decades, but by the 1970s, a new Gregory-Lincoln school opened a short distance north. The 1926 palace of a school for the Black children of Fourth Ward closed in 1980 to sit vacant for decades.[61]

The dream of Houston Mayor Lee Brown and others was to preserve the school and turn the long abandoned landmark into something useful. On April 28, 2008, Freedmen's Town residents joined then-Mayor Bill White for a groundbreaking, and today a preserved school lives on as the African American Library at Gregory School.[62]

Children playing at the new Gregory School 1920s.
HHRC

GREGORY SCHOOL

See Gregory Institute

Bond issue as seen by *Informer*

"SCHOOL BOND ISSUE FOR $3,000,000"

Informer, Saturday, April 21, 1923

A bond issue for $3,000,000 for school purposes will be submitted to the voters of the Houston Independent School District on Monday, May 7.

At this election, the voters will also decide whether future school boards, under provisions of the amended charter, are to be appointed or elected by popular vote.

In issuing a detailed statement some weeks ago, the school board stipulated how the money would be spent in event the bond issue carries and included in the proposed school program a junior high school for colored children residing in Fifth Ward.

Nothing was said about improving conditions around the ward schools for colored children, despite the fact the Colored High, Gregory, Dunbar, Langston, and other such schools are totally inadequate and unfit for school purposes and are really a menace and a hazard.

Take the Colored High School: The present enrollment is about 1,000, with an average attendance of 900 students. There are seats for only 500, forcing practically 400 to stand or sit cramped up in a seat with another pupil all day. The children are compelled to play out in the streets, doing so at a hazard, oftimes, to their very lives. Classes are held in a low, dark, and damp basement, wholly unfit and totally inadequate for school purposes; while the building would hardly do credit to a town of 10,000 population.

The other three colored ward schools enumerated above are frame structures, one of which is likely to fall when a good gust of wind strikes it a center blow; while all of them are in a dilapidated condition and one is situated in the center of a young lake, which undermines the health of both the teachers and the pupils, with the result that more teachers have died out of Gregory School than any other school in the system.

The Booker T. Washington, Douglass, and Harper Schools are hardly any better, the teachers and pupils being forced to wade in water and mud to reach the latter during rainy spells. The buildings are frame and two of them have verily seen their best days. All of these schools constitute a menace to public health and with stoves for heating purposes during the winter, they are likewise a fire hazard, continually and constantly endangering the lives of pupils and teachers.

Just what the school authorities plan in improving these schools by replacing these old structures with modern buildings and in rendering and maintaining the conditions and environments more healthy and wholesome, has not been divulged through public print.

The colored voters should certainly manifest more than passing interest in this election, for it will profit the race absolutely nothing to wait until the election is over and then whine and belly-ache about what we ought to have.

We should organize our forces, appoint a representative committee to meet and confer with the school board with a view of ascertaining how much and where will this money be spent for colored schools.

Such procedure will be perfectly within our rights and we shall be exercising the prerogatives of citizenship to at least make an effort to find out "where we come in."

To vote $3,000,000 for school purposes and then spend practically $2,800,000 for White schools and about $200,000 for one school building for colored children or turn over to them an antiquated school building now employed by White children, will not have the remotest semblance of justice, a fair and square deal.

But unless we get busy, organize our forces and endeavor to get something tangible and concrete in appropriations for better and more commodious school buildings for colored scholastics, we shall have nobody to blame but ourselves.

People seldom get all they ask for and where they ask for nothing, nothing they shall receive. Selah!

C.F. Richardson

GRICE SCHOOL

John W. Grice, a native Texan farmer in the Hockley area of far northwest Harris County was the likely source of the name of Grice School that was operating in District 33 as early as 1889. It is intertwined with Binford that is the only other school appearing in the district, and though both names show up in records between 1891 and 1913, they do not seem to appear in the same year. Binford was located on today's FM 1488. In 1907, Grice is described as a very small box structure that has never been painted.[63]

Grisby School about 1890. Marie Neuman Gray

GRISBY SCHOOL

G.H. Grisby deeded an acre of land for a school to County Judge John Tod in 1895 with the standard reversion clause in case its use as a school ceased. The single room school, in County District 10, was located just east of the modern Highway 6 and north of Kieth Harrow Drive.[64]

GUM GULLY SCHOOL

Gum Gully opened on the Huffman Road just over three miles north of Crosby in 1914. It was closed and students rolled into Crosby in September 1925. The building is now adapted into a residence.[65]

Gum Gulley School building in the 2010s. Mike Vance photo

GUM ISLAND SCHOOL/ FAIRBANKS SCHOOL

See Fairbanks School

Schools Habermacher – Horn

HABERMACHER SCHOOL

Habermacher was a small community and railroad stop on the Texas Western Narrow Gauge in far southwest Harris County just past where modern day Westheimer Road veers south into Westheimer Parkway to the west of Highway 6. It had a school operating prior to the Civil War. Today the site sits within Barker Reservoir and George Bush Park. The Habermacher family came to the area about 1841 after some years in Pennsylvania following their emigration from Germany.[1]

HAMILTON J H S

When it opened as the capstone of Heights Boulevard in September of 1920, the beautiful, three-story, neo-gothic building with turrets flanking the front entrance was trumpeted as "a credit to all concerned." One year later, the $157,000 home of Heights Senior High School was said to be in a "portion of the city... growing so rapidly in population and in educational interests, that it has already outstripped facilities which had given promise of being sufficient for a number of years." The answer came in the form of a fire and a bond issue. [2]

It had opened with 24 classrooms, an auditorium and even janitors quarters, and within a year, the district administrators were calling for two more wings of four rooms each plus a gym and swimming pool. As those plans took place, the junior high, which had inherited the former Heights High School building at Yale and 12th, burned to the ground. Faced with a huge number of students with no school, the new Heights building went on a schedule of high schoolers in the morning and junior high pupils in the afternoon. It was an arrangement that lasted two years until bond money was used to construct the new, larger Reagan High School a few blocks away. At the same time that opened in 1926, the building on 20th and Heights was rechristened Alexander Hamilton Junior High.[3]

Hamilton JHS newly opened. HISD

The junior high flourished, including a high profile experiment in student government in the 1930s with an executive cabinet and captains and lieutenants that oversaw divisions of other students. Among the duties was directing the 1,200 pupils through the halls and lunch room, and a Good Cheer Department that collected and distributed money, groceries, fruit, and toys for the poor during the Depression and sent cards and letters to bereaved families. Hamilton thrives today as a Vanguard middle school.[4]

HAMILTON STREET SCHOOL
See Rusk

HARBOR SCHOOL
See Eliot

HARGRAVE'S SCHOOL
Hargraves was a small one-room school that switched back and forth with Lee's Schoolhouse for primacy in District 8 during the last two decades of the 19th century. Petitions to consolidated and to re-establish were presented to the county commissioners in the mid-1880s, but the Hargraves name, perhaps derived from area landowner Levi Hargrave, continued for at least another decade.[5]

HARLEM E S, BAYTOWN
Harlem School was built by the Goose Creek ISD in the African American McNair community north of Baytown in the late 1920s. Originally it had three rooms with dirt floors and outdoor toilets. Those conditions lasted into the late 1940s before renovations to expand and upgrade the facilities took place. It was renovated,

air conditioned, and integration was started in 1963. A new Harlem Elementary was built in 1992, and the old building was demolished a few years later.[6]

The Community Use of Schools

We were also careful to especially stress the idea that the school plant should be so constructed that the widest possible use may be made of it by the community as a whole. The doctrine was set forth that the schools belong to the people and should be used by them to the greatest extent possible... In several instances neighborhood improvement clubs were given permission to hold regular meetings at the school house. The only restrictions imposed were that there should be no discussions of a partisan political, or sectarian religious nature; that the clubs should be responsible for the care of the building, and should give some suitable remuneration to the regular school janitor for his extra work... At four buildings there was a series of lectures delivered by prominent physicians of the town on subjects relating to public health. These four buildings were the Rusk, Dow, Sherman, and Reagan... One lecture was on the care of the eye and ear, another was on the care of the teeth, a third was on the subject of proper milk supply and a fourth was on general hygiene... That there is also a need for them is attested by several little incidents that arose. In one case, a lecture had been delivered on the subject of the care of the teeth. At the close, the meeting was thrown open for questions and for discussion. One old lady arose and stated that she had been much interested in what she had heard, but intimated that she had some doubts as to the accuracy of some of the statements. She particularly doubted the statement that it was conducive to good health to brush one's teeth regularly. "For", said she, "I am in as good health as anybody, I am seventy years old, and I ain't never brushed my teeth yit!"

Houston City Schools Report 1910

HARLOW SCHOOL

In 1897, the new town of Etta wanted to have Houston streetcars run south from the town of Brunner, across the Shepherd's Dam to connect with the cars that ran out San Felipe Road. At the time, Etta could boast a new post office, a "growing population," the Houston Negro College, and a county school in District 23 which later changed to District 4 which also contained Platte, Burke, and Post Oak Schools. According to city directories, the school was located four blocks south of the area's main throughfare of the San Felipe Road. Among the students there in 1903 were young Burton and Ruby Harlow, children of English-born building contractor

Edwin Harlow who would be honored with his name on the school that served the neighborhood. Etta School is last listed in 1912, and Harlow appears the following year. Whether it was a new, nearby location or the same plot of land is unclear.[7]

Harlow School just off today's busy West Gray. HHRC

Harlow School sat on a small lot in a rather rural setting at what would eventually become the south side of Peden at Harlow Street which became Elmen. The street grid that Houstonians know today as the River Oaks shopping area grew up around it. In October 1913, when the Houston city limits expanded, bringing Harlow from County District 4 into the city school system, streets such as nearby West Gray did not even extend as far out as the building. By 1921, the school for the first five grades had four rooms and 70 desks. Shortly thereafter, growing population in the area brought the school closure and incorporation into nearby campuses.[8]

HARMONY GROVE SCHOOL

Mr. and Mrs. Kemp were the first teachers at this school that started at the Harmony Grove Methodist Church on the west bank of Goose Creek, just north of today's Missouri Street in Baytown. It opened in 1859, and the Kemps were replaced by Rev. C.C. Preston early during the Civil War. Preston petitioned to start the Bayland Orphanage in 1866, and the Gaillard's Landing School began to serve the needs of the area children.[9]

HARPER SCHOOL

Shiloh Colored School was operating by 1886 when Pink Parker had charge of the single room building at the northwest corner of Center and Court Streets. It was serving the Chaneyville community, a majority-Black neighborhood that grew up near the burgeoning industrial area along Washington Road and today's Montrose Boulevard. By the mid-1890s, the school was going by the Chaneyville name. Following Parker at the schoolhouse was John Henry Yates, Jr., son of the city's most famous Black preacher, and the popular Yates, Jr. was at the center of a small firestorm when the county decided that the $60 a month salary he had been promised was too high and went to court to fire him while he continued to teach for another year.[10]

In 1904, the City of Houston extended its city limits and split Chaneyville in two, bringing the Black school and its 85 children there into the city system. Six years later, the two-room building was replaced with a new four-room frame school raised above ground to create a basement, and the name was changed to honor the Baltimore poet and abolitionist Frances Harper. That building was destroyed by the 1915 Hurricane and rebuilt on the same spot, next to Damascus Baptist Church. The principal at that time was Georgian George B.M. Turner who spent most of his 35 year career in Houston schools at Harper.[11]

Harper School doorway in 2010s. Laurie Feinswog photo

When the bond-fueled building boom of the latter 1920s arrived, the Harper School community was rewarded not only with a brand new Hedrick & Gottlieb designed building in 1927 but an upgrade in status as junior high grades were added to the elementary. In the late 1930s and 40s, Harper was also the location of night classes for Houston's Black adults. The historic building was changed to use as an alternative campus years later. By the early 2000s, the Harper site was put up for sale by HISD. The initial transaction was placed on hold, and the district again voted to list the property in late 2024.[12]

Home Economics

Home Economics for female public school students, also known as Domestic Science, followed a rise similar to that of industrial science, or shop classes, for the boys. Officials believed it prepared the young women for their proper role in American life.[13]

Houston and the larger Harris County schools, such as Harrisburg and Fullerton, all felt strongly about the course. One department supervisor in Houston made clear that homemaking "is as distinctly a profession as many that we have long considered so—that it is more far reaching and more vital in its scope than any other, since on the efficiency of the home and homemaker depends the efficiency of the members of that home."[14]

Domestic science rooms began to show up in Houston schools roughly five years into the 20th century, starting with the White and Black high schools and Fannin, Allen, Taylor, Hawthorne, Sherman, and Rusk elementaries, the latter benefitting from the work of the Settlement House. By 1909, the subject continued to expand in both Black and White grade schools, with Langston, Travis, Jones, and Austin gaining home ec kitchens and sewing rooms. Two more White elementaries, Reagan and Lubbock, and African American Dunbar were in the works. The total number of girls in the department topped the two thousand mark during that school year. In addition, a few dozen students took the courses in night schools at Rusk and Sherman.[15]

The sewing programs sought to teach young women a practical knowledge in grade school including "practice of the simple hand stitches, and their application to plain garment making; also buttonhole making, patching, darning and mending." County school officials added that they wished the girls to "secure the best value at the least expenditure." The city school policy was that each student could purchase her own work at cost, though it was not required. The accounting for the school year in Houston said that $157.25 was raised in that fashion, leaving a net cost of sewing supplies for the district at roughly twenty-six dollars.[16]

Unlike cooking that required a working kitchen, the sewing classes meant only acquiring a Singer machine or two. Since the school board was slow in bringing the equipment into African American grade schools, a few decided not to wait. Mother's clubs at Douglass and Booker T. Washington elementaries purchased and donated machines, and the former even paid to hire an instructor.[17]

Booker T. Washington HS trained girls for domestic service. HHRC

High school pupils got a more advanced course of study. They began by reviewing the chemical composition of food and how it related to health and nutrition. Sewing came in the second half of the term, moving beyond the practical to "the development of the artistic and beautiful." The full domestic science course also included "invalid cookery, special diets, home nursing, and first aid to the injured; house planning, furnishing and sanitation, and a full course in sewing and dressmaking."[18]

Each of the city's segregated high schools prepared luncheons for the superintendent, school board, and faculty during the 1909-10 year. Both were said to show "evidence of sound, practical training." The White High School also prepared a buffet luncheon for the graduating class of Texas A&M. None of that matched those girls' highlight the previous year when they hosted Dr. Charles W. Eliot of Harvard.[19]

Domestic Science classes, led by Mabel McBain, pulled their weight during World War I in Harris County. Not only did they hold classes on cooking, canning and sewing for the public, they opened their facilities for all. Supervisor Ada Gause reported that "The equipment has been open to the use of the public at all hours when not actually in use by the day school program. The housewives in the community, the Red Cross workers and the Food Administration representatives have all been made welcome."[20]

One year later, after the Armistice had been signed, the annual report carried a different recommendation: "Because of large gas bills, and damage to domestic science equipment during last summer, the advisors suggest that these rooms be used only upon permission from Mr. Morgan."[21]

As women began to enter the mainstream work force more frequently following WWII, home economics began to fade from favor. The women's movement of the 1970s primarily viewed it as a way to bind American women to household and maternal roles, away from competing for jobs with men. That thought process, coupled with the expense of building and maintaining teaching kitchens, led to the gradual demise of home ec as the 20th century gave way to the 21st.[22]

HARREL SCHOOL

Harrel School in County District 8 was located on what is today FM 1960, first east, then after a fire, west of Kuykendahl Road. County records reflect a confusing warren of name changes in the 1880s and 90s with the previous names of Hobson and possibly Lee's giving way to the Harrel name for good by 1894. Harrel, spelled both with one or two Ls, continued to serve the area until 1935 when it merged with Spring School to form Spring ISD.[23]

HARRIS COUNTY SCHOOL FOR BOYS

Harris County opened a School for Boys, meaning delinquents, in Seabrook in 1910. Almost immediately, several of the school's sixteen charges began attempting to escape by "taking advantage of the sleeping watchman" and trying to swim their way to anticipated freedom. All were quickly caught. County Judge Ammerman was ecstatic about the investment, though members of the Houston Police Department noted that the number of petty thefts downtown suggested that not all of the area's delinquent boys had been corralled.[24]

In 1914, the school was relocated to South Houston, but in 1925, the now 63 boys were moved back to a site on Clear Lake, three miles west of Seabrook on the north side of what is today NASA Road 1. Aside from a large three story building, the farm site had barns and shops, and the boys raised chickens, pigs, and registered Holstein cows, some of which went to supply other county homes. The county's juvenile probation department oversaw the facility in an army-like fashion. Boys wore uniforms, took regular school classes, and were offered training in "printing, baking, shoe repairing, blacksmithing, poultry and dairy husbandry, vegetable gardening, garment making, automobile mechanics, calisthenics, military drill and band music." [25]

The school portion of the operation was combined with the Webster ISD in 1934, and in 1936, the county ceased using the School for Boys name. The younger boys stayed at what became solely referred to as the Bayland School which had moved to Clear Lake, but the older ones were sent to the State Training School for Boys at Gatesville. The Clear Lake site was renamed Harris County Youth Village in 1972.[26]

HARRIS COUNTY SCHOOL FOR GIRLS

Harris County opened a facility for delinquent girls in September 1914, styling it the Harris County Training School for Girls. It was under the supervision of Ethel Claxton who became an institution unto herself, staying at the helm for 37 years. The location was a large parcel of land on what would become Chimney Rock Road, northwest of the new town of Bellaire that had been donated by Joseph Meyer. The campus had a collection of buildings including four large houses called "cottages". It once topped 80 acres of property with plenty of room for gardening, farm work, and baseball, swimming, and basketball to go with the academic courses and vocational subjects like cooking, laundry, and sewing. The baseball games were real hardball in the earliest years, and former Major Leaguer Chappie McFarland, who had retired in Houston as manager of the Queen Theatre on Main Street, volunteered as the girls' instructor.[27]

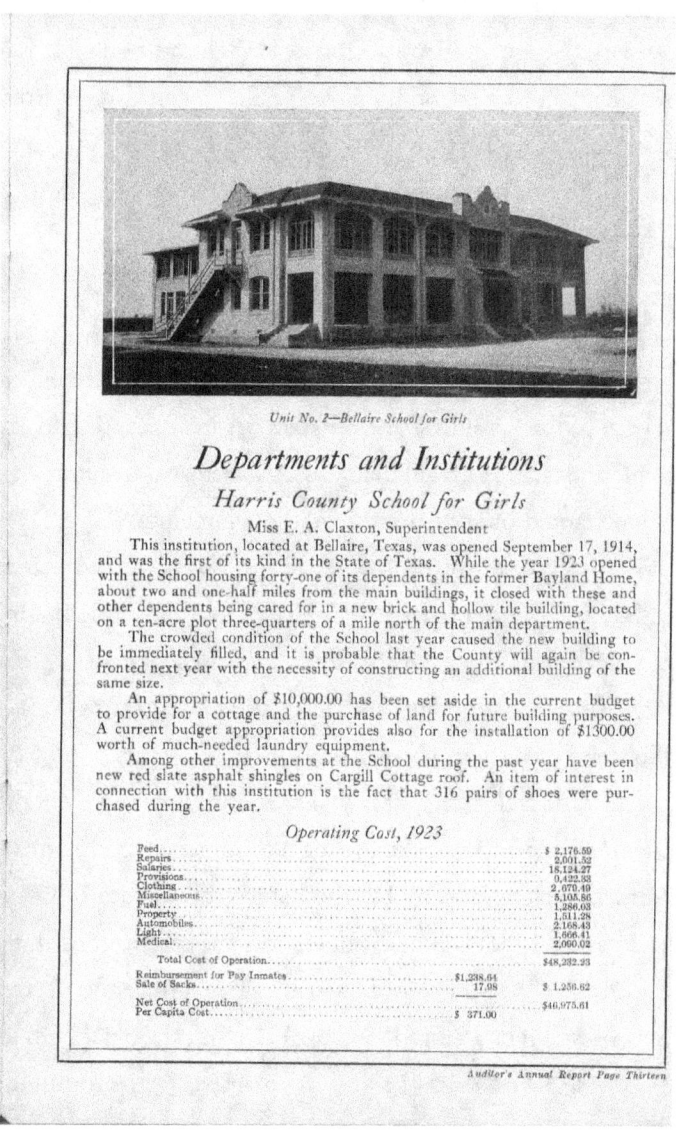

Unit No. 2—Bellaire School for Girls

Departments and Institutions

Harris County School for Girls

Miss E. A. Claxton, Superintendent

This institution, located at Bellaire, Texas, was opened September 17, 1914, and was the first of its kind in the State of Texas. While the year 1923 opened with the School housing forty-one of its dependents in the former Bayland Home, about two and one-half miles from the main buildings, it closed with these and other dependents being cared for in a new brick and hollow tile building, located on a ten-acre plot three-quarters of a mile north of the main department.

The crowded condition of the School last year caused the new building to be immediately filled, and it is probable that the County will again be confronted next year with the necessity of constructing an additional building of the same size.

An appropriation of $10,000.00 has been set aside in the current budget to provide for a cottage and the purchase of land for future building purposes. A current budget appropriation provides also for the installation of $1300.00 worth of much-needed laundry equipment.

Among other improvements at the School during the past year have been new red slate asphalt shingles on Cargill Cottage roof. An item of interest in connection with this institution is the fact that 316 pairs of shoes were purchased during the year.

Operating Cost, 1923

Feed	$ 2,176.59
Repairs	2,001.52
Salaries	18,124.27
Provisions	9,422.33
Clothing	2,079.49
Miscellaneous	5,105.86
Fuel	1,286.03
Property	1,511.28
Automobiles	2,168.43
Light	1,666.41
Medical	2,060.02
Total Cost of Operation	$48,282.23
Reimbursement for Pay Inmates	$1,238.64
Sale of Sacks	17.98
	$ 1,256.62
Net Cost of Operation	$46,975.61
Per Capita Cost	$ 371.00

Auditor's Annual Report Page Thirteen

In the mid-1920s, every girl on campus mourned the loss to breast cancer of Mary Burnett, a beloved teacher who had been at the school since its inception. The outcry was so great that county officials placed her name on the school, though the generic Harris County School for Girls continued to be used, as well.[28]

The school, along with the Boys School, became independent school districts in 1932 to take advantage of state tax money. By that time, girls ages six through juniors in high school lived at the campus. Their final year, the young women were sent to a public Houston high school. By the 1950s, they attended Bellaire-area schools for even more classes. In 1952, the Girl's School ended, and the campus officially became the Burnett Bayland School, a co-educational operation. All of the original school buildings at the site had been demolished by the mid-1960s. An interesting postscript remains: despite the fact that girls at the school were committed by the courts, many of them wrote tender letters of thanks to the staff after they had moved on to adult life.[29]

HARRISBURG COLORED SCHOOL

The location listed as 762 Elm between San Marcos and San Antonio, backed up to Brays Bayou next to Gilfield Baptist Church, is no long part of the modern street grid in Harrisburg. It was at least the second location for the Harrisburg Colored School, whose trustees had sold the previous lot in 1907. This school was one of the first in the county for African Americans outside of the city of Houston, predating the new school laws of 1876. There was a separate Black board of trustees by the late 1880s, and the school was employing multiple teachers by that time. [30]

Though the enrollment at Harrisburg Colored fluctuated due to a large number of seasonal farm workers who lived south of the area, the Black school population often outnumbered the White in the town. The entire community had suffered a hit when the railroad shops in Harrisburg burned then moved to Houston in the 1870s, causing a major downturn in population. By the early 20th century, however, Harrisburg Colored School employed four teachers for almost 200 students, and the building was large enough to include an auditorium.[31]

In 1909, a young teacher with six years' experience in Montgomery County came to Harrisburg. She was a native of Victoria and a graduate of Prairie View named Savannah Kay. Three years later she succeeded B.W.

Petteway as principal, a post that she held for over three decades. Kay lived in a house on John Street and became a major cog in the community including involvement in the Asbury M.E. Church, YWCA, the Eastern Star, the statewide union for African American teachers, and the Interracial Commission that operated in the late 1920s.[32]

HARRISBURG SCHOOL

The town of Harrisburg at the confluence of Brays and Buffalo Bayous predated Houston by a dozen years, and was the port that served the settlers along Buffalo Bayou and southwest to the Brazos. Young Dilue Rose wrote of her father fetching a schoolteacher from a boat at Harrisburg to serve their community near modern day Stafford. Though some would-be historians have placed the school, taught by an Irishman named David Henson, in Harrisburg, the first preserved record of a schoolhouse at that town itself comes a bit later. The prospering community had some sort of education by at least the 1850s, but it seems almost certain that there was a small school earlier.[33]

The town was an economic rival of Houston, and was home to the first railroad in Texas in the early 1850s, an industry that brought jobs to the community. When the state constitution called for reorganized public schools in 1876, Harrisburg duly registered both the White and the Black schools that were already in operation. Trustees for the White school included Andrew Birdsall Briscoe, a direct descendant of town founder John Richardson Harris, who was living in the family home at the time. He was joined by John Curry, O.C. Mulligan, and G. Bennett. When county schools were reorganized again, Harrisburg became the primary school in District 20. Another name that surfaced as a longtime trustee was Charles H. Milby.[34]

Among the teaching staff at Harrisburg were two of the three Dullahan sisters, Margaret and Kate, who taught in Harris County schools for decades. The school building was located on four blocks at Medina and Elm streets by 1890 with about 90 students taught by two teachers, but enrollment began to increase. At the end of the century, the citizens of District 20 purchased a full block, bounded by Harrisburg, Magnolia, Frio, and Orange, and built a new brick school on it complete with a second floor auditorium that was called the "social center of the community." The lots on Medina were sold early in 1900.[35]

The population at Harrisburg waxed and waned in the 19th century, but as the 20th dawned, moves to secure a deep water port were underway, and the turning basin on the channel was smack dab in a position to bring thousands of new jobs to the area. The electric streetcar from Houston was extended to Harrisburg, and residents began to consider themselves part of the "great commercial city" of Houston. By 1906, the school auditorium was needed for more classrooms, and in 1912, four additional rooms and the accompanying teachers were added to handle the influx of children belonging to the dock and construction workers.[36]

In spring of 1911, the people of district 20 passed a bond for $15,000 to build a new brick high school on the large school block. With eleven grades provided, it would be one of only three full-fledged high school run by Harris County schools. Support was so strong that there was but a single vote against. When the new four year high school opened in September 1912 with 35 students, it included a manual training shop for the boys and domestic science classes to teach girls to "feel the dignity of household work." One year later, a science lab was added. The library of over a thousand books was a joint venture of the school and the community, staying open year round. Plans for athletic fields were said to be in the works.[37]

Harrisburg HS class 1924. Mike Vance Collection

The growth in district 20 was not done, however. By 1914, the year the new deep water port officially opened, the school age population had risen by 50% over the year prior. Again the citizens went to the polls, this time approving $50,000 for upgrades to the existing buildings plus three brand new schools at Park Place, Brookline, and Magnolia Park. For two years, the children in those small but growing communities had been brought to Harrisburg schools each day by wagons.[38]

The town of Harrisburg was annexed to Houston in 1926, but it took another year of wrangling for the Harrisburg ISD to join Houston ISD. When they did so, the merger happened in three parts and included 46 teachers and roughly 800 students. It was under HISD that the grade school at Harrisburg became J.R. Harris Elementary in 1942.[39]

HART SCHOOL

Hart School may have originally been a replacement for Green Pond, but it operated throughout the 1930s and 40s. It is listed as such, located on Westheimer, near modern day Weslayan, by Ira Bryant's history of Black schools in the city.[40]

HART'S SCHOOL

Hart's School, an African American institution east of Houston, dated to at least 1886 when it was part of District 20 with the Harrisburg schools, but within the next three years Hart's and Oates Prairie had formed their own District 34. The school was named for Henry Hart, an Alabama-born farmer and an in-law of C.W. Oates for whom the White school in this area along Wallisville Road was named. Many descendants of the slaves brought by Oates and Hart took those surnames and remained in the neighborhood after Emancipation. In the 1940s, it was being called Oates Prairie Colored School.[41]

HARTMAN'S SCHOOL

See Winkler's

HARTWELL SCHOOL

Hartwell, located on a 2.26 acre lot near the southwest corner of today's FM 1960 and Aldine-Westfield, started as a multi-teacher schoolhouse in the early 1900s. In 1913, it was upgraded to a two-year high school. Hartwell was gone by the time schools in District 29 became Aldine ISD in 1935.[42]

HARVARD E S

The planned community of Houston Heights was up and running in the early 1890s, and by the end of the decade, the area was thriving enough to need a second school. Harvard Street School opened on September 18, 1898 on two small lots at the northeast corner of 8th and Harvard that had been donated by Heights founder O.M. Carter's real estate company. The first teacher was Miss Annie Thielen, and when she moved to nearby Cooley School, she was replaced by her sister Alice.[43]

The old frame Harvard School remained in use on campus for many years.
HISD

Though rooms were added to the wood frame school, by 1912, a two-story brick structure with a basement rose to replace it, and the original wood house was moved to the other side of the Heights to become the Black school called Eighth Avenue. The school was brought into HISD when Houston Heights was annexed by the city in 1918. Because the steam pipes and other services ran through the center of the basement, Harvard was not refitted for classrooms as many other schools of the time were. Students did enjoy the tall fire escape slides as play areas after school let out.[44]

The word "Street" was dropped from the school name early on, to the potential benefit of many Heights natives. Once longtime Harris County Commissioner Squatty Lyons found himself among a gathering of what some Texans might term fancy East Coast types who were discussing their upbringing and education. Without a single iota of untruth, Lyons was able to say, "I went to Harvard."[45]

Vandalism

Owing to the fact that quite a number of our larger buildings are far removed from both fire and police protection it is found that considerable damage and loss has resulted each year, mostly during the vacation, or summer months, through the recklessness and mischievous inclinations of our "Young Americans."

A hurried visit, recently made to several such buildings disclosed the fact that at one building forty window and door lights have been broken out since the close of school. This damage has been done from day to day, and is of continual occurrence. At other buildings similar damages have been done, while all kinds of annoying misdeeds of a greater or less degree are easily visible at each building where an investigation has been made. In several instances door locks have been forced open, with seemingly no object than just to show that it can be done. It may be discovered that there was a more serious object, but no outward losses from this source has been discovered yet.

I have found upon investigation that other cities have adopted the plan of erecting a two or three-room house upon the campus of most of their outlying buildings in which the janitor resides, and that in such instances the salary is so adjusted that it allows a fair remuneration as rent to the school board. I can see no reason as to why this policy could not or should not be adopted here. In order that we might meet conditions I would suggest that for the immediate present we erect two such houses where most needed, to cost not more than $500 each.

Houston City Schools Report 1906-07

HARVEY SCHOOL

The name of Harvey School in District 17 near Crosby shows up in one County Report in 1910.[46]

HAWTHORNE E S

When Houston organized its own public schools under the new constitution and accompanying codes in 1877, they were set up by wards with a White and a Black school in each. The school for the First Ward, meaning west of Main and north of Congress, was for a time located a mere block from the line of demarcation, in George Hermann's building at 87 Travis. In the late 1880s, there was an African American schoolhouse in what Houstonians today consider the First Ward, but the White students went to classes on Washington Avenue. Finally, in 1893, the Houston Avenue School, a raised two-story, T-shaped building, opened at the southwest corner of Houston and Bingham. Neighborhood residents thought they had truly come up in the world. It was the first brick grade school in the city's history.[47]

In less than a decade, the school was so crowded with children of the downtown workers and industrial or railroad laborers that classes were held in half day shifts. The tiny principal's office had even been converted to hold classes. A four-room wooden addition was added in 1904. Crowding continued until the state-of-the-art Crockett School was opened in 1912, and Hawthorne for a time served only pupils of the first four grades. It was an arrangement that allowed them to concentrate on improvements aimed at the younger children. In 1915, they built a miniature grocery store to teach the lessons of commerce. Outside play area remained tight until adjoining property was purchased from Third Presbyterian Church in 1929.[48]

Hawthorne also proved to be a pioneer in the arena of low scholastic attendance. The 1921-22 school report lists it as the only school in the city with an unused classroom, caused by striking workers moving out of town. By 1959, the First Ward had an aging White population, and the school was closed, at least for a few months. That fall, when a new year started, an overflow of African American children from nearby Brock Elementary was moved down Bingham Street to what was termed the Brock Annex. As segregation disappeared a few years later, it was the old Hawthorne site that received a new school called Richard Brock. Elementary classes ended there in the mid-2000s, and for a time it was an early childhood center before being abandoned by HISD entirely.[49]

Hawthorne ES faculty 1911. Mike Vance Collection

HEGAR SCHOOL

The Hegar School, in a small community named for the storekeeper there, dates to the late 1800s and continued as a school in District 11, sitting near the intersection of today's FM2920 and Cormier Road until sometime after 1914.[50]

HEIGHTS ANNEX SCHOOL

This was a short-lived small rectangular building on a single lot at the northwest corner of 14th and Alexander in the 1920s that provided overflow for a shifting school landscape in the neighborhood.[51]

HEIGHTS HIGH SCHOOL

The town of Houston Heights was growing just after the start of the 20th century. By 1904, there was a total enrollment of 497 pupils at all the Heights schools, and the board decided to build a separate home for the high school. It opened that fall with eight rooms and adjoining cloak rooms at a cost of roughly $12,000. A ten-room annex was added later. As the neighborhood continued to flourish, the school designed for 300 was eventually almost double that number, and money was raised to build a new high school at 20th and Heights. The old high school building at the northwest corner of 12th and Yale became Heights Junior High.[52]

Though Heights HS played Cleburne to a scoreless tie in the first ever state football championship in 1920, both schools claimed the title. HHRC

About 6:30 A.M. on the morning of Thursday, March 13, 1924, a pedestrian saw a fire in upper floor of the building and called for some newsboys to alert the firemen at station 14 across the street. It was to no avail. Only the outer walls of the school remained along with temporary shacks in the yard. Three fire fighters were injured, and 603 students were left without a school. While the seventh graders stayed in the two shacks, the other students attended the new Heights High on a half day rotation. When Reagan High opened, the junior high children inherited the building on 20th. The name was revived in 2016 when board trustees voted to remove the Reagan name from that high school.[53]

HELMS E S

Houston Heights was a thriving community at the time that it was annexed to the City of Houston, and Houston city schools, in 1918. That same year, a new elementary school opened at 503 W. 21st, named for the recent Heights Board of Education president James Frank Helms. From the get-go, the eight-room, single-story building was too small and ill-received. The Ladies Advisory Committee scathed in their inaugural inspection that Helms was "a striking example of what not to build. The faults are glaring—and we urge the board to view the atrocities there displayed." Within three years, there were two "improvised" rooms inside the building and four temporary shacks in the yard. Additions were forthcoming, and by the mid-1930s, the student body had more than tripled in size to over 700.[54]

One noted feature of the early 1920s at Helms was a unique wrinkle in student government. Instead of the usual committees to enforce punishment and encourage citizenship, Helms organized a "student municipality" called Hornville in honor of the city superintendent. "The rooms of the building were designated as districts, the aisles became streets and the desks were homes; the corridors serving as avenues and boulevards, and the playground assumed the dignified name of park and athletic fields." There was even indoctrination into the racially restrictive voting practices of the time as students "were taught that while it is possible for a man or woman to reside within the city limits without meeting the full obligations of citizenship, all men and women who wished to take part in the problems which every city has to face, must pay their poll taxes" in order to vote for the school officers such as mayor, councilmen, health commissioners, and fire chief. The school was rechristened as the Helms Community Learning Center in April of 2001.[55]

Newly opened Helms ES. HISD

HENDERSON SCHOOL

This was a tiny one-room, wood school for African Americans that sat on a 50' x 100' lot in what the City School Report of 1922 said was an all-White neighborhood of Brooksmith. Holding only about 30 desks, with no lights, and stove heat in the early 1920s, it lay immediately north of Hollywood Cemetery on Temple Avenue on a site that today would be just east of I-45. It is possible that this property was where the old Hollywood School had previously sat. It appears to have been discontinued by the mid-1920s.[56]

HENDERSON, J P E S

James Pinckney Henderson was elected as the first governor of Texas after it joined the Union. The school named for him opened at 1800 Dismuke at Barrymore in the East End in September 1929, one of six elementary schools of that time that used the same Harry D. Payne architectural plans but with a different exterior. Using money from the third bond issue of the decade, it had 12 classrooms, a clinic, and a play-lunchroom on six acres. Henderson also boasted gas, thermostatically controlled heat. Its safety patrol of older boys and girls was also recognized.[57]

HERMANN SCHOOL

The great Houston philanthropist George H. Hermann donated land to County District 25 for the location of a 26' x 50' raised wood frame schoolhouse for the first four grades that was constructed by James Shapely in 1898 in Ryon Addition on the north side of Hays Street between Cochran and Hardy. It was absorbed into the city school system about 1904 and closed not long after.[58]

HIGGS SCHOOL

Higgs School, also known as Durdin according to Humble historian Robert Meaux, was located on modern-day Lee Road at Garner's Bayou, just south of the Humble-Westfield Road, today's FM1960. It was in operation prior to 1876 when school laws were reorganized. It operated as part of County District 29 for many decades, still appearing on a county map in 1934, the year before the formation of the Aldine ISD.[59]

HIGGS COLORED SCHOOL

Higgs Colored School operated in District 29 in the Humble area from at least the mid-1880s. With a small African American population, the school went through periods of operation and temporary closure during which the children and a small amount of tax money were sent to other districts. In 1907, the building near Westfield, was described by county school officials as being in "very good shape."[60]

L. L. Pugh

When he died at Hermann Hospital in May of 1951, the *Houston Post* obituary called him "a real old-timer." There were those who had racked up greater longevity in local schools, but few who had such an impact on both Harris County and HISD schools as Lee L. Pugh.[61]

He was born in Parkersburg, Illinois in 1872 and attended Valparaiso University in Indiana. Later in life, he worked to get a degree from Sam Houston State Teachers College at Huntsville.

Universally known by his initials L.L., Pugh moved to Harris County to teach school before November 1899 when his daughter, a Texas native, was born. Soon after, he secured the job as head of the county's schools where he would stay for over a decade. County superintendent of schools was an elective office by the latter reaches of the century's first decade, and, to keep his job, Pugh placed ads in several local papers, including the *Jewish Herald* where he solicited "the support of my friends." [62]

As superintendent, he regularly made school visits on horseback. Pugh instituted organizational up-grades preparing and distributing a brochure for teachers and parents alike, and formalizing a calendar for monthly reports from each of the county's school houses.

The year 1904 brought another incident for Pugh who was mugged by a man waiting at his wagon gate when he returned home one night in September. Two tussles ensued, but the school boss was able to retain his pocket book which contained fifteen dollars.

A story repeated in his obituary was that he "once handled the sale of a farm where the Shamrock (Hotel) now stands – the land sold for nearly $60 an acre."

After leaving the county's employee in 1915, he went on to become one of two supervisors of rural schools for the Texas Department of Education as part of a comprehensive overhaul pushed by Governor Jim Ferguson. Pugh became a regular speaker at state conferences and institutes, backing the one million dollar investment in education, saying that those who opposed the measures were "mere 'politicians' and men who profit on child labor." He also urged teachers to organize into unions.[63]

L.L. Pugh. HHRC

When he decided to return to Houston, Pugh went to work for Houston schools, starting as principal at Anson Jones Elementary just northeast of downtown. During the Depression years, Pugh brought innovations to the school including helping neighborhood residents with sewing and canning, even going so far as to leave the school unlocked on cold nights to provide a heated place to stay. Pugh was also chosen to oversee a book-length history of Houston's White schools for the Texas Centennial celebration of 1936.

Following his stint at Jones, Pugh moved to Harrisburg Elementary, one of the few schools with an even older pedigree than Jones. He retired from HISD in 1942, preferring not to work past age 70 as some other educators had done.[64]

Pugh was married to Ada May Kelly of Illinois about 1897, and the couple had one daughter, Ruby. He was active in multiple local organizations including the Knights of Pythias, Woodmen of the World, and First Christian Church on Main and Bell. L.L. Pugh's death came one day after his 79th birthday.[65]

Economic Realities For Some Black Families

"The attendance of children is always low on Monday and Friday, and the cases of tardiness are correspondingly high. Why? Because many of the children come from homes where the washing of clothes is done for a living. The children go after the clothes on Monday, and frequently take them back on Friday. When they go for the clothes on Monday, the White family is frequently at breakfast. The lady tells the Negro children to wait till she can gather up the clothes. She takes her time, and when the clothes are gathered up, it is too late for the Negroes to get to school on time, even if at all, that day. It is quite possible that some of our good women who take an active interest in missionary work for the education and Christianization of the heathen in foreign lands are, by a little thoughtlessness on their part, standing in the way of the education of the little Black children at home, who perhaps need it quite as much."

Superintendent Paul W. Horn, *Houston Schools Report 1909-10*

HIGHLAND HEIGHTS E S

Prairie View alum Rosa Mosely moved from the small White Oak School on Montgomery Road in Acres Homes to head the new location of Highland Heights School on Yale Street Road in 1932. The school grew quickly, reaching 180 pupils in 1934. Among the teachers around that time was Lulu White who would go on to become an important NAACP leader. In the still rural area northwest of the Houston city limits, many students rode horses or mules to school. Albert Williams recalled that he and his sister rode to class on a horse that then returned home on his own. In the early 1940s, HISD named the school for Mabel Wesley, but four years later, a new campus, farther north, was opened for Wesley Elementary. The younger three grades remained at Highland Heights, and the older three moved to Wesley. Eventually, the two were zoned as separate elementary schools. A new Highland Heights building was built at 865 Paul Quinn.[66]

HIGHLANDS COLORED SCHOOL

African American students around the town of Highlands, originally known as Elena, in East Harris County had a small school on East Houston Street in that community, near the site of today's Hopper Elementary. It was taken over by Crosby ISD then transferred to Goose Creek ISD in 1936.[67]

HIGHLANDS E S

Elena was a small community on the east bank of the San Jacinto River that subsequently became known as Highlands. Though a station on the Beaumont, Sour Lake and Western Railroad, it remained a sleepy community of but a few hundred until the booming industrial war effort in the early 1940s ballooned the population to several thousand. The small Elena School, serving County District 17, was built in 1911 on the east side of Crosby Lynchburg Road at Houston Street and replaced with a new four-room building in the mid-1920s. Children in grades eight and up went to school in Crosby. In 1936, Highlands schools were de-annexed from Crosby ISD and taken over by Goose Creek ISD. Highlands Elementary was replaced with a new building in 1993.[68]

HILDEBRANDT SCHOOL

Shortly prior to 1910, a portion of District 2 in far north Harris County was designated as District 47, Hildebrandt. The one-room school, located on John Hildebrandt's land near today's Hildebrandt Road, operated in a heavily German community until the Klein ISD was formed as Rural High School number 1 in 1928.[69]

HILLEBRANDT SCHOOL

See Jefferson

HILLENDAHL SCHOOL

Hillendahl, named for an influential family in the Spring Branch area, was a one-room school in District 27.[70]

HINE'S SCHOOL

When existing schools sent representatives to the courthouse to register under the new 1876 school law, there were only four African American schools in Harris County outside of the city of Houston. One of them was Hines in the area of Little White Oak Bayou that became part of District 25. Among the first students and trustees were members of families that included the Hicks and Stewarts. Hines was also one of Mabel Wesley's first teaching posts as early as 1886 and continuing into the mid-1890s. This may have been replaced by, or even connected to the Hollywood School.[71]

HOBSON SCHOOL

Hobson was an original, pre-1876 county school named for trustee J.W. Hobson, a Virginia-native who lived in District 8 in northwest Harris County. School names in that district changed often in the late 19th century, and in a confusing manner. County Treasurer notes show Hobson changing to both Harral and Hargraves.[72]

HOCKLEY SCHOOL

Hockley, on the Houston & Texas Central Railroad, dates to 1857 and, for one year, went by the name of Houseville. The school there seems to date to a period near the start of the Civil War, and was definitely in operation prior to the 1876 law revision. By 1890, there were about 70 young scholars under the tutelage of Professor H.D. Norton there. Hockley operated a school in District 11 at least into the 1930s.[73]

Harris County Library bookmobile at Hockley School 1930s. HCPL

HOCKLEY COLORED SCHOOL

District 11, at Hockley, operated a Black school at least as early as 1886, continuing into the 20th century. In 1907, the *Post* back-to-school stories noted that this was a "very good school" with a teacher who had been there for seven years.[74]

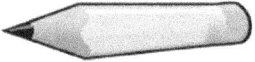

The Anatomy of a Rural Bond Election

In June 1884, Harris County Commissioners reorganized their schools, approving twenty common school districts that would provide the structure of rural schools for decades. Some schools within these rural districts were underwritten quite informally by groups of neighbors to set aside a place for a hired teacher to educate their children on land that was sometimes provided for and named after an area farmer.

If that sort of grassroots effort didn't fully cover the needs, however, much like today, bond elections were held. In Harris County, each of the common school districts managed their own. A typical case in point was an election held in Common School District 11 on the 3rd of March, 1916.

District 11 served the town of Hockley with three schools, two for White students and one for Black. The county school report of 1913 repeats verbatim the thoughts voiced in 1910 about the districts' facilities: "This district has two school buildings and maintains a six and eight months' term of school. They have a local tax for supplementing the State fund, and each school has a library valued at about $300. I would suggest that the trustees of this district add another room to the building at Hockley and add another teacher so as to divide the work, instead of requiring one teacher to do the work of two." Note that the report refers only to the two White schools, Hockley and Hegar. As in many other county district reports, the African American schools were not even mentioned.[75]

The boundaries of district 11 were reworked in 1915, and late that year, prominent residents petitioned Harris County Judge W. H. Ward for permission to hold a bond election. They wanted to raise $6,000 to replace the wood frame school building for Whites at Hockley with one of the brick designs that had been opening in other common districts around the county.

The denomination of the bonds was set at $1,000 each, an extremely high amount. Most school bonds of the day were sold in denominations of $100 or $250. The implication may have been that merchants of Hockley had already committed to the purchase.

The law demanded that County Sheriff M. F. Hammond post three notices in public places at least three weeks prior to the election. He submitted paperwork on February 9, 1916 showing that he had posted the notices at J.M. Piel's store, J. P. Rayder's store, and R. Leon's store. A decade later, publication of the notices in newspapers had largely replaced the hand nailing process. In the 1910s however, the sheriff's notices were still posted at local landmarks, including some reports showing that they were regularly nailed to a tree at a low water ford, the town filling station, or a telephone pole or fence post to be read by passers-by.[76]

On Friday, March 3, 1916, twenty-four voters went to the existing schoolhouse at Hockley. All of them voted in favor of the school bond, adding twenty cents per hundred dollars to their property tax bill.

The turnout in Hockley is not out of line for the era. A vote in Penn City was four to zero, and at Deepwater a bond election in the same year of 1916 brought out only three voters, all of whom opted to tax themselves in the name of education.

HOFFMAN SCHOOL

Hoffman School shows up briefly in the County Treasurer's ledgers for District 5 with Rose Hill in the early 1890s, but there are no expenditures, and the money is transferred to Rose Hill.[77]

The entrance foyer at the new Hogg JHS. HISD

HOGG J H S

Hogg Junior High, at 1100 Merrill in the Woodland Heights, opened with 29 classrooms and a manual training shop in 1926 as relief for nearby Hamilton. Before it was named for the popular progressive former governor, it was designated as Norhill Junior High School. W.S. Brandenberger was the first principal, overseeing about 900 pupils. In the fast-growing Heights, though, it was not enough. Two additions and ten years later,

Hogg sported 53 classrooms, over 1,500 children and one of the largest PTA organizations in Texas. Today, the Razorbacks at Hogg live on with programs for a STEM magnet and International Baccalaureate.[78]

HOHL E S

The school at 5320 Yale that bears the name of Minnesota-born businessman Henry Hohl has a fascinating architectural story. Hohl donated the plot of ground where a one-room frame building was opened in 1901 then replaced by a two-room brick school in District 25 in 1914. At the start of the following decade, Hohl, with only about 20 students, a majority of them with Italian surnames, joined HISD as the city limits encompassed it. The area grew quickly, and parents took pride building a baseball diamond, new outhouses, and arguing to keep it from being closed in the mid-1920s. A breezeway for use as a dining area was put at the back of the school, two rooms were added and an auditorium built. By the mid-1950s, well water was abandoned in favor of city water that had finally come close enough to the school. The most interesting feature at the new school today are Rooms 101 through 104. They are the old brick school that was completely absorbed into the new construction, still maintaining closed up transoms and tall wood-beamed ceilings that loom above the drop-down acoustical tiles. Even the old front steps and a crawl space lurk beneath the floors causing a big rise in elevation.[79]

The original building at Hohl ES. Hohl School archives

HOLLYWOOD SCHOOL

Hollywood Cemetery's entrance today sits northeast of the intersection of North Main and I-45, but when the cemetery opened in 1895, those coming to pay respects entered the cemetery from the east, off Montgomery Road, today's Fulton, and across a bridge over Little White Oak Bayou. Close to that entrance was a small frame school for African American children in the neighborhood which took its name from the new cemetery next door. It began as part of County District 25, but when Houston's city limits were extended about 1903, it became the smallest Black school in the Houston public school system. There were two rooms and 78 children that school year. Complaints started as soon as the city took over. In 1906, officials reported it to be "so dilapidated in its condition as hardly to be worth even minor repairs." Still Hollywood, which handled only the first four grades, had two legendary educators as principals in the first decade of the 20th century: E.O. Smith and Mabel Wesley. It was a remote section of town. No city water was available, but there was a "substantial cistern." Its students were not well-off. When library contributions were sought in 1910, Hollywood had the lowest return in town at only $2.65. The school burned during the 1912-13 year and was rebuilt with Wesley still in charge. Any woes were rendered moot when it was replaced by Crawford during WWI.[80]

Lettie Smith

This is the story of Lettie Smith. I do not know that I can tell it better than by quoting the exact words of a personal letter which I received last winter from a Houston lady of culture and refinement:

"I think that, as Superintendent of the Houston schools, you would perhaps be interested if I were to tell you some of the things I have noticed about Lettie Smith, the little colored girl who now works for me as nurse and house girl. She is a pupil of the High Third grade at Hollywood School.

"My attention was first called to her school work by the respectful manner in which she spoke of her teacher, and her childish longing for school. Next I found her recognizing the portraits of Longfellow, Whittier, and other American poets, which she saw on the walls of our library. She would tell little stories of their childhood, which she said she had read at school. She noticed some raffia mats that I have, and readily told how and of what they are made. She often sings little patriotic songs to the baby, and tries to teach her rhymes, and memory gems. She usually gets good grades on her report cards, and she says she can't bear to hear children 'mouth' over their reading.

"She has evidently had a good, earnest, sensible teacher. It is remarkable to me that the public schools are doing so well for the colored children—and for the White children, too, for that matter. I think that Lettie compares at least fairly well in advancement with the average White child of her age and grade."

The fact that an educated Houston woman, a housekeeper, and the wife of one of Houston's good citizens, thought it worth while to write the Superintendent this letter, speaks well not only for her own kind heartedness and appreciation, but also for the work our colored schools are doing.

Superintendent Paul W. Horn

Houston City Schools Report 1909-10

Note: The teacher at Hollywood School at the time was Mabel Wesley

HOLY GHOST SCHOOL

The City of Bellaire and environs officially got its own Catholic Parish in June 1946 when two masses were held in the town's City Hall for most of the 35 families registered there. Parishioners opened their own building two years later, and a temporary school was also opened for 69 students.[81]

HOLY NAME SCHOOL

Holy Name Church opened at 1917 Cochran on the near Northside in 1920, and five years later, when a new building was erected, Father G.A. Wilhelm oversaw the opening of a four-room parish school in the old church. Many of the parishioners were Italian, Irish, Polish, or Czech immigrants. Classes were full, and in 1928 another teacher was added followed a year later by four more classrooms. Sisters teaching there commuted first from Incarnate Word Academy downtown and then from the convent on Bissonnet until the old church rectory was converted into housing for them in 1938. Holy Name parish school closed in 2009 in spite of having roughly 180 pupils only a decade before.[82]

Holy Name Catholic School 1937. HHRC

HOLY ROSARY SCHOOL

The Dominican Sisters taught at the parish school at Holy Rosary, opened in 1913, the same year as the church, in the 3600 block of Milam on what was then the South End of Houston. With other Catholic school options located nearby and residential population in Midtown dropping, the school closed in 1986.[83]

HORN E S

Longtime Superintendent Paul W. Horn was honored with an elementary school at 4535 Pine Street in Bellaire in 1949.[84]

Paul Whitfield Horn

When the Houston School Board started inviting applications for a new school superintendent in 1904, it was certainly a slap in the face to the man who already had the job, Professor W.W. Barnett. In fact, Barnett even reapplied for his own job along with aspirants from places as far flung as California, Missouri, Colorado, and Virginia. In the end, none of the out of state applicants made the final cut.[85]

After the first ballot to select a candidate to head the city's schools, Barnett was tied with Professor Paul Horn of Sherman, Texas at three votes apiece. Professor Jameson, the principal of the city's Fannin School, got a single vote. On the second vote, Horn emerged the winner, and the result was made unanimous. He arrived in town within the week and immediately "occupied the superintendent's chair."[86]

Paul W. Horn, a Missouri native with a degree from Central State College there, was 34 years old. He had been the school superintendent at Sherman, Texas for seven years and high school principal there for two years before that.[87]

A decade in, it seemed that a vast majority of Houstonians were quite pleased with the choice. A *Houston Chronicle* editorial was effusive: "Superintendent P. W. Horn is not only a man of exceptional scholastic ability, but he has proved himself a diplomat, a manager and a splendid executive. He has... maintained a degree of efficiency that has been the talk of the state. A man of P.W. Horn's exceptional ability would be drawing anywhere from $10,000 to $20,000 per year if he had devoted his life to some other line of professional work. There is hardly a head of any big corporation in the city of Houston who does not draw a larger salary than will be paid the head of Houston's great school system – the one thing in Houston in which every taxpayer, especially every father and mother, is vitally interested."[88]

Houston Post cartoon of Paul Horn

He headed Houston's city schools during a time of rapid growth overseeing a jump in student population from just over 9,000 to almost 38,000 during his 17-year tenure. Horn advocated an aggressive building plan for the city in those days before HISD became a separate entity, and the number of schools rose from 23 to 55 by the time he left in 1921 to head the American schools in Mexico City.[89]

After a short stint as president of Southwestern University in Georgetown, Horn resigned to accept the presidency of the brand new Texas Technological College in Lubbock, today's Texas Tech. He was so respected in the field of education, that when he died at age 64 following complications after appendicitis surgery, the Texas flag atop the capitol in Austin was placed at half-staff. Paul Horn was buried in Lubbock, not on campus as many people wanted, but in a small family plot. A Houston ISD elementary school was named in his honor in 1949.

Schools Houston – Humble

HOUSTON ACADEMY

The city directory of 1866 began its article on education in Houston by opining that "The city of Houston is not as well supplied with permanent educational facilities as its wants demand." There was one somewhat large school of the day, however - the Houston Academy, not to be confused with an earlier college preparatory school of the same name that Henry Gillett operated for about two years in the mid-1840s.[1]

Two years after Gillett left town in 1846, a group of ten trustees was formed to fill the void with a coeducational, non-denominational Houston Academy. It was finally chartered on August 19, 1856. The main force behind the charter was a bequest of $5,000 in the will of former mayor, grocer, and railroad entrepreneur, James H. Stevens. He promised the money whenever the citizens of Houston could match it with another $10,000. Seventy stockholders rose to the challenge by raising $20,000, and construction began for the two-story brick school on September 17, 1857 on the block bounded by Austin, Caroline, Capitol, and Rusk.[2]

One bequest from the Stevens will underlines the proclivity of the rich to send their children to private teachers no matter where their community largesse went. He left a large sum of money for his daughter, the interest on which was to "be used and expended for the proper support and liberal education… so that she may enjoy every reasonable advantage and facility, but private tuition is by all means preferred to Public or Boarding School education."[3]

Houston Academy and surrounding buildings. HHRC

Stevens had been elected mayor in 1855, running on a "Railroad" ticket along with alderman candidates that included William Marsh Rice and Thomas William House. As mayor, he gained permission from the State to run a tap line from the Buffalo Bayou, Brazos & Colorado Railway so that Houston could steal some of the highly lucrative cotton shipping business away from the rival city of Harrisburg, a few miles downstream. He died of consumption in July of 1856, but when the tap line opened that October, the locomotive was named the James H. Stevens.[4]

Rice and House were also among the first incorporators of the Academy, as were other leading merchants and politicians such as Cornelius Ennis, the man who succeeded Stevens as mayor, and Peter W. Gray, a legislator and attorney who had founded the Houston Lyceum, precursor to the Houston Public Library, in 1848. Prominent men such as these realized that Houston was lagging behind in the area of education, and though Houston might not have free schools, an inexpensive alternative was a priority.

Dr. Ashbel Smith was the first principal of the new Academy. By the time he took the job in 1858, Smith had one of the best resumes in Texas. He had served as Surgeon General of the Army of the Republic of Texas shortly after his arrival in the new nation in 1837. He negotiated a treaty between Texas and the Comanches, served as Texas' Secretary of State, spent two years as Charge D'Affaires representing the Republic in England and France, had one term representing Harris County in the state legislature, helped found the Democratic Party in Texas, negotiated another treaty in which Mexico recognized the independence of Texas, served in the United States Army in Mexico under Zachary Taylor, and spent several years as Sam Houston's roommate. Following his brief stint with the Academy, Ashbel Smith would serve in the Second Texas Infantry during the Civil War, sustaining an arm injury at Shiloh, and eventually rising to unit commander. He then resumed his work in education, serving on public school boards in Harris and Galveston Counties, and as one of three commissioners who established the school which is now Prairie View A&M University. To many Longhorns, his biggest legacy is as the "Father of the University of Texas", championing the cause of establishing "a first class state university" and then becoming the first president of its Board of Regents in 1881.[5]

Smith was followed at Houston Academy by a Prof. Pettit and then Rev J. R. Hutchison, D.D., who was overseeing 150 students of both sexes and a staff of three or four by the fall of 1860, the year Sam Houston gave a famous anti-secession speech in the building. School stayed in session during the early years of the Civil War, but in the summer of 1864, the Confederate military authorities took over the school and converted it into a soldiers' hospital. The convalescent soldiers are said to have made good use of the school's 600 volume library.[6]

When the War ended, the Houston Academy reopened with 203 students and six teachers, and with what the city directory described as "flattering prospects of usefulness." The classrooms were described as "large and airy" and well suited for their purpose. On the faculty was Matilda J. Young who remained a prominent Houston teacher for the rest of the century and later operated a girls' school on the second floor of the Academy Building.[7]

When a handful of Houston citizens voted 65 to 9 to take the state legislature up on its offer of local control of schools, the Academy building became part of the public school system. Its library was donated to the Houston Lyceum. The old building was remodeled in 1878, losing its cupola and bell, which had been taken from the captured Union ship *Harriet Lane*. It was renamed the Clopper Institute in honor of Prof. E. N. Clopper. The City of Houston acquired the ground in 1880, and eventually the original five-room brick building was demolished and replaced with a new Houston High School on that block in 1894. That plot remains property of HISD to the present day as the home of the High School for the Performing and Visual Arts.

HOUSTON ACADEMY - GILLETT'S

Though still in his late twenties, Henry Flavel Gillett was "already a well-known teacher" when he opened his Houston Academy in the *Telegraph* newspaper building at the southwest corner of Preston and Main Street in 1844. The Connecticut-born Gillett, a cousin of Ashbel Smith, taught at another private school in Houston in 1840 before moving to Independence in Washington County where he worked at Union Academy. He was the brother of a prominent minister, and the two of them would soon be found among the leaders of the Friends of Education, an unsuccessful movement to bring free public schools to the new State of Texas. His Houston Academy of 1844 advertised college preparatory work, with Gillett promising "to teach all branches necessary to enter all colleges in the United States" In addition to the two brothers, Mrs. M.H. Bigelow headed the female department.[8]

A monthly fee of two dollars was charged for reading, writing, and orthography. Courses in currency, arithmetic, grammar, and geography cost three dollars. It was four dollars for the most advanced courses which included Latin, Greek, sciences, and "the higher branches of English." Given his school's coincidence with the admission of Texas to the Union, tuition was accepted in "Par Funds" meaning that Gillett would divine "the actual gold value in the different varieties of currency then circulating in the United States, much of which had found its way into Texas." This first Houston Academy closed in 1846, when Gillett moved back to Independence to teach in the preparatory department at Baylor University. He had one more Harris County residency left in him when he numbered among the founders of Bayland Orphanage in 1867, and remained with that bayside institution for 15 years as superintendent.[9]

Scholarships

Miss Amy Longcope is due the first honor of the June graduating class, she having made the best average record of the year. Her total average was 96.05. This record entitles Miss Longcope to the scholarship offered by the University of Texas. While seven of the young ladies of the graduating class stood above 90, none of the boys was able to reach that mark.

Houston Post 7 June 1904

HOUSTON ACADEMY - WELCH'S

On of the longest-lived college preparatory academies in early 20th century Houston was that run by the large, mustachioed Christian W. Welch. He had come to Houston as principal of Houston High in 1888, launching himself into the educational landscape, teaching botany to teachers at the summer normal, before returning to his native South Carolina to become physics professor at a new college called Clemson. After a short term there, Welch returned to the Bayou City where he opened the Houston Academy for Boys and Girls in the former Tracy home at 1706 Polk at Jackson in 1896. The professor taught mathematics, Latin, and Greek, languages he believed essential to be truly educated. His daughter, Louise, was on the faculty, as were several others.[10]

In 1905, Welch's Academy moved south a few blocks to 2215 Caroline at Hadley. His students still enjoyed success, with a few earning acceptance to prestigious Eastern colleges including Yale and Harvard. His graduates included Harris County cattleman Sam Allen, Rufus Cage, who would become school board president, and James Baker, son of Captain James A. Baker and father of the future cabinet member. In spite of this, Welch was said to show no partiality toward his wealthier charges, allegedly telling one student, "If you think you and your bobbed tail horse and rubber tire buggy are ornaments to this school, just take them and get out." The professor became ill and the school closed about 1919. There was a brief attempt to reopen it under the supervision of his daughter, but that dream died in 1922.[11]

HOUSTON AVENUE SCHOOL

See Hawthorne.

HOUSTON BAPTIST SCHOOL (COLORED)

See Houston College for Negroes

HOUSTON CITY SCHOOL

See City School

HOUSTON COLLEGE FOR NEGROES

African American civic leader Jack Yates helped open a school for Houston Blacks at Cooper Place, a rented house on Bell at San Jacinto, from 1885 to 1894. The house school taught "Negro boys and girls during the day and Negro adults at night." Affiliated with Baptist Missionary Associations, the school moved to an ambitious college campus just north of the 3200 block of today's West Dallas, west of Dunlavy, that operated from 1894 to 1921. The campus, on what was then called San Felipe Road, was mostly on the north side of the road, but at least one building sat on the south side. A street named Terrell ran north to the biggest cluster of buildings that included two dormitories, a large laundry, and more.[12]

Houston Negro College in its house location. Rev. Jack Yates is standing at center. HHRC

Though it was called a college, the school also had non-college students, offering at times a more scholarly focus or a more industrial bent depending on who was in charge. It was termed an industrial school for part of its existence. On the other hand, in 1896 and 97, Professor J.H. Garnett was in charge bringing solid credentials in the world of early African American higher education. He had previously been president of Arkansas Baptist College and Guadalupe College in Seguin, and he left Houston College to become professor of Latin and Greek at Lincoln Institute in Jefferson City, Missouri by 1899, going on to Kentucky State University and the American Baptist College in Nashville.[13]

Kept afloat by donations from individuals and from Baptist organizations, the school was never very large. In March 1914, a faculty of nine oversaw 109 elementary students and only 18 termed secondary. Structure-wise there was a three-story central building, that included a mess hall, chapel, office, library and reading room, classrooms, and a dress-making department. Also on campus were a boys' carpentry work shop, a girls' laundry, shade trees, walkways, tennis courts, and playing fields.[14]

HOUSTON GARDENS E S

This small elementary school opened at 6820 Homestead in 1935, named for the African American neighborhood in which it was located. In the 21st century, the school is completely new and has been renamed in honor of longtime City Council Member Ernest McGowen.[15]

HOUSTON HARBOR SCHOOL

See Harbor School

HOUSTON HEIGHTS ANNEX SCHOOL

See Love

HOUSTON H S

The longest, mostly uninterrupted run in the history of Bayou City schools belongs to Houston High School, though it was also known by a handful of other monikers. At various times, it was also called Clopper Institute, the Normal and High School, Central High, and Sam Houston High. Sometimes these names were official, and sometimes it seemed to be merely usage, and getting the public to use the nom du jour was sometimes like herding cats.

When the public school system opened under the provisions of the Texas Constitution of 1876, the uninterrupted school system that remains in the state to this day, the City of Houston did not have enough money to include a free high school. On the first of October 1877 a high school, with a tuition of four dollars a month, was opened in the "old Houston Academy building" at Rusk and Caroline. It was under the guidance of school superintendent H.H. Smith and his daughter, Fanny Whiteside, with Gustav Duvernoy teaching English. The 20-year-old Academy building proved unsuitable, though, and the following year, the high school classes were held on the second floor of the Masonic Building which stood at the northeast corner of Main and Capitol. Girls sat on one side of the classrooms and boys on the other.[16]

The Masonic Building where school classes were held.

The following year, there was another move, to rooms at a building on Main and Prairie that later housed the Schulte Store. It was that year that Houston produced its first public high school graduate. Miss Lucy Brown constituted a class of one, and she had moved from out of town.[17]

In 1880, the city bought the old Academy building and the block on which it sat for $7,500 and spent a year renovating it into a high school, by this time supported entirely by tax revenue as opposed to tuition. There were five rooms, and the number of scholars each year during the 1880s ranged from about 50 to 106 by 1890. Improvements did come. A science lab was added. The first school newspaper, the *Aegis*, came in 1889 under the sponsorship of Professor Arthur Livermore who also started a football team the same year. The game was more akin to rugby, played intramural games only, and players were forced to order uniforms and equipment from back east. Parent complaints about the violent sports made football an on-again-off-again program for the next thirteen years.[18]

There were many more female than male students overall. Most of the graduates honored in the commencement ceremonies at the nearby Sweeny & Coombs Opera House were girls, and the city school board president Cesar Lombardi opined that, "One of the most discouraging features of our present high school is the very small proportion of male scholars. Either our young men do not appreciate the advantages of a high school education, or this institution, in spite of our best efforts, offers no attraction to them, and, in either case, something should be done to bring about a remedy."

The smallish Academy building, called "in dangerous condition" by the city, was demolished in 1892, and for the next three years, high school classes took place in five rooms on the upper floors of the old Kiam Building on Main and Congress. Sixth and seventh graders in Houston were relegated to six rooms at the city's Market House.[19]

While the students had been dispossessed, the city was finally getting a real high school building. Cesar Lombardi pitched his friend William Marsh Rice to pay for the structure as a "monument to his memory that would not crumble with time." Rice ultimately opted to donate his money to building a college for Houston instead.

A solicitation letter was sent out on September 1, 1893 for a three-story high school plus a half-basement which would hold toilets and two living rooms for janitors. There would be classrooms, recitation rooms, an assembly hall, library, museum, an observatory and lots of light, both natural and via gas fixtures. Forty-two sets of plans were submitted, yet Eugene Heiner's design was selected unanimously. Stadler and Lucas got the construction contract, J.R. Morris & Sons got plumbing, and the Cincinnati firm of Peek-Smead won the contract for heating and ventilation. When the building opened in 1895 at a cost of over $80,000, it was trumpeted as the best high school in the South.[20]

Houston HS was a popular subject for picture postcards. This photo was taken prior to the annex. Mike Vance Collection

By the turn of the century, the curriculum included typewriting, stenography, Spanish, and civics. Also added were many more students than anticipated. In 1904, the school board let a contract for an Olle Lorehn designed annex that added 14 classrooms, more bathrooms, and two study halls. By 1908, that addition had been expanded, ultimately providing 19 rooms plus other labs, a gymnasium, an elevator, and a newspaper office. The faculty added physical education coaches for both girls and boys. In spite of that, by 1913, with enrollment well over one thousand, calls began for a new "million dollar" high school building.[21]

As happened more than once in Houston schools history, the city got a reprieve in the form of a fire. On Tuesday night, March 18, 1919, Houston, or Central, High School burned down. Registrar and teacher Emma Duvernoy who had taken over the job upon her father's death, saved some of the records, but the building was a goner. The library salvaged only 115 books plus 25 more that were checked out at the time. Before the blaze was even extinguished, school officials announced a plan for South End Junior High to run a split schedule in which the junior high students attended in the morning and high schoolers from 1 to 5:30 P.M..[22]

The new Central High rose on the same block, but, though some $476,000 were spent, when it opened in January 1921, a budget shortfall meant that there was no auditorium, lunch room, gymnasium, or swimming pools. Those were postponed. There were, however, 65 rooms and 1,500 desks.

The rebuilt Houston (or Central) HS in the 1920s. HISD

In 1926, in preparation for three new Houston high schools opening, the name was official changed to Sam Houston High. One year later, the Black Battalion was organized by Verna Bunton as the first all-girls marching drill, drum and bugle corps in Texas. It was named in honor of popular school principal Frank M. Black, who had taught math at the school in 1905, served as head man at Longfellow and Travis Elementaries and South End Junior High before returning to Central as the boss. When Black died at the age of 52, the Battalion stood in formation by his grave.[23]

The most famous teacher in the city's history taught at Sam Houston in 1930. The young nephew of George D. Johnson, head of the history department, came to teach debate and public speaking. His name was Lyndon B. Johnson, and he went on to become the 36th President of the United States.[24]

In 1937, when Austin and Lamar High Schools opened, the enrollment at Sam Houston was cut in half. It was "especially ruinous" to the school's athletics. Adding to the woes were the school's surroundings that included seedy bars, prostitutes, and street people who occasionally rambled through the halls of the building.[25]

The final class downtown, in May 1952, had "only 162 graduates down from a high of around 600." The Sam Houston High name was resurrected at a new facility on Irvington in 1955, and the building downtown served as the HISD administration headquarters until the "Taj Mahal" opened at Richmond and Weslayan in 1970. After the administrators left, the old high school was boarded up, suffering a few small fires from vagrants. It was demolished in the mid-1970s and paved as a parking lot. That remained its use until HSPVA rose on that block.[26]

Public School Art League

Culture in 19th century Houston was sometimes scarce, and a major effort to improve the lives of the city's school children came from the Public School Art League. Formed in 1900 by some four dozen of the most civic minded women in town plus a handful of gentlemen, it quickly grew to be one of the city's treasures, and from its efforts grew the premier location for fine art that Houston has to offer.

The founders of the League included Mrs. Robert S. Lovett, Cora Redwood, Sybil Campbell, Gussie Howard, Edith House, Mrs. James A. Baker, and Adele Looscan. The hope was to enlist many Houston mothers in the effort. The ladies set annual dues at fifty cents and offered life memberships for fifteen dollars. Article five of their by-laws created three committees, one of which was charged with censorship and chaired by Emma Richardson Cherry, a well-trained, acclaimed artist in her own right.[27]

In spite of that precaution, the league ran into controversy quickly. Within their first year, a purchase, not to exceed $125 including transportation, was approved to bring a large copy of the Venus de Milo from the cast house of the Louvre in Paris and place it in the front hallway of the Houston High School. It went first to Fannin School where the students were thrilled, the parents less so. The High School again was singled out for the gift, but the idea of a barely clothed statue in full view of teenagers, warranted a committee to view the work first. The decision was a no.[28]

Ultimately, the Art League "disposed" of the sculpture when a few leading citizens purchased it for donation, and Mrs. Cherry presented the piece for an unveiling on the grand occasion of the opening of the city's new Carnegie Library in March 1904. The library patrons were much more open-minded than the school board, and the artwork was lauded and afforded a place of honor. In 1926, Houston's Venus made the move to the new building on McKinney and Smith, and there it remains, a treasure in the beautifully restored Julia Ideson Library Building.[29]

Venus de Milo in the Julia Ideson Building's second floor reading room. Wikimedia Commons

The Houston Public School Art League kept up a steady diet of donation over the years. In keeping with the climate of rigid segregation, the donations of art reproductions were made to the White schools only. In 1904, they concentrated on third grade classes, giving them "a series of pictures representative of some school of art." Of the early donations, some reproductions were in color, but most were in black and white. Fannin School, thought of as the ritzy area of town, had a handful of paintings donated directly by student's families, as well.

Some of the women went on personal quests to supply images that could expose some of the Houston students to new worlds. Jean Sherwood donated four large prints in 1905, including two photographs she had taken herself of cathedrals in Milano, Italy and Burgos, Spain. The same year, Cora Bacon Foster gave 75 steel engravings of works by British artists.

The artwork was decidedly European and American. Some women of the League in 1905, led my Mrs. Cherry, looked into expanding Houston's horizons through the donation of Japanese works of art, but no takers could be found. "It was concluded finally, after finding one teacher who was willing and glad to have Japanese art in her room, to place Japanese prints in one room at Fannin School. It soon morphed into an entire "reception with a Japanese program" part of which was filled with short talks by members of the Ladies Reading Club who had "made a comprehensive study of Japan." The League even went so far as to "tint" the walls of the room to complement the art, and the anticipated donation of Japanese armor "brought from over the seas" would enhance the learning experience even further.[30]

The ten year mark of the organization saw more participation by men. The first male officers appeared including William Marsh Rice, nephew of the benefactor of the planned Rice Institute, home builder William Wilson and Houston School Superintendent Paul Horn. Overall, League membership passed 600, and both funds to buy art, and creative ways to display it, kept coming.

By 1911, a report from Anson Jones School, just northeast of downtown, listed 48 copies of famous paintings with a notation that it was "substantially the same list that has been furnished all the schools." The school placed a value of over $600 on the artwork which had ranged in price from around a dollar to well over $10 apiece, not including framing and glass. Among the paintings represented were classics including Rembrandt's painting *Night Watch* and casts of Donatello's *Laughing Boy* along with historical subjects such as *Washington Crossing the Delaware* , *The Return of the Mayflower* and *Pilgrim Exiles*. There was the stuff of legend like Watts' *Sir Galahad* and the accessible heart warmers like Landseer's *Dignity and Impudence*. Along with others by Millet, were bucolic scenes including *At the Watering Trough* and a handful of religious works in the form of various Madonnas.[31]

In the early 1910s, the Public School Art League changed direction, or at least augmented it. They began holding annual exhibitions in conjunction with the American Federation of Arts. In 1913, for example, works by such up-and-coming artists as Childe Hassam, William Lathrop, Charles M. Russell, and William Merritt Chase were shown for two weeks in the ballroom of the Bender Hotel. Later that year, with the White public schools of the city largely filled with art, the group reorganized as the Houston Art League and began building the nucleus of a museum collection. They even received a building site from the city at Holman and Austin.

Unfortunately to some, the site, the Foegard Tract, was also to be the location of the new South End Junior High School. School board member Dr. S.C. Red, for one, claimed that the Art League, advocating for artistic placement of the school building, interfered with the board "to such an extent that there can now be no athletic field on the property." Even though plans were drawn up for a two story, columned classical art museum at the promised corner, the simmering controversy caused the project to be put on temporary hold. After a series of other delays, the Art League would eventually open a grand, permanent home for Houston's art collection at Montrose and Main in 1924.[32]

HOUSTON MALE AND FEMALE ACADEMY

This private school was one of the larger ones, operating at least from 1857 to 1862. James A. Bolinger was principal at the start. The male and female departments maintained separate entrances, classrooms, and recitation rooms. Among the instructors there was Mr. A. DePelchin whose widow became well known in educational and charity circles.[33]

HOUSTON, SAM E S, BAYTOWN

Sam Houston Elementary was opened on Lee Drive in Pelly in the 1920s and received additional rooms in conjunction with the large GCCISD bond in 1929. By the end of the 1930s, there were eight classrooms on a small five acre parcel. An active oil well that operated on campus blew on a Saturday afternoon in 1951, "spraying crude oil over homes, autos, trees and persons caught within half-mile of the" school and continuing the dowsing for six hours. Parents made demands to "stop all oil work on the campus at least until summer vacation begins." As the Goose Creek oil field played out, old pumping equipment was stacked next to the campus.[34]

HOUSTON SELECT ACADEMY

One of the many private schools in the 1840 time period, this one was run by Mr. W.J. Thurber. His school was de rigeur for the time, but he also offered night school for adults "who may wish to gain a knowledge of English Grammar."[35]

HUFFMAN SCHOOL

Huffman was a small school in District 30 on the Humble-Crosby Road just east of where the road makes a dogleg near Walraven Rd, north of the town of Huffman. It was operating by at least 1876, and a new building was constructed around 1912. At the end of the 1930s, it was still operating as a common school district with 51 students. Those continuing on to high school did so at Crosby.[36]

HUFFMAN COLORED SCHOOL

District 30 in the northeastern most section of Harris County operated a school for African Americans at least by 1886. It and the White school, also named Huffman, were the only ones in the district. At least in the early years, money was sometimes transferred to the Crosby Colored School, indicating that the Black scholastic population in Huffman did not warrant operating a separate schoolhouse. Classes were held in a private house for part of the first decade of the 20th century. In the late 1930s, the school enrollment had increased to about 20 in the one-room frame building.[37]

HUFSMITH SCHOOL

Anderson King, a freed slave, donated the land for a school serving the Black community near Hufsmith, a town that grew up around the International & Great Northern Railroad stop in 1902. The African American school was in County District 31. By 1907, it was operating a seven month term in a "very good" building. [38]

HUMBLE E S

This elementary school was opened at 340 Charles Street in 1949, remaining there until a new campus was built near Deerbrook Mall in 1999. The Humble ISD had purchased the land in 1938, and opened a football stadium there two or three years prior to building the school. There is a charter school operating on the campus today.[39]

HUMBLE SCHOOL

County District 28's first school was Joe Dunman's, an established institution that, while near the center of the district, was not so close to the new community of Humble that was growing along the East & West Texas Railroad tracks. In 1888, residents in the new town petitioned for a split in the district, and they remained Number 28 in the northern half while the southern section, and Dunman's School, went to a newly formed District 35. William Humble, son of the town's namesake, donated a parcel of land at the corner of today's Old Humble Road and Isaacks Road, and a one-room wooden building went up, dubbed West River School.[40]

The number of students hovered around the 20 to 30 range until the discovery of the Humble Field, one of the largest oil finds in the nation, turned things upside down. In 1904, enrollment soared from 32 to 68 in a year, forcing the hiring of a second teacher. By summer of 1905, a year in which the brand new oil field produced over 15 and a half million barrels, a second building was added. The following year, with 217 students, a third wooden schoolhouse was brought in.[41]

Humble School photo with fanciful birds and an airplane added to the negative by the photographer. Mike Vance Collection

Faced with the continuing influx of oil workers in the first decade of the 1900s, the people of County District 28 voted in favor of a $10,000 bond. The result was a two-story, six-room brick building to replace the wooden West River School. That property was sold and became incorporated in the town cemetery. The new school, now catering to students all the way up to ninth grade, was on a block bounded by Higgins, Herman, and Avenue F, an area that remained the center of education in Humble for decades. One year after the "magnificent" schoolhouse opened, district trustee J.W. Hall wrote this comment to the county board: "The people of this little town have various differences of opinions on public questions, but when it comes to the matter of schools, we put our shoulders together and march side by side for the benefit of the children of the future generations of this country."[42]

When the newer Humble Elementary opened in 1949, the old building provided overflow classrooms at bender High School, but in 1955, it was demolished to make room for a new cafeteria, band hall, and gym.[43]

HUMBLE H S

See Bender HS

HUMBLE PRIMARY SCHOOL

Humble ISD opened a primary school for the first two grades on the east side of Avenue F between Higgins and Herman in 1921. Combined with the grammar school and high school, it completed an education center in the town. Population in Humble fluctuated greatly in the early years of the 20th century due to WWI especially because of the volatility of employment in the adjoining oil fields. [44]

Texas and Harris County Schools Facts Circa 1896

Texas spent $4 million on public school compared to Massachusetts - $10 M, New York - $24 M, Pennsylvania - $18 M, Illinois - $16 M.[45]

In 1895-96, Texas expenditures from the $4.02 M was $3.3 M on teacher salaries with the next four highest items $110k on furniture, $90k on supervision of schools, $59k on clerks, janitors and other employees, and $56k on repairs to buildings. State Superintendent Carlisle complained about no expenditures on new buildings.

Put another way, Texas spent 84% on teacher salaries compared to 48% in Pennsylvania, 56% in New York, 63% in Louisiana. Closest to Texas in that regard were Virginia and Kentucky which each at 77% spent on teachers.

For the 1894-95 school year, Houston had a listed enrollment of 6,488 White students and 4,533 African American. In statewide statistics there were 526,101 White students and 167,651 Black.

Harris County schools used $13,004 in state funds and $2,000 in county funds. The City of Houston schools used $38,573 in state funds and $64 in county funds. La Porte also had a school district listed in the state report with less than $1,000 in expenses, of that $685 was teacher salary.

Harris County had 40 districts with 51 White schools and 33 Black schools. They built five schools during the 1896-97 school year, three White and two Black. Of the total number of Harris County schools, 42 were owned by deed (28 White/14 Black) and 48 were leased (29 White/19 Black), many from small property owners in the neighborhood.

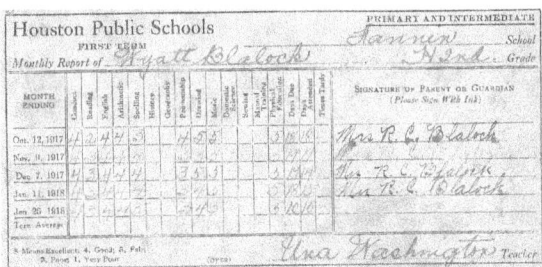

A 1917 report card from Fannin ES. Courtesy of
Virginia Blalock

Endnotes

The Start of Free Public Schools in Texas

1. Eby, Frederick. *The Development of Education in Texas*. MacMillan (New York) 1925; Jones, Selma. *Schools of the Republic of Texas*. Southwest Texas State University Master's Thesis. 1948

2. *A School History of Texas*. Barker, Eugene C., Potts, Charles S., and Ramsdell, Charles W.; Bonewitz, Edwin. HMRC MSS25 1:9; Eby

3. *Houston Chronicle* 5 February 1939; *A History of Public Education in Houston, Texas*. Keller, Katharine. M.A. thesis (University of Texas at Austin, 1930); *Houston*. American Guide Series. WPA. Anson Jones Press (Houston) 1942;

4. *Telegraph* 28 January 1846

5. http://www.educationbug.org/a/history-of-public-schools.html   accessed 25 March 2016; https://www.raceforward.org/research/reports/historical-timeline-public-education-us   accessed 25 March 2016;

6. https://tshaonline.org/handbook/online/articles/fpe08   accessed 25 March 2016;

7. *State Gazette* (Austin) 1 December 1855

8. White, Clifford. *Texas Scholastics 1854-55* (1979); *Republican Compiler* (PA) 12 February 1855

9. *State Gazette* (Austin) 1 December 1855; White; *Telegraph* 16 December 1857

10. *Harris County Commissioners Court Minutes* November 1856; Eby

11. *HCCCM* May 1858, June 1858, August 1858; November 1858, February 1859, May 1859

12. *HCCCM* May 1860, June 1862, January 1864

13. Bonewitz

14. Bonewitz; *Telegraph* 25 January 1860; *Telegraph* 8 December 1863

15. Eby

16. Handbook De Gress; Eby

17. *Public Education and Texas Reconstruction Politics, 1871-1874*. Moneyhon, Carl H.. *Southwestern Historical Quarterly* Vol. 92 No. 3 January 1989 p 393-416

18. https://tshaonline.org/handbook/online/articles/fde64 accessed 19 December 2015

19. *General Laws of the Twelfth Legislature of the State of Texas, First Session – 1871*. J.G. Tracy, State Printer. (Austin); James M. Carlisle, State Superintendent of Schools in the Biennial Report of the State Department of Education 1897, p xix

20. Moneyhon; *Democratic Statesman* (Austin) 18 November 1871; *Handbook of Texas Vol I*, p 640-641

21. Bonewitz

22. United States Census 1870 Ft. Bend County, Tx.; Yelderman, Pauline. *The Jay Birds of Fort Bend County*. 1979; United States Census 1880, 1900 Harris County, TX; Texas Legal Directory 1876-77

23. Bland, Kathleen. *History Notes Show Old School Problems. Post* 19 June 1950; Bonewitz

24. *Galveston Daily News* 17 August 1871

25. Bonewitz

26. *Galveston Daily News* editorial 24 February 1865; Campbell, Randolph. *An Empire For Slavery*. LSU Press 1991

27. *Telegraph* 31 May 1870; *GDN* 1 February 1871

28. *First Annual Report of the Superintendent of Public Instruction of the State of Texas* - 1871. DeGress, J.C.. J.G. Tracy, State Printer (Austin)

29. *Semi-Weekly Brenham Banner* 25 August 1871

30. *San Antonio Daily Express* 26 August 1871

31. *Letters Received, Office of Superintendent of Public Instruction of the State of Texas*. William Houston to J.C. DeGress 21 August 1872

32. *William Carey Crane and Texas Education*. Thompson, E. Bruce. *Southwestern Historical Quarterly* Vol. 73 No. 3 January 1955. P 417-18

33. *Second Annual Report* DeGress

34. *San Antonio Daily Express* 10 February 1872

35. *Telegraph* 15 October 1871; *Telegraph* 28 October 1871; Lavender, Mary Alice P. *Social Conditions in Houston and Harris County, 1869-1872* M.A. Thesis, Rice Institute, 1950 pp. 164-65.

36. *Telegraph* 25 September 1872; Lavender

37. *First Annual Report*. DeGress; Winegarten

38. *Second Report* De Gress

39. Bonewitz

40. *Second Report* De Gress

41. ibid

42. James Pearson Newcomb Papers, BTHC, William T. Clark to Newcomb, 2 June 1871

43. *Flake's Daily Bulletin* (Galveston) 19 July 1871

44. *Journal of the Senate of the Twelfth Legislature of the State of Texas*. 1871. J.G. Tracy State Printer.

45. ibid

46. *General Laws* 1871

47. *General Laws, Second Session*, 1872

48. *Second Report* DeGress

49. Bonewitz

50. *General Laws, Thirteenth Legislature* 1873, John Cardwell State Printer (Austin); *GDN* 9 May 1873

51. Moneyhon

52. Handbook DeGress; Wiki list Austin Mayors

53. *Constitution of the State of Texas*, 1876, Article 7, Section 3

54. *Development of Education in Texas*. Eby, Fredrick.1925. Macmillan Co.(New York); *General Laws, Fifteenth Legislature*. 1876

55. Young; Bonewitz

56. Young

57. *Houston Age* 2 October 1877

58. *Telegraph* 3 March 1876

59. Young; Bonewitz

60. Bonewitz; Harris County ledger book, Texas Department of Education, 1877, Harris County Archives

61. *The Clarion* (Jackson, MS.) 6 June 1877, p 2

Schools A

1. Hickman, Ella Smith. *Private Schools of Houston from 1900 to 1936* (1939); Lavender, Mary Alice P.. *Social Conditions in Houston and Harris County, 1869-1872* (M.A. Thesis, Rice Institute, 1950); *Telegraph and Texas Register* 26 September 1872; "Scrapbook on Education" found at Houston Public Library in 1939 and quoted by Hickman.

2. Hickman

3. City Directories; HCCCM F285. 14 May 1891; Harris County School District 25 Minutes ledger; Digital Sanborn maps 1907;

4. *Post* 17 October 1913; County Reports; Digital Sanborn Maps 1924; *Houston City Directories*, various years; *Houston City Schools Report* 1913-14; HISD Wiki; Pugh, L.L. and Denison, Lynn. *A History of Houston Schools*. 1936

5. *City Report* 1913-14, 1914-15, 1918-10, 1920-21, 1921-22; Author interview with Sammy Patranella 2008; *Houston Post* 17 December 1962

6. Harris County Schools Report 1912, 1913;

7. Cy-Fair ISD websites; *Brookshire Times* 4 November 1938; *Brookshire Times* 14 April 1939; *Valley Star Monitor-Herald* (Brownsville) 25 May 1941; *Brookshire Times* 13 August 1948

8. Edwards, Margaret Hopkins. Handbook of Texas. Accessed 12 June 2016; Howard, Margaret Ann and Freeman, Martha Doty. *Inventory and Assessment of Cultural Resources at Bear Creek Park, Addicks Reservoir* (Austin: Prewitt and Associates, 1983); *Chronicle* 15 July 1970; USGS map 1916

9. *County Report* 1910; Perkins, John Cody. *A General Survey of Rural Schools of Harris County, Texas.* Master's Thesis. University of Texas. June 1933

10. County Reports; *Brookshire Times* 14 April 1939; *Post* 5 September 1907

11. *County Report* 1912

12. ibid

13. Cole; USGS Topographic Map, Crosby 1919

14. City Directories; Pugh and Denison; Bush, David. Greater Houston Preservation Alliance. April 2010

15. GCCISD websites' Henson; Scott, Barney Harold. *An Administrative Survey and Proposed Plan of Reorganization of School in Eastern Harris County*. M.E. Thesis. University of Texas, August 1940.

16. Texas State Historical Marker. Aldine. 1999; County Reports; Author correspondence with Mark McKee in May 2016; Blackmon, Durward Harvey. *An Educational Survey of a Portion of North Harris County, Texas* (Master's of Education thesis at UT-Austin, 1939)

17. ibid

18. ibid

19. McGee; Blackmon; *Brownsville Herald* 27 July 1947; *Mexia Daily* 18 November 1948

20. Davis, Sandy. *History of Dairy (Alief), Texas.* Alief 130 Anniversary Celebration Commission, 1991; HCCCM P193. 17 February 1910; HCCCM P440. 19 December 1910; Alief ISD Dedication. Charles Burdette Boone. 27 September 1984; Alife. Vertical files, HMRC. HPL; *The Horizon* 8 Mar 1989; *Southwest Advocate* August 27-September 2, 1986 Vol XVIII #52; HC Auditor's Report 1930; HC 17 August 1947

21. *County Report* 1912

22. Harris, Dilue Rose. *Reminiscences*. Quarterly of the Texas State Historical Association IV, October 1900, p 124

23. Preston, Josephine Corliss. *The Teacherage*. Journal of Education, Vol, 84, No. 8. 7 September 1916. P 215-216

24. Maxcy, Spencer J.. *The Teacherage in Rural American Education*. Journal of General Education, Vol. 30, No. 4. Winter 1979. P 267-274

25. Preston

26. Archdiocese of Galveston-Houston; Digital Sanborn Maps; City Directories; GDN 6 October 1922

27. Digital Sanborn Maps; City Reports

28. City Reports; *Chronicle* 17 February 1941; *Valley Morning Star* (Harlingen) 28 November 1931

29. City Reports

30. HISD websites

31. http://law2.umkc.edu/faculty/projects/ftrials/conlaw/schoolprayer.html   accessed 25 February 2016; http://www.allaboutpopularissues.org/prayer-in-public-school.htm accessed 25 February 2016

32. *City Report* 1907-08; *Post* 16 September 1915

33. *City Report* 1921-22

34. *Chronicle* 7 June 1934

35. http://caselaw.findlaw.com/us-supreme-court/333/203.html   accessed 25 February 2016

36. Andrews, Rose. *Down Yonder in Almeda, Texas*; Texas State Historical Marker, County Treasurer Ledgers; *Post* 15 May 1897; *Post* 19 March 1899

37. County Reports; HC Deed V 329:29

38. Andrews; HISD websites

39. *Post* 19 March 1899; HISD directory 1942-43

40. McHugh, Sister Mary Sebastian. *History of the Order of the Incarnate Word and Blessed Sacrament in Houston, Texas* (M.A. Thesis, University of Houston; 1948); *GDN* 22 June 1894; *GDN* 26 June 1895; GDN 8 June 1905; Archdiocese of Galveston-Houston

41. SD 25 Minute book

42. Archdiocese records

43. City Directories; *GDN* 20 September 1915; *Suburbanite* 8 March 1918; Bryant; Johnson

44. Bryant; *Chronicle* 10 April 1945; *Chronicle* 12 November 1994

45. City Directories; Digital Sanborn Maps 1907, 1924; City Reports

46. City Reports; Pugh; *Post* 7 December 1962

47. Laurentz, Carleen Riemen. *A History of Stephen F. Austin Senior High School*; HISD Websites;

48. Author interview with Moises Villalpando

49. *Post* 25 October 1916

50. Vance, Mike. *Houston's Sporting Life 1900-1950*. Arcadia (Charleston, SC) 2012

51. *Chronicle* 23 October 1929

52. *Thresher* 4 March 1932

53. Kaplan, David. *Chronicle* 22 June 2008

54. Houston Arts and Media. N2N Interview with Ann Malone. HMRC/ Woodson Research Center

55. *Informer* 2 June 1923

56. *Informer* 10 June 1933

57. Digital Sanborn Maps 1924; Pugh; http://www.findagrave.com/cgi-bin/fg.cgi?page=gr&GRid=91246 766 accessed 29 September 2016; *GDN* 3 June 1924; *GDN* 10 January 1925; *The Municipal Book of the City of Houston, Period Ending December 31, 1928*; Aulbach, Louis. *Buffalo Bayou: An echo of Houston's wilderness beginnings.* Houston 2012

58. Howard, Alexander. *Hearing Aids: Smaller and Smarter. New York Times.* 26 November 1998

59. *City Report* 1914-15

60. *HISD History Outline* 1976

61. *City Report* 1916-17; *City Report* 1921-22

62. *City Report* 1921-22

63. *Chronicle* 28 October 1924

Schools B

1. City Directories; County Treasurer ledgers; Porter Map of Houston 1890; HCCCM E625. 15 May 1889; HCCCM F285. 14 May 1891; *Post* 15 May 1897; *Post* 19 March 1899; Worrall

2. https://tshaonline.org/handbook/online/articles/hvf03   accessed 10 September 2016; HCCCM 21 May 1854; Handbook https://tshaonline.org/handbook/online/articles/eqh09%20accessed%206%20October%202017 ; GDN 11 November 1900; County Reports; http://www.cfisd.net/en/about/know-your-district/history/   accessed 10 September 2016

3. http://bane.cfisd.net/en/about/know-your-school/history/   accessed 10 September 2016; Daniels

4. HCCCM F434. 14 May 1892; HCCCM F419. 13 February 1892

5. USGS Maps 1914; County Reports; HCCCM Q170. 12 March 1912; HCCCM Q373. 11 December 1912; Dimon, Atha Marks. Handbook https://tshaonline.org/handbook/online/articles/hlb08%20accessed%2029%20September%202016 ; Sizemore, Deborah Lightfoot. *The LH7 Ranch in Houston's Shadow*. 1991

6. Hickman; Keller; U.S. Census Harris County 1910, 1920; Texas Death Records; *GDN* 9 May 1911

7. Hickman; *GDN* 25 May 1905, *GDN* 27 May 1910

8. Texas Death Certificate; Hickman; City Directories

9. Cole, Edith Fae Cook. *Crosby's Heritage Preserved: 1823-1949*. Self 1986; County Treasurer ledgers; Texas Historical marker. Barrett's Station; *Post* 5 September 1907; *Chronicle* 16 December 2019; TSHA Nadbook Online. Barrett, TX. https://tshaonline.org/handbook/online/articles/hgb03   accessed 16 December 2019

10. Cole; County Treasurer ledgers; Texas Historical marker. Barrett's Station; *Post* 5 September 1907

11. ibid

12. http://es.houstonisd.org/barrickes/home.html accessed 29 September 2016

13. Bland, Kathleen *Post*. 26 October 1948 "Pupils Aplenty; Short on Teachers; School Head Tells of Primary Faults"

14. Hickman Based on interview with founder's granddaughter and *Chronicle* article, 25 September 1932

15. HISD websites

16. County Reports. County Treasurer ledgers; *Post* 15 May 1897; *Post* 19 March 1899; HCCCM G233. 8 April 1895; Upchurch, Leslie. *Welcome to Tomball: A History of Tomball, Texas*. D. Armstrong. 1976

17. Texas Historical Marker text; WPA Guide to Houston; GCISD text; County Treasurer ledgers; Harris County Archives records various; https://www.fold3.com/page/2552_bayland_orphan_home_186719 48#description accessed 27 August 2016; *Post* 2 September 1907

18. Harris County Archives, Juvenile Probation Records, Children's Homes, Ethel Claxton Scrapbook, V. 1, Pt. 1, 1914-1930; Currlin, Alice Bruce, *Community Welfare: Houston, Texas* (Houston: The Community Chest and Council of Houston and Harris County), 1946

19. Henson; Scott

20. Henson; GCCISD websites; Scott

21. County Treasurer ledgers 1889-1893; HCCCM F:344 13 August 1891

22. Harris County Schools original ledger 1876; Texas Historical Marker file. Bear Creek Methodist Church and Cemetery. 1994;

23. HCCCM February 1882, E:98 18 June 1884, Country Treasurer ledgers 1886-1895; Post 15 May 1897; Post 19 march 1899; GDN 19 November 1893

24. County Treasurer ledger 1886-87

25. County Treasurer ledgers 1889-1894; *Post* 19 March 1899

26. *County Report* 1910, 1912, 1913, 1914

27. Humble ISD archives; Meaux; County Reports; Montgomery T. S. *Report of the Summary of the Humble Public Schools* in Bulletin of the Sam Houston State Teachers College (May, 1926); HC Auditor's Report 1925

28. Meaux; Humble ISD archives; Blackmon, Durward Harvey. *An Educational Survey of a Portion of North Harris County, Texas.* (Master's of Education thesis at UT-Austin, 1939)

29. Humble ISD archives

30. County Treasurer ledgers; HCCCM F285. 14 May 1891; HCCCM F436. 14 May 1892; *Post* 15 May 1897; *Post* 19 March 1899

31. County Reports; City Directories; Suburbanite 8 March 1918; HISD Reports; Pugh & Dennison

32. HISD websites; Author interview with Juan Regalado 29 June 2007

33. City Directories

34. Cy-Fair ISD Websites; County Treasurer ledgers; Author correspondence with Jane Ledbetter January 2009 and August 2016; Cypress Top Historical Society archives; *Post* 15 May 1897; *Post* 19 March 1899; County Reports; Sullivan

35. Sullivan, Ledbetter; Cypress Top

36. USGS Map Waller quadrant 1916; HCCCM F285 14 May 1891; County Treasurer ledgers; *Post* 15 May 1897; *Post* 19 March 1899; County Reports; HC Deeds 297:140 27 November 1912

37. County Treasurer ledgers; SD 25 Minutes ledger; GDN 10 November 1889; HCCCM F436. 14 May 1892; GDN 1 June 1895; GDN 15 May 1897; GDN 19 march 1899; City Directory 1895-96

38. City Reports; Bryant; https://tshaonline.org/handbook/online/articles/fbl71 accessed 4 September 2016;

39. Digital Sanborn Maps 1924; McHugh; Archdiocese of Galveston-Houston

40. Pugh & Dennison; City Directories;

41. Meaux; Kleiner, Diana J.. Handbook https://tshaonline.org/handbook/online/articles/hrb81 accessed 2 October 2016

42. City Reports; *Post* 9 February 1905; City Directories; *Post* 24 February 1905

43. City Reports; *Post* 10 October 1905; *Post* 14 November 1905

44. City Reports; Fonville, R.H.. *Growth of Northside Schools*. Article, late 1920s

45. *Chronicle* 14 May 1925; HISD Minutes 9 May 1955; HISD document Brackenridge School

46. *City Report* 1908-09; *City Report* 1909-10; *Post* 1 September 1909

47. Chapman, Betty https://houstonhistorymagazine.org/wp-content/uploads/2014/07/Kuhlmann-Family.pdf accessed 02 October 2016; City Directories; County Treasurer ledgers; County Reports; HC Deeds. 7 September 1855; Harris County School Census 1855' Original HC schools ledger 1876; HCCCM E98. 18 June 1884; HCCCM F203. 15 November 1890; HCCCM F285. 14 May 1891; HCCCM F419. 13 February 1892; Post 15 May 1897; Post 19 March 1899; Post 25 January 1914

48. County Treasurer ledgers; Bryant; City Reports; City Directories; 1931 Harris County Schools Map; HISD Directory 1942-43; *Post* 5 September 1907

49. Labay, Allen F.. Texas Abstract Co. for CFCISD. 30 March 1965; Harris County Deeds 106:613; Author interview with Jane Ledbetter, Kleb Woods County Park; *County Report* 1910, 1912, 1913, 1914

50. Ledbetter; Sullivan, John Bernard. *A Historical Perspective of the Cypress-Fairbanks Independent School District, Houston, Texas, 1884-1984*. Dissertation, Southern Illinois University, 1988. Author notes that "much of this information was drawn from an unpublished manuscript: B. Crews, *Brief Notes on the Cypress-Fairbanks I.S.D.* (1964); and from newspaper articles in the *Waller County Record*; and a few old school yearbooks."; Perkins

51. Pugh and Denison; http://es.houstonisd.org/briscoees/briscoehomepage/aboutourschool.htm accessed 17 March 2012; City directories

52. HISD Collection. HMRC

53. USGS Map Park Place quadrant 1922; City Directories; Pugh & Dennison; County Reports; *Chronicle* 13 November 2024

54. Lavender; *Telegraph* 23 January 1869

55. *Suburbanite* 8 March 1918; City Reports; County Reports; Pugh & Dennison; *Post* 8 February 1918

56. *Mexia Daily News* 20 April 1953

57. County Reports; Harris County road map 1934; Perkins

58. *Telegraph* 26 September 1872; City Reports; City Directories; *GDN* 20 December 1883; 27 September 1884; Digital Sanborn Maps 1896

59. City Reports; Post 19 September 1897; Dealy & Baker Guide to Houston 1895

60. City Directories; Johnson; Bryant; City Reports; Prather, Patricia. *Nathaniel Q. Henderson*. TSHA. Handbook of African American Texas

61. City Reports; Digital Sanborn Maps 1907; Prather

62. Bryant; City Reports; *GDN* 14 June 1922; Prather

63. *Chronicle* 22 September 2007; Swamplot 10 August 2009

64. City Directories

65. *Chronicle* 13 November 1989; SD 25 minutes ledger; HCCCM E607. 14 February 1889; City Directories

66. HCCCM J301. 1 December 1900; HCCCM J395. 7 March 1901; City Directories; *Post* 19 March 1899; *GDN* 14 August 1898; *GDN* 16 July 1896; *Post* 15 May 1904; HC Deeds 174:103. 8 March 1905; HC Assessor's Abstract Vol 3

67. City Reports; City Directories; Digital Sanborn Maps 1907, 1924

68. City Directories; *HISD Report* 1924-30; *Post* 16 September 1929

69. Pugh and Dennison; Burbank School History. HISD Collection. HMRC; Author interviews at school 29 June 2007

70. Author interviews

71. City Directories; Burbank School History. HISD Collection. HMRC; *Chronicle*. Bayou City History. 19 August 2010

72. City Directories; *Post* 19 March 1899; HCCCM N:463 14 May 1907

73. County Treasurer ledgers

74. City Directories; City Reports; Pugh & Dennison

75. Henson; GCCISD websites; Scott; Beverly, Trevia http://www.baytownhistory.org/images/Wooster_School_Brochure-NEW.pdf accessed 10 October 2016

76. Texas Historical Marker. Independence Heights; Handbook Online. O.P. DeWalt; *Suburbanite* 8 March 1918

77. City Reports; From http://indepheights.rice.edu/schooldays.htm   accessed 19 July 2013; Bryant; Johnson;

78. *Chronicle* 17 May 2008

Schools C

1. City Directories, City Reports; County Reports.

2. Pugh & Dennison; HCCCM P293. 10 June 1910; County Reports; GDN 27 May 1910; HISD websites; *Chronicle* 20 May 1918

3. *Chronicle* 3 July 2011. Lisa Gray; GDN 16 June 1923;

4. U.S. Census Bureau historical records, various; Cochran, J. Chester. *The Municipal University as a Community Service Institution, Especially as Exemplified in the Aims, Organization and Growth of the University of Houston*. The University of Texas (Austin) 1950

5. Cochran

6. Census Bureau

7. ibid

8. USGS Map 1914; HCCCM E98. 18 June 1884; County Treasurer ledgers; HCCCM E625. 15 May 1889; *Post* 15 May 1897; *Post* 19 March 1899; County Reports; HCCCM M546.16 Feb 1906

9. County Reports; County Treasurer ledgers; *Post* 5 September 1907

10. County Treasurer ledgers; Author interview with Debra Sloan 5 January 2010

11. King, Major James King. *The History and Development of White Oak Colored School, Aldine Independent School District, Houston, Texas* MA thesis, Texas Southern University. 1961; Texas Historical Marker. George Washington Carver School; County Reports; United States Census Harris County 1900; Post 5 September 1907

12. Texas Historical Marker George Washington Carver School; City Directories; HISD websites; Author interview with Debra Sloan and Jewell Simpson Houston 5 January 2010

13. http://www.gccisd.net/carver/   accessed 02 October 2016

14. Archia, Ernest Alvin. *A Ten Year Follow-Up Study of the Sixty Graduates and Ninety-Two Drop-Outs of the George Washington Carver High School, Goose Creek, Texas with Implications for Curriculum Organization.* M.S. thesis at Prairie View State Normal and Industrial College, 1942; *Baytown Sun* 13 July 2008; GCCISD websites

15. Cy-Fair ISD websites; Cypress Historical Society archives; Ledbetter

16. Clayton, Baytown Museum; Texas Historical Marker. Cedar Bayou Masonic Lodge; 1876 HC schools ledger; HCCCM E98. 18 June 1884; County Treasurer ledgers; *Post* 15 May 1897; *Post* 19 March 1899; County Reports; Cartier, Robert J. & Hole, Frank. *History of the McCormick League and Areas Adjoining the San Jacinto Battleground.* 1972; Harris, R.O.. *Houston Mercury* 9 July 1873; Research of Chuck Chandler

17. Goose Creek CISD website; County Reports; USGS Maps 1914; Scott

18. County Treasurer ledgers; *Post* 19 March 1899; Author interview with Reggie Browne, Jr. July 2015; Henson, Margaret Sweatt and Ladd, Kevin. *Chambers County: A Pictorial History.* Donning Co. 1988; *Post* 5 September 1907

19. Maggie Walterine Johnson Birth Certificate; United States Census Harris County 1900, 1910, 1920; HMRC Hicks Family Collection MSS.0190

20. HMRC Hicks

21. Scott; https://tshaonline.org/handbook/online/articles/hfc06%20accessed%208%20October%202017 ; Perkins

22. *Telegraph* 26 September 1872

23. Digital Sanborn maps 1896, 1907, 1924; Johnston; Johnston; Marguerite. *A Happy Worldly Abode: Christ Church Cathedral 1839-1964.* 1964; City directories

24. Archdiocese records

25. County Treasurer ledgers; HCCCM E625.15 May 1889; United States Census Harris County 1900, 1920; *Chronicle* 7 September 1932;

26. WPA Guide to Houston; Young; Post 19 June 1950; Keller, Katharine. *A History of Public Education in Houston, Texas* M.A. thesis (University of Texas at Austin, 1930); Bright, Margaret Dorothea. *The Social Development of Houston, Texas 1836-1860.* M.A. thesis (University of Texas at Austin. 1940)

27. SHQ V34:4 April 1931. University of Texas at Austin; Telegraph 4 May 1842; Eby, Frederick. *The Development of Education in Texas.* MacMillan (New York) 1925; Davis, Flora Agatha. *The Early History of Houston Texas 1836-1845.* M.A. Thesis. University of Texas. August 1940

28. TTR 21 August 1939; Keller; https://tshaonline.org/handbook/online/articles/iep01 accessed 21 April 2016; https://www.tsl.texas.gov/arc/passports.html accessed 21 April 2016; *Star* (Houston) 2 March 1843

29. *Chronicle* 5 February 1939; Keller; WPA Guide

30. *Morning Star* 16 February 1843; *TTR* 17 October 1845; Keller; Eby; *Morning Star* 31 January 1846

31. Author interview with Don Ramsey 2008; USGS Map 1914; County Reports; Cole

32. City Reports; *Post* 24 December 1912

33. Pugh & Dennison; City Directories; HISD websites; *Post* 1 December 1942

34. *City Report* 1888-89

35. *City Report* 1892-93; *United States Census, Harris County* 1900

36. *Post* 11 August 1914

37. *City Report* 1916-17

38. *City Report* 1919-20

39. HISD web history; Johnson; HISD Directory 1942-43; *Chronicle* May 2005

40. http://www.galenaparkisd.com/campuspages/clf/history.htm accessed 23 September 2017

41. *Spring Times* undated; Beverly

42. City Directories

43. County Treasurer ledgers

44. Dunn, Jeffrey. Bellaire, TX. Handbook of Texas. https://www.tshaonline.org/handbook/online/artic les/heb05 accessed 19 June 2016; County Reports 1913, 1914; City Directories; *Post* 25 January 1914; Hays, Mrs. Robert N. and Hawks, Mrs. J.W., Eds.. *Bellaire's Own Historical Cookbook*. Bellaire Women's Civic Club, 1969

45. *Post* 25 January 1914

46. San Antonio Express 27 January 1924; Wilcox, Annie Roberts. *Student Participation in School Government: An Experiment at Bellaire, Texas.* Master's thesis (University of Texas, 1933)

47. ibid

48. Wilcox

49. *Cookbook*; *City Report* 1924-30; *Post* 12 April 1927; *Post* 28 April 1927; Texas Death Certificate Alfred J. Condit 19 April 1927; *Chronicle* 19 April 1927; Pugh and Dennison

50. *Cookbook; Chronicle* 7 January 2010

51. City Directories; Digital Sanborn Maps 1924; Archdiocese archives; Currlin, Alice Bruce, *Community Welfare: Houston, Texas* (Houston: The Community Chest and Council of Houston and Harris County), 1946; GDN 24 February 1924

52. Digital Sanborn Maps 1924; City Directories; Texas State Historical Marker. Cooley School. 2013; SD 25 Minutes ledgers; Harris County Assessor's Abstract of Town Lots and Additions Vol 3. 1900-1905; Pugh; Author correspondence with Dr. Gayle Davies. 27 July 2012

53. State Marker; Sr. M. Agatha. *History of Houston Heights 1891-1918*. Premier Printing Co.(Houston) 1956; City Reports; Pugh

54. Reynolds, James W. https://tshaonline.org/handbook/online/articles/fob02 accessed 13 February 2016

55. *Post* 11 April 1924; *Post* 12 August 1923; *Chronicle* 8 April 1924

56. Benjamin, Karen. *Progressivism Meets Jim Crow: Curriculum Revision and Development in Houston, Texas, 1924-1929*. Paedagogica Historica. Volume 39, Number 4, August 2003, pp. 457-476 Rutledge; *Houston Post* 10 February 1926.

57. *Post* 24 February 1934

58. Benjamin; Bryant

59. Rodriguez, Ruth. *Daily Cougar*. 12 November 2007; *Houston Chronicle* 8 April 2001; Reynolds

60. County Treasurer ledgers; County Reports; USGS Maps 1914; *GDN* 5 June 1894; HCCCM F442. 15 June 1892; *Post* 19 March 1899; *Post* 28 October 1922

61. School register 1876; HCCCM E98. 18 June 1884; County treasurer Ledgers; HCCCM F436. 14 May 1892

62. City Reports; Bryant

63. United States Census 1870, 1880 Harris County; Mabel Wesley Texas Death Certificate; Jackson, Andrew Webster. *A Sure Foundation*. Houston 1939; Mabel Wesley Obituary 24 May 1941

64. Harris County Treasurer Records, 1886 – 1891; *GDN* 14 September 1890

65. United States Census 1900, 1910 Harris County; Harry Wesley Texas Death Certificate.

66. *Post* 20 February 1906; *Post* 18 November 1913; *Post* 7 December 1913; *Post* 9 August 1910; *Post* 11 August 1914; *Post* 10 August 1915

67. *Post* 13 September 1904; United States Census 1880 Harris County

68. *City Report* 1909-10; *Post* 9 October 1908; Wesley obituary

69. Wesley obituary; Jackson; United States Census 1910, 1920, 1930 Harris County; *Houston City Directory* 1932

70. City Reports; City Directories

71. City Reports; *Chronicle* 18 December 1943; *Post* 18 December 1943;

72. Scott

73. County Treasurer ledgers; County Reports; Cole, Edith Fae Cook. *Crosby's Heritage Preserved: 1823-1949*. Self 1986; USGS Maps 1914; County Auditor's report 1923

74. ibid

75. Cole; Author interview with Don Ramsey June 2008

76. Ramsey; Cole; http://www.yourhoustonnews.com/lake_houston/news/crosby-isd-breaks-ground-on-n ew-high-school/article_48086770-9e5d-509d-989e-0499dfe67b33.html   accessed 11 September 2016; Scott

77. School District 25 Minutes; County treasurer Ledgers; County Reports; HCCCM G256. 19 July 1895; *Suburbanite* 8 March 1918

78. SD 25 Minutes

79. City directories

80. Sullivan, John Bernard. *A Historical Perspective of the Cypress-Fairbanks Independent School District, Houston, Texas, 1884-1984.* (Dissertation, Southern Illinois at Carbondale, 1988.); http://www.cfisd.ne t/en/about/know-your-district/history/   accessed 24 August 2016

81. Cypress Historical Society records; Hickman; HC original 1876 schools ledger; United States Census Harris County 1880; County treasurer ledgers

82. County Treasurer ledgers; Daniels, Jack. *An Educational Survey of a Portion of Northwestern Harris County.* (Dissertation. UT Austin. 1940); Cypress Historical Society records

83. CY-Fair ISD web history; Sullivan;

84. Culivan; Cy-Fair ISD web history; Post 31 March 1951

Schools D - E

1. Davis

2. Pugh; Fonville; City Directories; City Reports

3. Pugh

4. *Post* 8 July 1925; *Post* 14 July 1925; *Press* 5 July 1925; *Press* 9 July 1925; *Chronicle* 7 July 1925; Pugh

5. *Press* 18 October 1930; *Post* 18 October 1930;

6. *Press* 19 October 1930; *Post* 19 October 1930

7. HISD Scrapbooks RG B1 HMRC; *Press* 19 October 1930; *Press* 21 October 1930; *Post* 21 October 1930

8. *Post* 23 May 1933

9. City directories

10. Digital Sanborn maps 1924; Pugh; City Directories

11. San Miguel, Guadalupe, Jr.. *Brown, Not White*. Texas A&M Press. 2001; McClymer, John F. *War and Welfare: Social Engineering in America 1890-1925*. Greenwood Press. 1980.; Hill, Howard C. *The Americanization Movement*. American Journal of Sociology V24:6. May 1919

12. Author interview with Felix Fraga; San Miguel; City Reports; De Leon, Arnoldo. *Ethnicity in the Sunbelt*. Texas A&M Press. 2001; Steptoe, Tyina. *Houston Bound: Culture and Color in a Jim Crow City*. University of California Press. 2016

13. Pugh;

14. Pugh; *Chronicle* 5 May 1925; *Chronicle* 30 October 1928

15. GCCISD websites; Archia; Henson; Texas Historical marker. Baytown Mexican School; Scott

16. Pugh & Dennison; City Directories; HISD web sites; *Post* 3 September 1942

17. Vance, Mike and Lomax, John Nova. *Murder and Mayhem in Houston*. History Press (Charleston, SC) 2015;

18. *Post* 16 June 1904

19. *Post* 25 April 1904; *Post* 18 May 1904

20. *Post* 10 October 1933

21. ibid

22. *Chronicle* 13 March 1934

23. *Post* 15 May 1897; *Post* 19 March 1899; County Reports; https://tshaonline.org/handbook/online/articles/hrdwr   accessed 26 August 2016; Dorris, Charles Albert. *Adjusting the Social Studies Curriculum to the Needs and Facilities of the Deer Park, Texas, School and Community* (M.A. thesis at UT-Austin, 1941)

24. Dorris; Ford, James; *Post* 5 September 1907

25. Dorris; Weidig, Barbara Yeary Weidig, *Deer Park: A History of a Texas Town*. Naylor (San Antonio.(1976)

26. Weidig

27. County Reports; Weidig;

28. HMRC Vertical Files. Deer Park; Weidig

29. City Reports; City Directories; Johnson; Digital Sanborn Maps 1924

30. Digital Sanborn Maps 1924; City Directories; Pugh; http://cw39.com/2014/08/25/students-of-closed-dodson-elementary-learning-about-blackshear-elementary/ accessed 4 September 2016;

31. Author conversation with Debra Blacklock Sloan; HISD websites; HISD Directory 1948-49

32. *Patriotism at Home*. Report of the Houston Foundation, Houston. 1917; Thomas, Jesse O.. *A Study of the Social Welfare Status of the Negroes in Houston* (Houston: Webster Richardson) 1929

33. *GDN* 31 July 1920; *GDN* 5 April 1921; *GDN* 27 April 1921; *GDN* 24 May 1921; HC Auditors Report 1930; *GDN* 3 May 1930

34. County Treasurer's ledgers; HCCCM E:372. 9 May 1887

35. Houston Age 2 October 1877; Bryant; City Directories; *GDN* 20 December 1883, 27 September 1884

36. *GDN* 16 July 1885; City Directories

37. Bryant; City Directories;

38. City Reports various; Sanborn maps 1896 & 1907;

39. City Reports; Informer 17 April 1937; Texas Death Certificate W.S. Francis 11 April 1937; Johnson

40. City Reports

41. *Chronicle* 15 August 1913

42. *Houston Post* 4 January 1904

43. *Post* 24 January 1905; *Post* 13 September 1904; *Post* 11 June 1906

44. Houston City Schools Report 1904-05. Report of Superintendent P.W. Horn

45. City Report 1885-86; Johnson; City Directories; Pugh and Dennison

46. Sanborn Maps 1890, 1896; City Directories; Pugh and Dennison;

47. City Reports various

48. City Reports, Sanborn Maps 1924; *Post* 7 December 1962

49. City Reports

50. Pugh; City Reports; Digital Sanborn Maps 1924; Chronicle 8 October 1990; HISD websites; http://www.meca-houston.org/meca-history.html   accessed 08 October 2016

51. *Houston Post* 4 June 1918; *Historic Houston Streets*. Hinton, Marks. Archival Press (Houston) 2006

52. *World War I and Academic Dissent in Texas*, Nicholas, William E. *Journal of the Southwest*, Vol 14, No.3, Autumn 1972 pps 215-230; *Rice's Student Rebellion*, HAM Slice of History. http://www.youtube.com/houstonartsandmedia accessed 02 January 2016

53. Nicholas

54. *City Report* 1917-18; Keller; *City Report* 1917-18

55. *Houston Post* 2 October 1918; *Houston Post* 3 October 1918; *City Report* 1917-18

56. *City Report* 1917-18

57. *City Report* 1917-18

58. *City Report* 1917-18

59. *Houston Chronicle* 18 February 1918

60. *City Report* 1917-18

61. *Houston City Directory* 1913; *Houston Post* 1 October 1916

62. *Houston City Schools Report* 1918-19

63. *City Report* 1918-19

64. *Hermann Park Trees*, HAM Slice of History. http://www.youtube.com/houstonartsandmedia%20accessed%2002%20January%202016 ; Hinton

65. *Post* 19 September 1897

66. Bryant; City Directories; City Reports; http://www.libraries.wright.edu/special/dunbar/biography   accessed 2 August 2016

67. *The Red Book of Houston.* Soutex Publishing. 1915; Bryant; Johnson; City Reports; *Informer* 9 February 1938

68. City reports; HISD websites; HISD Collection HMRC

69. Valentine Bennett Scrapbook; Harris County School Census 1854-55; Hickman; Meaux, Robert. History of Humble. To be published; http://www.humblemuseum.com/index.php/about/humble   accessed 2 August 2016; HCCCM C237. 30 May 1873

70. HCCCM E371. 9 May 1887 and E507. 11 June 1888; Meaux

71. https://www.findagrave.com/cgi-bin/fg.cgi?page=gr&GSln=dunman&GSfn=joseph&GSmn=w&GSbyrel=all&GSdyrel=all&GSst=46&GScntry=4&GSob=n&GRid=27561950&df=all&   accessed 2 August 2016

72. County Treasurer ledgers

73. United States Census Harris County 1860; County treasurer ledgers; *Telegraph* 11 January 1862;

74. HC original 1876 schools ledger; Meaux http://www.humbleisd.net/Page/57723 accessed 19 December 2015

75. *Post* 27 June 1897; SD 25 minutes book; HISD websites; City Directories; County Reports; City Reports; USGS maps 1922

76. *Post* 25 June 1917; City Directories; Lallier, Charline. *Houston High School*. 1938

77. *Post* 25 June 1917

78. *Morning Star* 1 May 1839

79. *City Report* 1888-89; Eby; City Report 1900-1901

80. *Post* 12 March 1899; *HISD History Outline*, internal, 1976; *City Report* 1915-16

81. County Reports; HC Deeds V294.p160; *Post* 27 June 1910

82. USGS Maps Settegast Quadrant 1921; City Directories; County Reports; HCCCM P516. 19 April 1911; *Post* 27 June 1919

83. Blackmon, Durward Harvey. *An Educational Survey of a Portion of North Harris County, Texas* (Master's of Education thesis at UT-Austin, 1939); *Baytown Sun* 10 April 1954

84. Blackmon; County Reports

85. City Directories; City Reports; *Post* 21 February 1932

86. City Report 1924-30; *Post* 21 February 1932

87. City Reports; City Directories

88. U.S. Census 1910, 1920 Harris County; HC Block Book 17:162

89. Sr. Agatha; HC Deeds V199. P 580-81

90. Digital Sanborn Maps 1924; Sr. Agatha; Bryant; City Reports; City Directories

91. HISD

92. City Directories; Suburbanite 8 March 1918; City Reports; http://www.houstonisd.org/Page/29054 accessed 18 September 2016; Pugh; *GDN* 5 April 1922; Fonville

93. Author interview with Ann Malone. HAM N2N; Pugh; http://www.houstonisd.org/Page/29054 accessed 18 September 2016

94. County Reports

95. USGS Maps 1914; County Reports

96. HC 1876 schools ledger; GDN 5 August 1883; McComb, David G. *Houston: A History*. UT Press. 1981; Wheat, Jim. *Postmasters & Post Offices of Texas 1846-1930; Brenham Inquirer* 19 January 1867; *Tri-Weekly Telegraph* 19 April 1867; Worrall

97. City Directories; Digital Sanborn Maps 18885, 1890

Schools F

1. City Reports; City Directories; Digital Sanborn Maps 1896, 1907, 1924; Dealy & Baker 1895 Guide to Houston

2. WPA Guide; City Report 1909-10; *Chronicle* 4 May 1903

3. City Reports; *Chronicle* 22 November 1929; Author correspondence with Jim Durkee and Ray Frazier. 25 July 2006

4. http://americanhistory.si.edu/lunchboxes/ accessed 23 November 2015; *Recollections of Early Schools.* Kenney, M.M.. *Southwestern Historical Quarterly*, Vol. 1, No. 4. April 1898 Pps 285-296

5. Houston City Schools Report, Superintendent Report 1906-07; *Chronicle* 27 December 1927

6. *Post* 7 December 1906 *Hygienic Lunches* p3

7. Houston City Schools Report 1906-07; *Post* 7 December 1906 *Hygienic Lunches* p3

8. *Chronicle*. 22 November 1929 *Longtime School Principal Dies;* Houston City Schools Report 1912-13; Houston City Schools Report 1913-14

9. Report of Supervisor of School Lunch Rooms, 1 June 1917; Houston City Schools Report 1917-18, Report of School Dietician

10. Houston City Schools Report 1917-18, Report of School Dietician

11. *City Report* 1913-14; *City Report* 1914-15; *City Report* 1918-19

12. *City Report* 1919-20, Report of Malnutrition Survey, Miss Lou Stallman, Director, Home Welfare Department, Young Men's Business League

13. *City Report* 1920-21; *Houston Independent School District Report* 1924-30

14. *HISD Report* 1924-30

15. *Post* 15 September 1930

16. *Chronicle* 23 October 1929, 4 June 1933, 8 June 1933, 13 September 1933; *Press* 5 June 1933

17. *Chronicle* 14 October 1929, 15 October 1929, 16 October 1929, 18 October 1929; *Post* 14 October 1929, 18 October 1929, 19 October 1929, 27 October 1929, 23 November 1929, 27 November 1929; *Press* 19 October 1929, 14 November 1929, 21 June 1930

18. *Report of Lunch Room Department. HISD.* 1936

19. Levenstein, Harvey. *Revolution at the Table: The Transformation of the American Diet*. Oxford University Press (New York) 1988. p.119

20. County Reports; SD 25 Minutes ledger

21. County treasurer ledgers; County Reports; Ford, James. Texas Historical Marker Narrative. 2007; *Post* 1 June 1961; City Directories; USGS Maps 1922; *Post* 5 September 1907

22. Pugh; City Reports; *Post* 21 July 1985

23. Vance, Mike. *Houston City Hall Timeline*. 2015

24. *City Report* 1921-22

25. *Chronicle* 20 October 1928; *Press* 21 December 1927; *Press* January 1930; *Chronicle* 23 July 1930

26. *Chronicle* 17 December 1924

27. *Press* 5 June 1927; *Chronicle* 12 November 1928; *Chronicle* 15 October 1929; *Post* 14 November 1929; *Chronicle* 23 July 1930

28. County Treasurer ledgers

29. *Telegraph* 28 October 1857; Keller; *WPA Guide*; Hickman; *Post* 19 June 1950; *Telegraph* 20 February 1839; Davis

30. *Telegraph* 4 May 1842; *Telegraph* 29 December 1841; *Telegraph* 26 December 1843; King, Judy. *Except the Lord Build: The Sesquicentennial History of the First Presbyterian Church, Houston, Texas. 1839-1989*. Houston, 1989; Texas Presbyterian 15 January 1848

31. *Telegraph* 28 October 1857; *Telegraph* 5 December 1855; *Telegraph* 7 March 1856; *Telegraph* 5 November 1856; *Telegraph* 10 March 1856

32. HISD websites

33. *Post* 17 August 1949; HISD websites; City Directories

34. http://www.old6ward.org/   accessed 10 October 2016; *GDN* 27 September 1884; City Reports. City Directories; Johnson; Bryant; *GDN* 18 October 1888

35. City Directories; City Reports

36. *Houston Age* 1 October 1877

37. Pugh; City Directories; City Reports; *Chronicle* 16 February 1941; http://es.houstonisd.org/franklines/School%20History/history.html%20accessed%2010%20October%202016 ; Author interview with Charles Saunders. N2N

38. *WPA Guide*; Elliot, Claude. *The Freedmen's Bureau in Texas*. SHQ 56:1 July 1952

39. Bryant; Elliot; Sorelle; Hornsby, Alton. *The Freedmen's Bureau Schools in Texas*. SHQ 76:4 April 1973; Keller

40. ibid

41. Hornsby; Keller

42. HC 1876 school register; HCCCM E213. 9 June 1885; County Treasurer ledgers; https://www.kleinisd.net/default.aspx?name=hf.photo.escho accessed 25 August 2016; HC Deeds 274:431. 9 August 1911; County Reports; Heritage of North Harris County

43. Cole; Scott

44. Allen F. Labay. Texas Abstract Company 30 march 1965; HC Deeds 17:209. 7 March 1877; HC Deeds 101:518. 22 November 1897; County Reports; Jane Ledbetter; Perkins

45. County Reports

46. City Directories; Digital Sanborn Maps 1924

47. County Reports; *Post* 17 December 1962; City Reports; Pugh & Dennison

48. *Post* 17 December 1962; Pugh & Dennison

49. *County Report* 1910; *County Report* 1912; *County Report* 1913

50. *County Report* 1912

51. *County Report* 1914

52. *County Report* 1912

Schools G

1. GCCISD websites; Harris County Historical Commission narrative. *Gaillard-Mitchell Cemetery*. Beverly, Trevia and Chandler, Chuck. 5 February 2020; Harris County Original School Ledger 1876

2. City Directories; http://www.galenaparkisd.com/campuspages/gpe/history.htm accessed

3. City Directories; http://www.galenaparkisd.com/campuspages/gphs_campus/history.htm accessed 25 August 2016

4. http://www.galenaparkisd.com/campuspages/gpms/history.htm accessed 25 August 2016;

5. City Directories; *Chronicle* late 1939 undated article;

6. Pugh & Dennison, City Directories; Perkins; https://www.gardenvillas.org/history-of-garden-villas.html accessed 9 March 2025

7. County Treasurer Ledgers; HCCCM F419. 13 February 1892, F451. 9 August 1892, G045. 19 August 1893

8. *Post* 19 March 1899; Pasadena ISD history; City Directories; County Reports; USGS Map 1914; Lewis; Perkins

9. Pasadena ISD history; City Directories; Lewis

10. Vance, Mike. *Mud & Money: A Timeline of Houston History*. Bright Sky Press. 2019; Kreneck, Thomas. *Del Pueblo*. Texas A&M Press. 2012; De Leon

11. Kreneck, De Leon; *GDN* 1911; Vance

12. Houston City Schools Reports. Various

13. Kreneck; De Leon; Houston City Directories. Various

14. De Leon;

15. Vance; De Leon;

16. Steptoe; Vance

17. Texas Historical Marker Application. Frost Town; Aulbach; Author interview with Kirk Farris

18. San Miguel, Guadalupe. *Brown, Not White*. University of Houston. 2001; De Leon; Kreneck; Vance

19. San Miguel; Houston Schools Reports; Vance

20. U.S. Census 1900 Harris County, TX.; County Treasurers Ledgers; HCCCM E98. 18 June 1884; *Post* 15 May 1897, 19 March 1899

21. Jane Ledbetter. Kleb Woods County Park; County Reports

22. County Treasurer Ledgers; *Post* 5 September 1907

23. City Directories; Lisa May, Archdiocese Archives;

24. ibid

25. WPA Guide; Lavender; *Telegraph* June 1869; *Telegraph* 13 October 1873; *Telegraph* 30 January 1875; *Chronicle* March 1934

26. WPA Guide; Carroll, B. H. Jr. ed. *Standard History of Houston: From a Study of the Original Sources.* H. W. Crew & Co.,(Knoxville) 1912; City Directories; Lavender; von der Mehden, Fred R., ed. *The Ethnic Groups of Houston.* Rice University Studies, 1984; Chapman; *Telegraph* 26 September 1872

27. WPA; City Directories; Digital Sanborn Maps

28. City Directory 1877-78

29. County Treasurer ledgers

30. County Treasurer ledgers; City Directories; City Reports; County Reports; Bryant; Bracey's Block Book 1919-20; HCCCM N603. 14 August 1907; HCCCM P103. 21 October 1909

31. *Recollections of Early Schools*, Kenney, M.M.. Southwestern Historical Quarterly, Vol. 1, No. 4. April 1898, p 285-296

32. *Biennial Report of the State Department of Education*, 1897. James M. Carlisle, Superintendent

33. *Bryan Morning Eagle*, 30 April 1907; *BME* 9 May 1907;

34. *City Report* 1907-08

35. *Post* 14 October 1913

36. *City Report* 1914-15

37. *City* 1914-15

38. *City Report* 1913-14

39. City 1914-15

40. http://www.tlc.state.tx.us/pubsconamend/constamend1876.pdf   accessed 24 November 2015; House Joint Resolution 37, 35th Texas Legislature,

41. Senate Joint Resolution 24, 44th Texas Legislature

42. Pasadena ISD archives; City Directories

43. HISD websites; *Post* 17 August 1949; http://www.golfcrestcountryclub.com/Default.aspx?p=dynamic module&pageid=391011&ssid=312086&vnf=1   accessed 5 September 2016

44. Harris County School census 1854, 1855. United States Census. Harris County,. 1850 and 1860; Research of Chuck Chandler; *Telegraph and Texas Register* 4 July 1850; Looscan, Adele. *Harris County 1822-1845.* SHQ 19:1 July 1915; Hickman; Texas Historical marker application. The Schools at Cedar Bayou.

45. HC original 1876 schools ledger; County Treasurer ledgers; Hickman; HC School Census 1855; GCCISD websites; Henson; County Reports; Jones, Mary Smith (1819-1907). *Letter from Mary Jones to Cromwell Anson Jones, October 28, 1875 - Page 1.* October 28, 1875. Special Collections, University of Houston Libraries. University of Houston Digital Library. Web. September 5, 2017. http://digital.lib.uh.edu/c ollection/p15195coll9/item/313/show/311 ; Jones, Mary Smith McCrory. Letter to [Cromwell Anson Jones,] [October 1875], letter, October 1875; *Baytown Sun* 1975; Chandler; (https://texashistory.unt .edu/ark:/67531/metapth2523/ : accessed January 28, 2020), University of North Texas Libraries, The Portal to Texas History, https://texashistory.unt.edu; crediting University of Houston Libraries' Special Collections.; Note - Although the School land deed was filed May 4, 1880 the Date of Instrument was January 18, 1879, two days before the Date of Instrument of the deed selling the rest of her land to David Wiggins. The Wiggins deed mentions the school land and the existence of the school in 1876, as well as her comment to her son that she "thought he had already filed it" indicates her intention of donating the land in 1876.

46. Beverly and Chandler; County Treasurer ledgers; *Post* 16 September 1904

47. Henson; GCCISD websites

48. HCCCM D145. 14 February 1878; HCCCM E213. 9 June 1885

49. Pugh, County Reports; City Reports; City Directories; http://www.georgiaencyclopedia.org/article s/arts-culture/henry-w-grady-1850-1889%20accessed%2002%20October%202016 ; *Brookshire Times* 27 November 1925; USGS Map 1921; *GDN* 15 May 1910; http://ms.houstonisd.org/gradyms/about%20 Grady.htm accessed 18 April 2011

50. County Reports

51. HCCCM E98. 18 June 1884; HCCCM E213. 9 June 1885; County Treasurer ledgers; City Directories; Digital Sanborn Maps 1924: Bryant; County Reports; City Reports

52. HCCCM E98. 18 June 1884; County Treasurer ledgers; *Post* 15 May 1897; *Post* 19 March 1899

53. County treasurer ledgers

54. *Telegraph* 24 January 1869; *Telegraph* 14 April 1869; Lavender; Bryant; Keller; Porter Map of Houston 1890

55. Bryant; Lavender; Sorelle

56. *Telegraph* 22 December 1869; *Telegraph* 18 January 1870; Tri-Weekly Houston Union 17 January 1870

57. *GDN* 27 September 1884; City Reports; Bryant

58. Lewis, J. Vance. *Out of the Ditch*. Rein Co. (Houston) 1910

59. City Reports; Bryant; *GDN* 6 April 1893; *GDN* 19 April 1893

60. City Reports; Bryant

61. *Chronicle* 25 May 1913; City Reports; United States Census. Harris County 1900; Johnson; City Directories; Informer ; Sorelle; Digital Sanborn Maps 1907, 1924

62. *Chronicle* 3 March 2008; *Chronicle* 6 May 2008

63. County Treasurer ledgers; HCCCM E625.15 May 1889; HCCCM F285. 14 May 1891; United States Census Harris County 1870, 1880, 1900. *Post* 19 March 1899; County Reports; HCCCM N464. 14 May 1907; *Post* 5 September 1907

64. HC Deeds 84:174. 3 October 1895; County Reports; USGS maps 1914

65. Cole; USGS Maps 1914; County Reports

Schools Habermacher - Horn

1. Hickman; School Census Harris County 1855; Worrall

2. City Directories; Digital Sanborn Maps 1924; City Reports

3. Pugh; City Reports

4. Wilcox; Pugh; *Chronicle* 13 October 1929; http://www.alexanderhamiltonms.org/History.htm   accessed 18 September 2016

5. HCCCM E98. 18 June 1884; County Treasurer ledgers; HCCCM E213. 9 June 1885; HCCCM E240. 10 August 1885; HCCCM E283. 11 February 1886; HCCCM E371. 9 May 1887; United States Census Harris County 1880

6. Wilson, Anna Victoria and Segall, William Edwin Segall. *Oh, Do I Remember!: Experiences of Teachers During Desegregation of Austin Schools*. SUNY Press. 2001; GCCISD official history; Scott

7. *Post* 25 August 1897; City Directories; HC Deeds V114:353. 24 July 1899 and V275:92. 26 July 1911; County Reports; *GDN* 28 July 1901; *GDN* 29 December 1903

8. City Directories; Digital Sanborn Maps 1924; County Reports; City Reports; Baines, Mary Harper. *Houston's Part in the World War*. 1919; United States Census Harris County 1910

9. Beverly and Chandler; *Weekly Telegraph* 25 May 1859; *Post* 7 September 1907; *Post* 1 January 1908

10. City Directories; County Treasurer ledgers; County Reports; City Reports; *GDN* 14 September 1895; *GDN* 29 October 1896; SD 25 Minutes ledger; Heritage Society. Yates House files; Author correspondence with Betty Chapman 23 August 2012

11. *Post* 22 June 1904; City Reports; United States Census. Harris County 1910, 1920; Digital Sanborn Maps 1907, 1924; Johnson

12. City Reports; *Chronicle* 13 November 2024

13. http://kids.britannica.com/comptons/article-202129/home-economics   accessed 20 February 2016; http://rmc.library.cornell.edu/homeEc/masterlabel.html   accessed 20 February 2016

14. *City Report* 1914-15

15. *City Report* 1906-07; *City Report* 1907-08; *City Report* 1909-10

16. Ibid; *County Report* 1914

17. *City Report* 1908-09

18. *City Report* 1909-10

19. *City Report* 1909-10; *City Report* 1908-09

20. *City Report* 1917-18

21. *City Report* 1918-19

22. http://hearth.library.cornell.edu/h/hearth/about.html accessed 20 February 2016

23. HCCCM E98. 18 June 1884; County Treasurer ledgers; *Post* 19 March 1899; County Reports; HC Deeds 466:114, 1000:382; USGS maps 1914; Smith, Margaret Mallott. *Spring Through the Seasons*. Sunbelt-Eakin Publishing. 2001; Perkins

24. https://tshaonline.org/handbook/online/articles/hgs04 accessed 29 August 2016; *Chronicle* 15 August 1910; *Chronicle* 18 August 1910; Harris County Archives files various

25. Currlin; HC Auditors Reports 1925, 1933; *Chronicle* 25 August 1929;

26. Harris County Archives; HC Auditors Report 1939

27. Harris County Archives. Various reports including Ethel Claxton Scrapbooks; *Patriotism at Home*. Report of the Houston Foundation, 1917; Currlin; HC Auditors Reports 1933, 1939; Vance, Mike, Ed. *Houston Baseball: The Early Years, 1861-1961*. Bright Sky (Houston) 2014; Honnette, Alyssa; Jackson, Sarah Canby

28. Honnette; Jackson; County Archives

29. ibid

30. Digital Sanborn Maps 1924; Bryant; City Reports; HCCCM M371.16 September 1905; HCCCM N400. 12 March 1907; HC original schools ledger; County Treasurer ledgers; *Fort Worth Daily Gazette* 10 February 1888; County Reports

31. Muir, Andrew Forest. Handbook Online https://tshaonline.org/handbook/online/articles/hvh27 accessed 4 July 2016; County Reports; *Informer* 8 May 1920

32. Bryant; Johnson; United States Census Harris County 1900, 1920; 1930, 1940; City Directories; County Reports; *Texas Standard* April 1935

33. Harris, Dilue Rose. SHQ Vol 4. October 1900, January 1901; Muir Handbook Online; Hickman

34. County Schools ledger 1876; HCCCM E98, Jun 18, 1884; HCCCM E625 15 May 1889; HCCCM F#)* 2 July 1891; County Treasurer ledgers;

35. Digital Sanborn Maps 1924; City Directories; County Treasurer ledgers; *Chronicle* 10 March 1952 Margaret Dullahan obituary; HCCCM I934 12 January 1900; Pugh and Dennison

36. *County Reports*; Pugh and Dennison

37. *County Reports*

38. ibid

39. *County Reports; Houston Report* 1924-30; HC Auditor's report 1923

40. Bryant; City Directories; City Reports; HISD Directory 1942-43, 1948-49

41. County Treasurer ledgers; HCCCM F436. 14 May 1892; United States Census Harris County 1900; Oates School history. HMRC. HISD Collection; HISD Directory 1942-43; *Texas Standard* January –February 1948; *Texas Standard* May-June 1949; *Post* 5 September 1907

42. HC Deeds 21 July 1913; County Reports; McKee; *GDN* 16 July 1913

43. City Directories; Digital Sanborn Maps 1924; Sr. Agatha; HC Assessor's Abstract Vol 3

44. Pugh; City Reports; Sr. Agatha; Author interview with Charles Saunders. HAM N2N. 9 July 2007

45. HAM N2N interview with Everett Lyons

46. County Reports

47. City Directories; Johnson; HISD websites; *Post* 19 September 1897; City Reports; Digital Sanborn Maps 1896; Pugh

48. *Post* 7 October 1904;

49. *Post* 15 September 1959; HISD websites

50. County Reports; HCCCM undated 1887

51. Digital Sanborn Maps 1924

52. Sr. Agatha; *Post* 3 April 1904; *Post* 8 April 1904; *Post* 17 April 1904; *Post* 24 April 1904; City Reports

53. City Reports; *Chronicle* 13 March 1924; *Chronicle* 14 March 1924; *Post* 14 March 1924

54. City Directories; Digital Sanborn Maps 1924; City Reports; HISD websites; *Chronicle* 13 October 1929; *Chronicle* 12 September 1932

55. Wilcox; Pugh; HISD websites

56. City Reports; Digital Sanborn maps 1924

57. City Reports; Pugh; City Directories

58. SD 25 minutes ledger; City Directories; City Reports

59. Meaux; USGS map 1919; United States Census Harris County 1880; County Treasurer ledgers; HC original 1876 schools ledger; McGee; Perkins

60. County Treasurer ledgers; County Reports; Meaux; *Post* 5 September 1907

61. L.L. Pugh Obituary, *Post* 18 May 1951

62. *Jewish Herald* 7 April 1910

63. Pugh obituary; *Brenham Daily Banner-Press* 14 September 1915; *Bryan Eagle* 9 July 1915; *Post* 14 September 1916; https://www.tsl.texas.gov/governors/personality/index.html accessed 15 March 2016

64. Gonzales, J.R.; *Bayou City History* 19 January 2013; Pugh Obituary

65. Pugh obituary; *Houston City Directory* 1932; United States Census 1910 Harris County

66. http://www.houstonisd.org/domain/4276%20accessed%2015%20October%202016 ; Author interview with Albert Williams HAM N2N; Bryant; Pitre, Merline. *In Struggle Against Jim Crow*. Texas A&M Press 1999; HISD Directory 1942-43

67. Cole

68. https://tshaonline.org/handbook/online/articles/hfh04 accessed 5 August 2016; County Reports; Cole; Scott

69. County Reports; *GDN* 3 September 1915; Severance, Diana. *Deep Roots, Strong Branches: A History of the Klein Family and Klein Community: 1840-1940.* HPN Books 1999

70. County Reports

71. HC original 1876 schools ledger; County Treasurer ledgers; SD 25 minutes ledger; United States Census Harris County 1880

72. HC original 18786 schools ledger; County treasurer ledgers; United States Census Harris County 1880;

73. HC original 1876 schools ledger; County Treasurer ledgers; HCCCM E98. 18 June 1884; Hickman; HCCCM E625. 15 May 1889; *GDN* 17 March 1890; *Post* 15 May 1897; *Post* 19 March 1899; County Reports; Perkins

74. County Treasurer ledgers; *Post* 5 September 1907

75. County Report 1913

76. Harris County Archives, School Bond Files

77. County Treasurer ledgers

78. City Directories; City Reports; Author interviews Ham N2N Lesta King, Charles Saunders 9 July 2007; Pugh

79. SD 25 minutes ledger; County Reports; City Reports; City Directory; Author visit to Hohl School 29 June 2007; Pugh; *Suburbanite* 8 March 1918; HCCCM R503. 8 October 1914; USGS Maps 1922

80. Bryant; SD 25 minutes ledger; City Reports

81. http://www.holyghostchurch.net/history accessed 03 April 2016; Archdiocese

82. Archdiocese; McHugh

83. Archdiocese; *GDN* 23 April 1944

84. HISD Websites

85. *Post,* 21 May 1904, 28 May 1904, 31 May 1904

86. *Post* 4 June 1904

87. *Post* 31 May 1904

88. *Chronicle* 3 June 1914

89. *Post* 14 April 1932

Schools Houston - Humble

1. Houston City Directory for 1866; W. A . Leonard, Compiler; Gray, Strickland & Co, 1866; David G McComb. *Houston: A History*; University of Texas Press; 1969; Johnston

2. Kleiner, Diana J. Handbook of Texas Online: Houston Academy; Pugh & Dennison; HISD Collection HMRC

3. Bright; Handbook

4. Beazley, Julia. Handbook of Texas Online: Thomas William House; Benham, Priscilla Myers. Handbook of Texas Online: Cornelius Ennis; Benham, Priscilla Myers. Handbook of Texas Online: James H Stevens; Cutrer, Thomas J.. Handbook of Texas Online: Peter W Gray

5. Silverthorne, Elizabeth. Handbook of Texas Online: Ashbel Smith

6. Pugh & Dennison; WPA Guide; Lavender; Hickman; Bright

7. Handbook; U.S. Census 1860, 1870 Harris County; City Directories; S.O. Young Papers. HMRC. MSS 10; Lavender; Hickman

8. WPA Guide; Bonewitz, Ed. HMRC MSS; Hickman; *Telegraph* 27 March 1844; *Telegraph* 17 September 1845; Davis; Grusendorff, Arthur A.. *Henry Flavel Gillette*. Handbook of Texas Online. https://tshaonline.org/handbook/online/articles/fgi29 accessed 1 June 2019

9. Hickman

10. United States Census Newberry Co, SC 1860, 1870, 1880 Harris Co, TX 1900, 1910; Hickman; Johnston; *Post* 14 June 1922; *GDN* 22 July 1889; *Post* 14 September 1897; Chapman, John A.. *Annals of Newberry*, 1892; Pope, Thomas H.. History of Newberry County 1860-1990;

11. ibid

12. City Directories; Digital Sanborn Maps 1924; HMRC Yates MSS0281, Box 4, folder 2:Report of Houston College for 1919-20; Red Book

13. Journal of American Baptist Home Missionary Society. 64th Annual Report. 1896;brawner, Anne. Handbook Online. https://tshaonline.org/handbook/online/articles/kbg19 accessed 20 September 2016; Official Manual State of Missouri. 1901; Missouri School Journal V16 August 1899; *The Crisis*. August 1917; https://garnettnabritlecture.wordpress.com/about/ accessed 20 September 2016

14. Dept of the Interior, U.S. Bureau of Education, Bulletin, 1916, no. 39: *Negro Education: A Study of the Private and Higher Schools for Colored People in the United States, Volume 2* (Washington, 1917)

15. HISD websites

16. *Houston Age* 1 October 1877; Johnson; City Directories; City Reports; Hayes, Daniel J.. *Houston High: An Informal History* 1981; Pugh & Dennison

17. Hayes; Young; *Chronicle* 1941 clipped article; *Chronicle* 8 October 1911

18. Hayes; Bonewitz papers. HMRC. MSS 0025

19. City Reports; Pugh & Dennison

20. City Reports; Young

21. *Post* 7 April 1904; City Reports

22. City Reports; *Post* 28 March 1961; Hayes; HISD Archives. HMRC. Cornerstone.

23. City Reports; Frank Black obituary

24. Hayes

25. Houston Arts and Media. N2N oral histories. Ann Malone. 18 August 2007. HMRC & Woodson Research Center; Hayes

26. Hayes

27. Scrapbook, 1900–1924, Part I, Section A. RG19 Houston Art League Records, MFAH Archives

28. *Post* 9 March 1902; *Post* 14 February 1903

29. *Scrapbook*; *Chronicle* 5 March 1904

30. *Scrapbook*

31. *Houston City Schools Report* 1910-11

32. *Scrapbook*

33. Hickman; Earl Vandale Collection at UT-Austin; copy secured from the microfilm collection found at Rice: *Confederate Imprints, 1861-1865*, reel 113, no. 3994 (New Haven, CT: 1974)

34. GCCISD histories; *Valley Morning Star* (Harlingen) 27 March 1951; *Chronicle* 1 March 1953

35. *Morning Star* 8 January 1844; Bright

36. USGS Map 1914; HC original schools ledger 1876; County Treasurer ledgers; County Reports; *Post* 15 May 1897; *GDN* 12 September 1899; HCCCM E98. 18 June 1884; Scott; Perkins

37. County Treasurer ledgers; Scott; *Post* 5 September 1907

38. Heritage of North Harris County, County Reports; *Post* 5 September 1907

39. Humble ISD archives; Dr. Robert Meaux

40. County Treasurer ledgers; Meaux; Humble ISD archives; *Post* 15 May 1897;

41. Meaux; Humble ISD Archives; Smith, Julia Cauble. Handbook Online https://tshaonline.org/handbook/online/articles/doh07 accessed 21 September 2016

42. Humble ISD archives; Meaux; Montgomery; County Treasurer ledgers; County Reports; HCCCM P229. 23 April 1910

43. Meaux

44. Montgomery; Meaux

45. Biennial Report of the State Department of Education, 1897. James M. Carlisle, Superintendent

Index

C

H